Out of the Blue

A BOOK ABOUT
RADIO AND TELEVISION
BY

John Crosby

19 52

Simon and Schuster · New York

ALL RIGHTS RESERVED
INCLUDING THE RIGHT OF REPRODUCTION
IN WHOLE OR IN PART IN ANY FORM
COPYRIGHT, 1946, 1947, 1948, 1949, 1950, 1951,
NEW YORK HERALD TRIBUNE INC.
COPYRIGHT, 1952, JOHN CROSBY
PUBLISHED BY SIMON AND SCHUSTER, INC.
ROCKEFELLER CENTER, 630 FIFTH AVENUE
NEW YORK 20, N.Y.

FIRST PRINTING

MANUFACTURED IN THE UNITED STATES OF AMERICA
BY AMERICAN BOOK–STRATFORD PRESS, INC.

TO

Mother and Father

CONTENTS

	FOREWORD	ix
1	*My First Exclusive*	1
2	*Some Rich, Wonderful Personalities—from Woollcott to Victor Mature*	21
3	*Here Come the Clowns*	41
4	*Sitting Ducks and a Few Dead Ones*	57
5	*Reasonably Serious Criticism*	79
6	*Witches and Plunging Necklines*	96
7	*Bless Their Little Hearts*	113
8	*Some Low Blows*	125
9	*What the Advertising Man Stands For and What We Stand For*	136
10	*Would You Like to Try for $64?*	151
11	*Whomsoever God and The General Electric Company Hath Joined Together . . .*	165
12	*Some General Observations*	180
13	*My Attention Wanders to Other Matters*	199
14	*The Animal Kingdom*	210
15	*Charms That Don't Necessarily Soothe the Savage Breast*	218
16	*Homicide, Plain and Fancy*	230
17	*An Era for the Ear*	237

18　*Hollywood and Other Foreign Lands*	252
19　*"But Seriously, Though . . ."*	269
AFTERWORD	289
INDEX	293

FOREWORD

SOME SIX YEARS AGO *I was entrusted—if that's the word I'm groping for—with the task of writing a radio column which later became, through the malign ingenuity of the Radio Corporation of America, a television column. In six years I have turned out about a million words, which is a terrible amount of wordage to devote to an industry so largely abandoned to trivia. The book which ensues is a selection from the columns. In assembling it, I was immeasurably assisted by three women —Jill Hellendale, Andrea Simon and Mary Crosby (to whom I'm occasionally married)—each of whom pored over my columns with such selfless devotion and zeal that the job took about five times as long as it should have.*

There was some loose talk when we started this volume about putting together a rounded and exhaustive study of the broadcasting industry. Fortunately, this worthy but dreary enterprise was abandoned. What follows are simply those columns which have given me or my three assistants the most pleasure. They are, in short, very personal, arbitrary and capricious selections. But then that is the nature of columnists— personal, arbitrary and capricious—and they get worse as they grow older. A column is a splendid place to vent one's grievances, one's hopes, one's opinions. A radio and television column is especially splendid because you quickly discover that you are emitting not only your own grievances, opinions and hopes, but everyone else's grievances, opinions and hopes. Especially grievances. Everyone has a grievance—usually four or five of them—against radio. In voicing your own criticism you are airing the secret despair of a great many million people. You become their champion, their friend, their fellow victim.

That is the nice part about being a radio columnist. There are many not-so-nice parts. For one thing, you are chained to a time schedule. A newspaper reader can read when she pleases.

A book critic can make his own schedule. Even a drama critic is altogether free on some evenings. But a radio critic is never wholly free or wholly unfree. Once when I was living on Fire Island, I would make up a schedule that would tie me up from, say, 7 to 7:30, 8 to 9, 9:30 to 10 and so on. That would have left two free half-hours. There isn't much you can do with a loose half-hour. I used to gallop down to the nearest saloon, a matter of two blocks, gulp a drink and sprint for home and radio two minutes ahead of broadcast time. Sometimes I'd be in and out of that saloon three or four times a night, always coming and going on a dead run. The drinkers thought I was insane.

The worst aspect of the job, I suppose, is the monotony. Nothing resists criticism so strenuously as radio. A radio columnist is forced to be literate about the illiterate, witty about the witless, coherent about the incoherent. It isn't always possible. My drawers are stuffed with notes about programs which are neither bad enough nor good enough to warrant comment of any sort. They hover, these programs, in a sort of nether world of mediocrity and defy you to compose so much as a single rational sentence about them.

Still, warts and all, it's not a bad job. Prowling through six years of these columns has reawakened a lot of memories and, on the whole, I've had a wonderful time with the Arthur Godfreys, the Kate Smiths, the Jack Bennys, the Jimmy Fidlers. What follows is not so much a record of what transpired on the air in those years as what went on in my mind. Some subjects have been treated far more extensively than others. Women, for example, have an entire chapter to themselves, while men have no similar distinction simply because I enjoy writing about women. Matrimony, too, gets more space than it deserves because the treatment of marriage on the air I find irresistibly ludicrous. Some of the worst programs ever broadcast —many of them long since departed—are described in ago-

nizing detail while some of the best programs are not mentioned. That's because bad programs make fairly entertaining copy. Therein lies the secret of the success of any radio or television columnist. If every program was a good program, I greatly doubt whether anyone would read us.

JOHN CROSBY

CHAPTER 1

My First Exclusive

The Age of Noise
[AUGUST 15, 1946]

"THE TWENTIETH CENTURY is the Age of Noise. Physical noise, mental noise and noise of desire—we hold history's record for all of them. And no wonder; for all the resources of our almost miraculous technology have been thrown into the current assault against silence. The most popular and influential of all recent inventions, the radio, is nothing but a conduit through which prefabricated din can flow into our homes. And the din goes far deeper than the eardrums. It penetrates the mind, filling it with a babel of distractions—news items, mutually irrelevant bits of information, blasts of corybantic or sentimental music, continually repeated doses of drama that bring no catharsis but merely create a craving for daily or even hourly emotional enigmas...."

The quotation is from the chapter on "Silence" in "The Perennial Philosophy" by Aldous Huxley.

The Age of Noise, eh? Well, not quite. It might be more proper to call it the Age of the Eye and the Ear. A sensory revolution took place in the 1920s, that decade that brought us not only the radio but the tabloids and later the talking motion pictures. Still later came the picture magazines. Today you may get through life virtually without reading at all. Much of our news and our information we acquire through pictures and sounds, at the movies, in the picture magazines, over the radio.

Learning by sight and ear leaves a different mark on the mind, if it leaves any at all, than the printed word, which requires an active use of the brain. Not long ago, I asked a housewife why she listened to soap operas. She said that soap operas were all she could get on her radio. Then why not turn off the radio? "It's a voice in the house," she said.

The Voice in the House, or to put it in Mr. Huxley's terms, the Noise in the House, has become indispensable. A reader wrote me once that dance music was just a method of getting around thought. "It blots out everything and leaves the mind perfectly empty," he said.

Too much radio is just a noise that blots out everything. I don't mean this as an indictment of the broadcasting industry. After all, the broadcasters are committed to putting noise on the radio sixteen hours a day. But we don't have to listen to it. Radio brings us music, entertainment, education, drama, news, just about everything. Each has its separate value. But put them all together and you have the Noise in the House, one of the worst evils of radio and something even the broadcasters—though probably not the advertisers—wish they could cure.

What on earth did our grandmothers do for a Noise in the House? They listened to the laughter of the children, the cackling of the hens, the whisper of the willows. It was noise enough. And there must have been hours and hours of deep, dark silence.

The Age of Noise has not only altered our thinking processes: it is even altering our personalities. I don't know if anyone has ever made a study of the effect on personality of constant repetitious noise. However, in my youth before radio was invented, I knew several trappers in northern Wisconsin, men who lived in a silence broken only by the occasional sounds of the woods. So keen was their auricular perception, they could distinguish one woodsman from another by the sound their axes made when they were chopping wood at a distance of miles. They were men of deep simplicity with a grasp of the essential facts of man and nature that too many irrelevant noises would have ruined.

"Thinking is something new to man and he does it very badly," said H. L. Mencken in "Life" magazine. "We have lost the sureness of instinct of the baboon and not yet perfected sureness of reasoning." Now that we have the radio we'll probably never get around to it. There is too much to listen to.

Bikini: The Build-Up
[JULY 2, 1946]

"There is no foreseeable defense against atomic bombs," Albert Einstein, father of the bomb, wrote recently. "Scientists don't even know of any field which promises any hope of adequate defense."

To anyone who read that, the broadcast last Saturday night in which General Dwight D. Eisenhower, Admiral Chester W. Nimitz and Secretary of the Navy James V. Forrestal did their best to explain what the atom bomb test was all about, must have seemed strange. All three men spoke firmly, almost convincingly, about the need for an A-bomb test to strengthen the "national defenses." All three warned that the information provided by the test would "save American lives."

The phrases "save American lives" and "national defenses" ran through the program with the persistence of a Pepsi-Cola jingle. The military mind has always run to stock phrases but this type of phrase is comparatively new. During the war, the Army and Navy were flooded with bright young advertising and broadcasting executives who taught the admirals and the generals that a stock phrase repeated again and again will sell an idea just as efficiently as it sells soap.

"Cost American lives" and "national defenses" are perfect phrases to sell an idea, as unassailable and unprovable as: "Even your best friend won't tell you." Fear advertising no longer carries the old punch in selling mouth washes, but it still works fine to sell a national policy. The national policy-makers have lagged far behind the dentifrice industry in the use of propaganda.

The Eisenhower-Nimitz-Forrestal program set the pace for the Bikini bomb test. We now had a slogan for the product. All that was needed was a name for the product and a pretty girl on the cover. That came on Able Day, Sunday. At about 11 A.M. a news commentator reported:

"The atom bomb has a name now. It's called Gilda. Painted on the casing of the bomb is a picture of Rita Hayworth. Crew members asked for five pictures of Miss Hayworth in order to get a good likeness. Miss Hayworth said she was so flattered she couldn't get back to earth."

It was an apt remark. The atom bomb is of the stuff that lights the stars and consequently an earth-bound metaphor would not have been suitable.

Able Day dawned serene and cloudless on Fire Island where we waited for what General Carl Spaatz referred to as "the main event." The day was as blue as a Norse god's soul; the sea as green as Vivien Leigh's eyes. The shimmering beach looked not unlike Bikini except there were no palm trees.

To while away the time, we listened to Dr. Dillon Ripley, of Yale University, describe the significance of the atom bomb test. The Pacific Ocean, he said, was the last great frontier, "the greatest of all oceans and the one we know least about." The Pacific, he said, abounded in birds, fish and mollusks "all in urgent need of attention" from the scientists.

Then, apparently feeling he was wandering quite a distance from atomic fission, he added hurriedly: "Let us hope the atom bomb blast will stimulate research in the Pacific, an area we know so little about."

Bikini: The Build-Up

A stiff southwest wind whipped up whitecaps on the Atlantic, an ocean whose birds, fish and mollusks have long since received the most careful attention of the scientists. To kill time, we listened to Paul Hindemith's new choral work to the words of Walt Whitman's "When Lilacs Last in the Dooryard Bloomed."

"Come lovely and soothing death," sang the Columbia Broadcasting System chorus.

"Undulate round the world serenely, arriving, arriving.

"In the day, in the night, to all, to each,

"Sooner or later, delicate death."

The dead poet seemed closer to the point than the live scientist, possibly a little too close. We switched over to the National Broadcasting Company where no poetry obtruded.

"The National Broadcasting Company presents—the National Hour! This is the mirror of public opinion. We must have an enlightened public opinion to put us on the road to peace and reconstruction. Our subject today—the atom bomb!"

There was no nonsense about death here. David Dietz, science editor of the Scripps-Howard newspapers, explained in a matter-of-fact way that an atomic explosion was not much different from a fire in your grate. The fire in the grate, he said, was energy resulting from the change in form of carbon molecules. Atomic fission changed the form of the atom, during which some of the atom's weight was lost. The lost mass was transformed into energy, quite a lot of energy.

"We take you now to Kwajalein where W. W. Chaplin observed the take-off of the B-29, Dave's Dream, which will drop the atomic bomb on Bikini Atoll. Come in Bill Chaplin."

Mr. Chaplin interviewed the members of the ground crew of Dave's Dream. "We've been nursing that plane like a baby," said a tech sergeant. "She's ready."

The photographic crew chief said the explosion would be the "most photographed event in history. . . . Three hundred cameras.

... 3,000,000 photographs.... eight B-29's and two C-54s carrying cameras."

The broadcast switched to the U. S. S. Appalachian where scientists of all sizes, shapes and intellects were gathered to observe the blast. A geologist from the University of Wisconsin said he wanted to find out if Bikini Atoll rested on an extinct volcano. If the blast blew away the coral which forms the island, he'd find out. Another scientist worried about the effect of gamma rays on cancerous mice closeted on one of the target ships.

Aboard his flagship, the U. S. S. Mt. McKinley, Vice-Admiral W. H. P. Blandy assured the families of those participating that there was no danger. "No tidal wave," he said. ... "no danger of radioactivity ... all possible precautions." ...

The wind got a little chilly on the beach and we moved back to the cottage. At 5:30 P.M., the big event moved suddenly from the realm of speculation to the realm of actuality.

"The National Broadcasting Company interrupts all its programs to bring you a special broadcast. We take you now to San Francisco." ...

Bikini: The Let-Down
[JULY 3, 1946]

AT 5:30 P.M. Sunday the N.B.C. Symphony was deep into Shostakovich's Fifth Symphony, in which the Russian composer tried to express man's tormenting doubts, his dreams, his aspirations and the ultimate assertion of his personality. The symphony was abruptly terminated to bring the world the noise of the explosion of an atomic bomb over which man may have some trouble asserting his personality and which today forms the basis for some of his most tormenting doubts.

"In a few minutes," said the announcer, "many questions will be answered. What is the destructive radius of the atomic bomb?

Bikini: The Let-Down

Will it cause a tidal wave? Will this new test make the world more conscious of the importance of atomic energy control?"

Aboard the U. S. S. Appalachian, fifteen miles from Bikini Atoll, Larry Todd, a radio correspondent, explained the metronome placed aboard the old battleship Pennsylvania. The metronome, he said, was standing next to an open microphone in the old battlewagon, now abandoned by every living soul.

"Listen to the ticking of the electric metronome," he said. "When the metronome stops, the atomic bomb has exploded. Remember, no one knows what the explosion will sound like. It may be a whisper, a wheeze, a roar. No one has ever heard the explosion of an atomic bomb by radio.

"Listen to the ticking of the electric metronome. . . ."

The broadcast switched to Columbia Broadcasting System correspondent Bill Downs aboard the observation plane behind Dave's Dream, the B-29 which was to drop the bomb.

"If you could fill a washtub with bluing and put some orange strips in it, you would have a picture of Bikini Atoll from the air," shouted Downs over the roar of the engines. "These few minutes we are talking are a sort of wake for the gallant ships in the lagoon below. Can you hear the metronome?"

As a matter of fact, you could hear it much too clearly. It sounded like something out of "The Perils of Pauline."

From the flagship U. S. S. Mt. McKinley, Don Bell reported that the task force commander, Vice-Admiral W. H. P. Blandy, was pacing the deck "like an expectant father."

"Expectant father," muttered a girl sitting next to me. "Of all the lousy metaphors! Like a nephew waiting for his rich uncle to die! This is a death watch, not a maternity ward."

"Ten minutes to the bomb drop," said somebody.

"Come in Bill Chaplin at Kwajalein."

Chaplin started to explain the immense relief that flooded Kwajalein when the B-29 Dave's Dream finally got the fourth atomic bomb off the island and out of harm's way. He was cut off suddenly by the voice of the bombardier aboard Dave's Dream.

"Bombs away and falling," said the bombardier.

Then there was nothing but the sound of the metronome, which cut clearly through the deafening screeching of the static. Seconds passed and then the metronome stopped. It started again, haltingly, like Billy Conn trying to rise in the eighth round of his last fight, and then stopped for good. The screech of the static continued interminably, but there was no other sound, no whisper, no roar. Apparently the explosion of an atomic bomb has yet to be heard by radio.

"It looked like a knockout," shouted Bill Downs. He must have had the phrase prepared in advance. A few moments later he said, "There was no tidal wave. The airplane did not receive any shock wave. I can't see any damage below." He sounded disappointed.

Don Bell came back on the air from the flagship. "I can see the palm trees. The island is still afloat. I can see the Nevada, too. She's still afloat. Another ship seems to be on fire." He sounded a little hurt, as if he had traveled a long, long way for nothing.

There was a babble of description of the big cloud. "Rose and white, beautiful but sinister," said one. "Mushroom-shaped, beautifully colored," said another.

"Scientists agree it's a big success," said Larry Todd. The scientists, of course, could have had no basis for any such statement. The only thing they knew for certain was that the bomb went off.

The broadcast switched back to San Francisco, where Elmer Petersen obviously discarded all the prose he had assembled for the occasion and hastily substituted something more appropriate. "A tense and waiting world heard the broadcast of the explosion of the fourth atomic bomb. The sound of the explosion was not nearly what people had expected." . . .

The big show was over. We settled back to wait for the crew of Dave's Dream to return to Kwajalein to tell what happened. The

General Electric Hour orchestra helped to fill the long wait, playing, among other things, "Over There," a song which distills in a few bugle notes the pre-atomic opinion of the United States twenty-nine years ago. Later the G. E. chorus sang the hymn: "The Night Is Long and I Am Far from Home," which seemed at the time to have a disproportionate significance. Night fell rapidly, as it always does on Fire Island, where I heard the broadcast, and the frogs sang their age-old threnody.

At 11 P.M. we returned briefly to Kwajalein to hear the B-29 crew relate their experiences.

"Major Swancutt, did you have any bad moments on the flight?" asked Bill Chaplin.

"No," said the man who piloted Dave's Dream. "The most tense moment was the fifteen seconds waiting for the shock wave. It was about what we thought it would be."

"Thank you, Major Swancutt. And now Major Wood, the bombardier." . . .

And so it continued—the undigested, carefully censored, totally meaningless information. Radio brings you information at the speed of light, but it has not increased the speed of thought by a single m. p. h. In the wake of sensation, wisdom still plods in the dust far to the rear.

"And now Colonel Blanchard, will you tell us what you saw?"

"I think the most interesting thing was the way that snow white cloud shot up toward the plane."

"Thank YOU, Colonel Blanchard." . . .

It sounded a little like the Marx brothers.

Would They or Wouldn't They and Who Cares?
[APRIL 22, 1951]

SEMI-ANNUALLY, I catch up on the fabulous doings of the Hollywood folk as sprayed throughout the Eastern seaboard by those two great ladies, Louella and Hedda, on their radio programs. If you don't know the last names of Louella and Hedda, then you've been out of touch too long to have much interest in Hollywood anyhow.

It was a bad night to pick, last Sunday. The girls got me even more confused than usual. The whole country was hanging, breathless. Would Lex make it up with Arlene? Was this irrevocable, this quarrel about who was to meet whom where and at what time? The first word came from Hedda: "Arlene Dahl and Lex Barker won't be married," said Hedda with what seems, in the light of subsequent developments, unwarranted confidence. "She kept him waiting outside a department store." He was furious, according to Hedda, lit into the girl and left her weeping.

"I don't believe in divorce," declared Arlene (according to Hedda). "It's a good thing we found out in advance."

In other words, everything was off and I, like millions of other sentimental Americans, was heart-stricken. I waited till 9:15, when Louella blows in. "My first exclusive," said Louella. "Lex flies in to take his bride back." It was, she said, just a misunderstanding. "They're going to get married."

Well, you can imagine my state of mind! Would they or wouldn't they? And who was left waiting outside the department store? There was considerable disagreement here. Press reports the next day seemed to concur that it was Arlene outside the department store, not Lex. She was supposed to meet Lex at a cocktail party at Ceil Chapman's but she couldn't find a taxicab. That's why she was late.

A great deal of print was expended explaining about girls always being late (and Miss Dahl, it was intimated, is especially prone to this weakness) and about boys getting terribly irritated about girls who show up half an hour late. I studied all the reports carefully, weighing things in my mind. After considerable deliberation, it seemed to me that Miss Dahl was no later than most girls ever get and that Lex got no madder than most men ever get under similar circumstances.

One point that neither Hedda nor Louella touched upon—and a

very important one, too—was the fact that Arlene was trying to get that cab at Fifth Avenue and Fiftieth Street at 5:30 P.M. on a Friday night. Now, any lawyer could tell you that Friday night is a terrible night to get a cab anywhere in New York, that 5:30 is probably the worst hour and that Fifth and Fiftieth is easily the worst street. Arlene had a strong case there. There isn't a district attorney in the country that could break it down.

But, at that point (9:17 P.M. E. S. T. Sunday), the issue was: could Lex explain? Would Arlene forgive? Louella said they'd get married. Hedda said they wouldn't. Millions of us tossed in our beds that night, wondering. We had to wait until the Monday papers to find out. Then, in the "Mirror," we found Miss Parsons trumpeting: "While you are reading this, they [Lex and Arlene] may already be aboard a plane, New York bound, for their wedding." "The News," Miss Hopper's paper, went even further, contradicting their own columnist, and said that Lex and Arlene *were* flying back to New York together and would get married. And they did. Even while you are reading this, they are living happily ever after.

It was touch and go for a minute, though, and, on the whole, I think both Hedda and Louella acquitted themselves well in covering one of the great news stories of our day. Of course, Hedda did get it wrong, but then she comes on earlier in the evening. A bride could easily change her mind forty-two times between 8 and 9 o'clock, could tell one columnist one thing and the other another.

Anyhow, best of luck, Lex and Arlene. Just take it easy, Lex. Next time she says she's going to show up at 5:30, arrive at 6:30 and you'll meet her coming in.

The Jet-Propelled News
[AUGUST 29, 1949]

GEORGE F. PUTNAM, the news commentator, is winging his way, as this is being written, to England, thence to Germany, on a weekend round-up of European news. He'll be back, brimful of opinions, information and newsreels, in two days, prepared to give his television audience on W.A.B.D. in New York what is generally referred to as a first-hand report on two widely different branches of the human race in Britain and Germany—the key people, the typical people.

"Jet-propelled news coverage in the jet-propelled age—that's what noted television commentator George F. Putnam will give Americans this week end," trumpets a press release. He plans to leave here on a Friday, lunch with a typical British family Saturday, ingesting along with his austerity rations its typical views on economic, political and social problems in the world. Then off to Frankfurt for dinner with another typical, this time German, family and its views on the world. In both Britain and Germany, along with the typical, he'll talk to the key people. Then back to America on Monday for that first-hand report.

Well, bon voyage, Mr. Putnam, and happy news-gathering. Frankly, though, I'm a little doubtful about this jet-propelled news coverage. I've met a good many of the key people and also the typical people in this country and sometimes it's hard to tell them apart. I'm not sure how the British typicals stack up with the American typicals but some instinct tells me there isn't much difference. You tell an American typical he's typical and he's likely to blast you right away from the luncheon table. He may tell you he don't believe in Truman, he don't believe in Dewey, he don't even believe the Dodgers got a chance this year.

And there's your first-hand report. "A sense of hopelessness and despair has settled on the American people," you report to your audience. "I lunched today with a typical American family and they have no faith in anything."

Another thing about these lightning interviews. I've found it's difficult to wrest any sort of coherent opinion out of the typical or even the key people over meals. They've just met you. They're wary. They're also hungry. In extreme cases, they may be snappish or perhaps just morose. In any case their opinions are conditioned more by the state of their stomachs and their nerves than by the state of the world.

"I hope," said Mr. Putnam on the brink of departure, "that this is only the beginning of a series of flights. In the near future I plan to interview Franco, the Pope, Premier De Gasperi, Marshal Tito and even Stalin himself. The day is not far off when a news commentator will cover a story anywhere in the world and be back home with a first-hand report and pictures in a few hours."

It's an ambitious schedule all right, fully in keeping with the jet-propelled age. I have an idea there may even be contests later to see who can leave La Guardia Field, interview Franco, the Pope, Premier De Gasperi, Marshal Tito and even Stalin himself, and be first back to La Guardia with the first-hand report.

The assimilation of all this information and opinion, the presenting of it in some coherent and meaningful whole, the contribution to the Wisdom of the American people—both the typical and the key—will have to be worked out later. The big thing is to get there and get back fast.

And get pictures.

The Easter Parade
[APRIL 10, 1947]

N. B. C.'s BROADCAST of the Easter parade on Fifth Avenue ought to serve as a warning to anyone who yearns to be an announcer. Stay out of radio, bub, or you might wind up in the same fix that confronted Ben Grauer last Sunday. Mr. Grauer was in an open car ornamented with one thousand tulips and Maggi McNellis, both, according to Mr. Grauer, spectacularly beautiful. Shortly after the broadcast started, the car turned right on Fifth Avenue, which Mr. Grauer described as the "most famous avenue in the world," a phrase which took quite a kicking around all day.

"Oh, it's a beautiful day!" shouted Mr. Grauer happily. "Here we are plumb in the center of Fifth Avenue." For a few moments he spoke feelingly of the colorful crowds. He described Miss McNellis's hat with some assistance from Miss McNellis, who last year was voted the best-dressed woman in radio.

Then things started to go wrong. "No, please lady!" A note of alarm was evident in his voice. "Yes, thanks but ... We're having a riot here." I'm not entirely sure what was going on, but I gathered that a number of ladies were busily plucking the tulips from Mr. Grauer's car. "I'm sorry, madam. ... No, no, you can't. No, please! Driver would you go along, please?"

It was too late, I gathered. Herb Sheldon, a fellow announcer who came along to help describe the parade, said: "Well, we lost our thousand tulips in about three seconds."

"Thousands of people wanted our lovely tulips," said Miss McNellis brightly.

Then Mr. Grauer and the N. B. C. car ran into a traffic block. "Inspector," said Mr. Grauer, summoning up all his charm, "could we go ahead there? We're from N. B. C. ... What? ... Oh! ... Oh, thank you, inspector, thank you."

There was a hapless pause. "That was the voice of a high police official you just heard," said Mr. Grauer bitterly. "We have now turned off Fifth Avenue—at the request of the Police Department. I hope I'm still smiling."

The car proceeded east on Fifty-second Street, which Mr. Grauer, for lack of anything else to do, described in considerable detail. "We're now in an eddy of the Easter parade. The inspector—and all remember him lovingly this Eastertide—suggested we take our N. B. C. car down a side street."

Soon the car was sailing down Madison Avenue. "We're now behind St. Patrick's Cathedral," said Mr. Grauer helplessly. He gave a vivid description of the rear of St. Patrick's. Miss McNellis chimed in with a few historical notes about the old Whitelaw Reid house across Madison from St. Patrick's. Mr. Grauer suggested that it was a nice day. Miss McNellis, who sounded restive, described a beautiful blonde climbing into a taxi.

"She isn't wearing an Easter bonnet," said the best-dressed lady in radio, who had been brought along especially to describe Easter bonnets. "In fact, she isn't wearing a hat at all."

"Maggi," said Mr. Grauer in desperation. "See that nice policeman with the nice Easter smile? Well, smile back at him and see if he'll open that lane for us."

I could visualize Maggi smiling prettily and determinedly at the cop. "We're trying to get back to Fifth Avenue," Mr. Grauer explained to his unseen audience. He needn't have bothered. By this time we had forgotten all about the Easter parade and were caught up in the drama of the thing. Would Mr. Grauer get back to Fifth Avenue? Would Miss McNellis get a chance to describe a hat?

Apparently the cop yielded to Miss McNellis, for a moment later Mr. Grauer shouted: "Now we're heading west on Fiftieth Street. People are waving at us. Now we're back on Fifth Avenue, right in the heart of Fifth Avenue." He sounded like Ronald Colman when he finally got back to Shangri-La.

It was a brilliant but short-lived triumph because the fifteen minutes were up. "This has been a broadcast of the Fifth Avenue Easter parade," said the announcer, stretching a point. "This is Ben Grauer returning you to N. B. C., the National Broadcasting Company."

Oh, well, you can hear a description of the Easter parade any year. This one was different.

Old-Fashioned Boyhood

[DECEMBER 23, 1949]

Now COMES the time when the existence of Santa Claus is reaffirmed, when comedians dust off their Christmas routines, their Yule jokes, when "White Christmas" tinkles like silver bells from C. B. S. to A. B. C., when Lionel Barrymore booms like an organ over Mutual and visions of sugar plums assault all the vice-presidents of N. B. C.

Christmas broadcasts, normally as traditional as plum pudding, offer a few new notes this year. Louella Parsons, for example, will spend the day at the Alan Ladds. At 9:15 P.M. E. S. T. on A. B. C., she will tell her spent, replete audience how a prominent Hollywood family passes the day. (Little swimming pools for the kiddies, I expect. A Cadillac carved out of solid emeralds for Mummy. Just like any normal American family.)

Overcome by seasonal spirit, W. N. B. C. in New York will broadcast an hour-long "Santa Claus Roundup" in which Ed Herlihy will interview Mrs. Claus, Ben Grauer will get a few pertinent comments out of Mr. Claus, and Bill Stern will describe the final loading of Santa's sled. Then H. V. Kaltenborn will analyze the implications behind Santa's yearly pilgrimage. Out in far Hollywood, where Christmas falls every day, N. B. C. will broadcast the Christmas morning activities at the homes of Frank Sinatra, Bob Hope, Phil Harris and Alice Faye, Gordon McCrae and Art Linkletter, each featuring the happy cries of the gilded children of these stars.

It'll be quite a holiday for the kiddies, all in all. For the tenth straight year, Amos of Amos 'n' Andy will explain the Lord's Prayer to his daughter Arbadella; a hidden microphone will broadcast the children's Christmas Eve remarks to Santa from Macy's; Santa will visit the Quiz Kids on their broadcast (and I do hope they don't make a monkey of the old gentleman); the three daughters of Red Foley—Shirley, fourteen; Julie, eleven, and Jennie, nine—will help Pop sing Christmas carols on the Grand Ole Opry program.

It all takes me back to my own boyhood Christmases, which were as normal and American as any boyhood Christmas could be. Up at daybreak, shivering a little in the frosty dawn, the microphone clutched securely in one childish fist, the script in the other.

"Wake up! Wake up!" I would shrill to my brothers and sister, directly following the N. B. C. chimes. "This is Christmas Day!"

This was the cue for the N. B. C. Symphony, huddled over in the far left-hand corner of the nursery to launch into "Adeste Fideles," which in turn was the cue for my brothers and sister to roll over and yawn (always a difficult bit for the sound effects man) and for the announcer to go into his bit.

"Good morning and Merry Christmas, one and all. This is Ed Herlihy, bringing you the normal American Christmas of a normal American family. And here are the Crosby kids. . . ."

It is one of the most poignant and ineradicable memories of my childhood that we always got Ed Herlihy. We wanted Ben Grauer like every normal American boy. I used to write Santa every year for Grauer but we never got him. The O'Reillys, rich kids from the right side of the tracks, *they* got Grauer. They got the Philharmonic too and a much better time break on C. B. S. and all the best stars like Bing Crosby. (We always got Sinatra.)

Gads, how it all comes back to me now! Opening the presents under the tree. Actually, we didn't. A sound effects man had a recording which sounded much more like the tearing of Christmas wrappings than the real thing. Our happy cries of delight at the presents, being careful not to get too close to the microphone. I remember the gaily trimmed cables running across the living room, the electricians festooned, as was the custom, with mistletoe, Herlihy losing his place in the script and fluffing the words "Santa Claus."

Today, it all sounds like a dreadfully old-fashioned Christmas. Today we have television. The modern child, I expect, will have to wake up with full make-up to the sight of cameras instead of the traditional Yule microphones. Probably have to rehearse for three solid weeks. We never rehearsed more than a couple of days.

The Pot and the Kettle
[OCTOBER 29, 1947]

BROADLY SPEAKING, Jimmy Fidler, "your Hollywood reporter," is against sin and, to somewhat lesser extent, in favor of virtue. About

80 per cent of Fidler's Sunday night broadcasts are concerned with divorce or shattered romances (he deplores them), Hollywood fist fights (he's shocked by them) and scandal of one sort or another of which he invariably disapproves. On the other hand, a marriage which has survived for any length of time wins his unqualified indorsement. He also approves wholeheartedly of actors who treat their aging mothers with civility. His approval of matrimony and motherhood occupies most of the other 20 per cent of his broadcasts.

Mr. Fidler's moral purposes are as intense as those of a small-town spinster and his methods are identical. He is, for example, strenuously opposed to Hollywood celebrities publicizing their misdeeds and he voices this disapproval (as well as a detailed account of the misdeeds) over two national networks every Sunday night.

"Open letter to Mark Stevens," he scolded recently in his high-pitched, rather prissy voice. "Dear Mark: Ever since the termination of your romance with Hedy Lamarr and your reconciliation with your wife, you've been indulging in public self-recrimination. You've declared to reporters that you made a fool of yourself, that you don't deserve a wife like Mrs. Stevens. . . . The point is will you let her forget? Certainly she can't if you continue parading your repentance in the newspapers." Mrs. Stevens, of course, will have even greater difficulty forgetting since Mr. Stevens's repentance was paraded before two or three million radio listeners. The difference between public self-recrimination and public recrimination is too delicate, I guess, to be understood anywhere outside Hollywood.

Fidler persistently scolds his fellow columnists for spreading scandal, unfortunately spreading it just a little farther in the process. "Columnists," he said recently, "who've been linking George Raft's name with that of Starlet —— (let's not spread it any farther) had better watch their step. (She's) married to a war vet who's attending college in Los Angeles." The word "link" has a special con-

The Pot and the Kettle

notation in Hollywood. Fidler wasn't linking the two names or unlinking them. He was merely disapproving the whole thing.

Fidler's intrusions on privacy are sometimes of so intimate a nature as to be astonishing to anyone outside the film capital. "Attention Mrs. Brian Aherne," he declared the other night in his mincing tones. "Your husband, who promised to stop flying airplanes, has kept his word but, holy smokes, he's now learning to fly glider planes." Presumably Mrs. Aherne didn't know.

Besides sin, Fidler has been crusading fervidly against Westbrook Pegler (who took a poke at him in a column not long ago) and against Hollywood Communism. His vitriolic campaign against the Soviet Union contrasts rather oddly with the singing commercial on the show, which is set to the tune of "The Song of the Volga Boatmen." Like a lot of gossip columnists Fidler widens his field occasionally to take in world problems. He takes his pronouncements on the international scene with extraordinary seriousness and phrases them almost as carefully as diplomatic communiqués: "Attention, please, to this editorial," he said the other night. "I am not in full accord with Walter Winchell's warnings of war."

Right now, Fidler is conducting his annual poll to determine "the most popular living man, woman or child in America." Since Fidler's listeners, particularly those who write him letters, are hardly representative of the nation, the poll indicates little except the dreamy set of values of the Fidler audience. At this writing, the leaders in the poll are in order: Bing Crosby, Frank Sinatra, Jackie Robinson, the Rev. Edward Flanagan of Boys Town, Neb., Eleanor Roosevelt, General Dwight D. Eisenhower, Al Jolson, General Douglas MacArthur, President Truman and Fulton Lewis Jr. Secretary of State George C. Marshall started out in seventh place but he lost ground steadily to Jolson and Robinson and last week slipped off the list entirely. He was replaced by Fulton Lewis Jr., whose solutions to world problems are easier to digest than the Marshall plan.

I don't know whether or not Mr. Fidler approves of this list but his stand on gossip is unequivocal. He's against it. Just the other night he sputtered with indignation about a girl who came back from Texas "and with an unprecedented show of bad taste announced the names of the six Texans whom she said had proposed to her."

"In my opinion," said Fidler stormily, "her tattletaling belongs precisely in the category with men who kiss and tell."

CHAPTER 2

Some Rich, Wonderful Personalities—from Woollcott to Victor Mature

Mature's Greatest Fight
[APRIL 18, 1950]

CECIL B. DE MILLE's great movie excess, "Samson and Delilah," which John Steinbeck reviewed succinctly in a single line ("Saw the movie. Loved the book"), contains one episode which has already attracted considerable well merited attention. That's the one where Victor Mature leaps out of a chariot in pursuit of a lion.

"You forgot your spear," Hedy Lamarr shouts at him.

"It's only a young lion," replies Mr. Mature, and forthwith dispatches it.

To you younger fight fans and even to some of you older ones who haven't followed Mr. Mature's fighting career, this bit may smell faintly incredible. The veterans among us who have watched the boy since his early days knew it was no contest to start out with. The lion never should have been matched against Mature. You wouldn't throw Willie Pep against Lee Savold, would you?

Me, I've been following Mature since way back when he was acting—well, appearing, then—in "1,000,000 B.C." which was loudly acclaimed on its first run as the worst motion picture ever made, anytime, anywhere. I consider that claim sweeping. There have been a great many motion pictures perpetrated since Thomas Alva Edison committed the error of inventing that terrible machine. I think it rash to elevate any single picture to such high honor. One of the ten worst, maybe. Not necessarily the worst.

Normally, pictures don't fall into my purlieu. (If you don't know what a purlieu is, you ought to be reading Nick Kenny. A purlieu, as any fool can easily discover by a trip to the dictionary, is afforested land, severed from the royal forest by perambulation, and disafforested so as to remit to the former owners their rights, subject to certain forest laws and restrictions. Let's press forward, men.)

I repeat. Normally, pictures don't fall into my purlieu. They fall, by perambulation, into the purlieu of the movie critics. However, there is a statute of limitations on these things. When a picture gets on television, the movie critics wash their hands of it. As far as "1,000,000 B.C." is concerned, the movie critics washed their hands of it the day it appeared, some of them washing their hands uninterruptedly for four days running. And anyhow, "1,000,000 B.C.," along with the other nine worst pictures ever made, is now on television, where, if you're sufficiently agile, you may catch the early fighting Mature. (If you want to refer to him as the immature Mature, go right ahead. But leave me out of it.)

He had three fights in this picture, all of them, if you're a student of the game, interesting. The first was with a saber-toothed buffalo, weighing in at 1,200 pounds. It was a great fight. The two of them, Mature and the buffalo, disafforested about half an acre of timber before Mature, in the first minute of the second round, severed the beast permanently from the royal forest.

You could tell the kid was green. He wouldn't keep his left up and his footwork was slow and uncertain. But he was game, aggressive and willing to learn. Trouble with the first fight was it made the kid cocky. He insisted next on a match with an elephant, weighing in at twelve tons and clearly out of his class. In the first ten seconds of the fight, the elephant pitched him 1,000 feet—straight down—into a river. The late Carole Landis had to wade out and rescue him.

That contest sobered him. He buckled down to serious work. His next time out he was matched—there were some pessimists like John Lardner who claimed he was over-matched—against a dinosaur. It was a fight that still brings a faraway look to the eyes of those few oldtimers who saw it. Outweighed, outreached, outclassed, Mature stayed in there punching, wore the beast down in the eighth and kayoed him in the tenth.

If Miss Lamarr had seen that battle, she never would have made that silly remark about the spear. She'd have shouted instead: "You come back here, you big bully, and leave that poor little lion alone."

He Was Too Good a Man to Be Sick
[OCTOBER 27, 1950]

I FIRST LEARNED of the death of Al Jolson in an afternoon paper, which carried the news in the left-hand column of Page 1. In the adjoining column were the late scratches from horse parks all over the country and I couldn't help thinking that Al would have glanced over the late scratches before he got to his own obituary.

He was an incurable horseplayer and a very good one. The last time I saw him he skipped up to me—Al never walked, he trotted, as if incessantly impatient to be somewhere else—and moaned in that odd speech of his wherein he managed to eliminate consonants almost entirely: "Nine'ee nine tuh one an' ah oney had twenney dollahs on dat hoss. Ah had dat hoss two mon's now but ah couldn' believe it. Nine'ee nine tuh one. Ah said 'Ah no. Nine-ee nine tuh one.'" The horse came in and paid $212 for $2 and Al couldn't forgive himself for winning only $2,120 when he could have made a killing.

I'll never forget the day Jolson took me to the races at Santa Anita. From his box, he held court to a throng that can only decently be described as motley. Movie executives, directors, movie stars, touts, race track attendants—they all stopped by from time to time and Al told jokes and passed out endless free advice on how to be a movie executive, director, movie star, tout or race track attendant —all in that booming voice that could be heard in the middle of the infield. You've never heard a horse rooted home unless you've heard Jolson bellow: "Come awn Bootstrap!" Of the 70,000 people booting home their horses in the stretch drive at Santa Anita, Jolson's, I'm convinced, was the only voice the horse could actually hear.

Jolson entered a horse park or a room or a stage or his own home with a skipping strut which automatically made heads turn. Even if you'd never heard of Jolson or never seen him, you would know that this was a person of importance. He was the most vibrant personality I've ever met on or off stage and he endowed every move, every utterance, with importance. It was fortunate that he could do this because, in his vivid stage career, he survived and even made hits out of some awfully cheesy musicals.

The moment Jolson walked on a stage, you got the impression that something terribly important was going to happen. Frequently, nothing important did happen but you kept feeling somehow that, in a minute or two, it would. Practically no one, except Ethel Merman, has that sort of vital stage presence in the theater any more.

Jolson belonged to a vanishing type in many ways. For one thing, he felt obligated to entertain all of the time—whether he was on a stage in front of 1,200 people or in a living room with three. Every time he walked out on the N. B. C. parking lot in Hollywood, it was a production number. The parking lot attendants drove up Jolson's car with a flourish that was missing on, say, Jack Benny's car. And while he was waiting, Al told stories and anecdotes for the benefit of the gas station attendants and out on the sidewalk a hundred or so people who apparently sprang out of the cement would press their noses to the wire and listen. It was quite a show.

"Who're you kidding?" declared Jolson when the end was drawing close and they were trying to tell him everything would be all right. "I've got no pulse." He was trying to get a laugh, even then, because a stage wait was unpardonable under any circumstances, including death. It wasn't the first time he'd joked about death. Once, he was driving down from Boston with Mitch Rawson and they passed a cemetery. "Some day," observed Jolson, "we ain' gonna pass." This time he didn't.

The newspapers said Al was sixty-four, but I don't know about that. He was palming himself off as sixty-four two years ago and there were grounds for suspicion even then that he was shaving off a year or so. I don't think anyone will ever know how old he was because I doubt whether Al knew. A couple years back, in St. Louis, I remember a teen-age girl—she was about sixteen—raving about this new singer, popularized by "The Jolson Story," called Al Jolson, whose albums were all the rage among her set. And I remembered wistfully that when I was sixteen I owned a Model-T Ford I called Jolson in honor of an actor who had just thrust talking moving pictures on the world by virtue of a movie called "The Jazz Singer." And sixteen years before "The Jazz Singer," he was nationally renowned as a stage comedian at the Winter Garden. And ten years before *that*, there was Jolson in Dockstader's Minstrels.

The end of his half-century career came without warning and the words used by director John Huston about the death of his father, Walter Huston, could very well be applied to Al: "He was too good a man to get sick. When the time came, he just died."

The '49 Model John J. Anthony
[FEBRUARY 25, 1949]

JOHN J. ANTHONY a new dynaflow 1949 model Anthony—is back on the air again after a rather longish pause for retooling. The former hack driver and eminent authority on agony has been missing quite a few years, which left an awful hole in radio. A girl who wanted to hear a little quiet suffering on the air was driven to soap opera which to your true connoisseur is synthetic stuff. For the real, honest, unexpurgated misery there wasn't anything like Anthony.

The '49 model Anthony, now edging toward fifty years, has a softer contour and more rounded lines than the old pre-war model though the inside of him is essentially the same. Anthony appears to have taken a course in benignity. He doesn't upbraid the petitioners as in the old days. ("What! You have been unfaithful to this woman!") More and more he lays the blame for their own frailty in the lap of God. Where in the old days he used to tell them to return to their husbands and stop playing around, he now invokes the assistance of God to straighten everything out. It's a full hour program and the Almighty, if He takes care of all these problems, is going to have His hands full.

Anthony, I should say, has as usual felt the pulse of the times and subtly changed his emphasis. "Good luck and God bless you," he told a woman the other night. The woman's husband had told her "in so many words" to get out. She was opposed to this project and had come to consult the good, gray, human relations counselor who is fully familiar with matrimonial problems, having spent some time thinking about it in alimony jail.

"Consult your pastor," he told the lady before dismissing her with that benign "God bless you."

A nineteen-year-old boy consulted him concerning his father who had suffered a heart attack and was now "in an institution." "You join with me in prayer," said Mr. Anthony. "Let's think about it hard. Let me hope and pray for you."

Years ago Anthony outraged all the recognized social agencies with his easy, unstudied and flippant solutions of the most complex problems of human relationship. Now he has escaped their jurisdiction by putting everything in the hands of the Deity where it's rather difficult to diagnose the results and sacrilegious to protest if there aren't any.

"The problem you present is really a prayer," he tells a mother who is worried about her truant son, "a prayer from a mother's heart."

Anthony, of course, is still working at the old stand of human suffering and he still can't quite prevent himself from smacking his lips with enthusiasm over an especially juicy case. He even gets this enthusiasm into the commercials which he rolls off his tongue sonorously, sanctimoniously and, at the same time, happily:

"We want you who suffer the agonies and tortures of arthritic pains to go to your druggist and ask for . . ." I didn't catch the name of the product. Something that gives "quick, lasting relief" from arthritis, which may surprise a great many doctors. Whatever it is you can't get it from God. That, at least, you have to get from the corner druggist.

Battle of Titans
[APRIL 10, 1950]

THERE LOOMS a financial struggle which threatens to eclipse the titanic battle between Jay Gould and Cornelius Vanderbilt for control of the Erie Railroad. Looms, hell. It's already on us, and any widows and orphans among you had better take to the hills. The issue is orange juice. The contestants are those two great financial typhoons—Bing Crosby and Arthur Godfrey. (A typhoon, junior, is a tycoon who sings. Then there's the buffoon, a tycoon who makes jokes. Like Bob Hope. What's a poltroon, you ask? Well, a poltroon is an eight-gaited comedian who sings, dances, makes jokes, makes faces, juggles, does high-wire acts, and makes a terrible amount of money. There's only one living poltroon—Milton Berle. For heaven's sake let's get on with this.)

The issue was joined last week when Arthur Godfrey, director and stockholder of the Hi V Corporation, makers of orange juice concentrate, took to the air for his—let's see now—third distinct and separate television show. He teaches the ukulele and merchandises, by a striking coincidence, orange juice. Way ahead of him in this business is Bing Crosby, director and heavy stockholder in Minute Maid, who sings and merchandises his brand of orange juice every morning. At least in New York he's on in the morning. Out of town you may find the program, which is transcribed, almost any time of the day or night.

Years ago, back in the Paleozoic Age when reptiles and radio comedians roamed the earth, a sponsor could procure the services of an entertainer by paying him, if you'll excuse the expression, money. Then there was a period, the Second Ice Age, when money was a joke. You offered a man money to appear on a radio program and he doubled up with laughter. Today, money has progressed—or, I suppose, degenerated is the word—even further. Money is no joke today. Money is an insult. To offer money to a comedian is like making derogatory remarks about his ancestry. Or even worse, about his ability.

The comedian wants stock in the enterprise. Or better yet, just turn the plant over to him and pay him dividends. Little by little the entertainers are going to wind up owning everything, like Rockefellers. The playboys of future generations won't be named Manville or Vanderbilt; they'll be Godfreys, Crosbys, Hopes and Jolsons. Inevitably, they'll start intermarrying like true aristocrats. You'll encounter names like Arthur Godfrey Crosby IV, of Sands Point, Deauville and Palm Beach. Arthur Godfrey Crosby IV will marry Hope Jolson, the most spectacular debutante of the year, daughter of Skelton von Bergen Jolson and great-great-granddaughter of *Al* Jolson, whose portrait hangs in the great hall of Aiken.

Well, let's stop wool-gathering.

The latest addition to Mr. Godfrey's empire is a fifteen-minute ukulele lesson. Godfrey has threatened to teach the nation how to play the ukulele for some time. He is now carrying out that threat.

The ukulele—this is for the benefit of the younger members of the class—is a stringed instrument which passed into what I consider a well-deserved obscurity for a number of excellent reasons twenty years or so ago. Godfrey's attempt to revive it strikes me as something like ordering the tide to recede. But you can't tell. Godfrey is a remarkable man. There is a body of opinion harbored by Arthur's more worshipful admirers that if it had been Godfrey instead of Canute, the tide *would* have receded.

Anyhow, the noted capitalist on this program strums his uke, explains basic finger movements, utters strong opinions about good ukes and bad ukes, which may cause a little consternation among ukulele manufacturers, and also demonstrates and drinks a little Hi-V orange juice. As a ukulele player, Arthur has twenty-one years of experience behind him and I suppose he is pretty good at it. I wouldn't know. I'm tone deaf to the charms of a ukulele.

Decades ago, popular myth held that a ukulele was potent courting equipment. My own experience never bore this out. The young blades in my vicinity considered a ukulele player no competition at all for the favors of young maidens. In fact, any one who couldn't elbow aside a ukulele player generally had some basic defect in his personality—like one eye in the middle of his forehead. However, we never ran up against Arthur Godfrey in these mating struggles.

The Coolest
[JANUARY 6, 1950]

DAVE GARROWAY, otherwise self-referred to as "the very low-pressure guy," "old tiger," and various other odd—or as he would probably say—incandescent labels, has made a fairly large splash on television. But N. B. C. also offers an awful lot of Garroway on radio, where you can sample the pure, undistilled Garroway.

The pure Garroway, I'm informed, is the embodiment of the bop movement. He is, as the bop crowd likes to describe it, a very cool guy. Or to put it in pure bop: "The coolest." The noun is unnecessary. The idea is to be as languid as possible about everything, and this is expressed by little shrugs, little liftings of eyebrows, and small flutterings of hands, by a general bonelessness both in physiognomy and in point of view. One must never get excited about anything. One must be terribly, terribly, terribly casual about everything and relaxed almost to the point of stupor.

This, if it's not too ambitious a word, is the philosophical basis for all the Garroway shows, both radio and television, and it must be admitted from the outset that this philosophy doesn't appeal to just everyone. A great many people are decidedly cool to this very cool guy. In Chicago, where Garroway first got his foot in the door and from which he still broadcasts his network shows, Garroway attracted many devout admirers. There were others—quite an impressive band too—who would like to wring his neck.

For this reason, I have small doubts that Garroway will ever win the popular acceptance of, say, Arthur Godfrey, which, it appears, is N.B.C.'s aim. He is a special taste, possibly a little fey for wide esteem. There have been visible efforts to tone him down, conceivably to avoid this charge. He once had an addiction for words like incandescent, tenuous, gruesome, serene, gauzy, protoplasmic, esoteric, hassel, carbohydrated, resilient. He used to address his listeners as "my lissome," "old delicate," "my translucent" and "my tawny." Of a singer he once remarked: "Listen how she holds that note and then she forces her hands around its throat and sort of shakes it."

There is a good deal less of this now, though Garroway still can't quite resist when some tenuous word wells up in his esoteric throat. "You'll find nothing big, nothing upsetting here," he tells his audience on his radio shows. The words, you'll note, are reasonably earthy; the philosophy is unchanged. Relax, kids. Nothing is worth getting excited about.

They are very quiet musical shows, featuring an instrumental quintet, a couple of singers—Connie Russell, who has one of those sex-starved voices, and Jack Haskell, about whom I don't appear to have anything at all in my notes—solos on various instruments and Mr. Garroway, his cool self. He engages more and more in philosophy of the mildest sort, little snippets of news that strike him as funny, and anecdotes about the cast.

Occasionally there are guests (Henry Morgan has been on a couple of times) and there are a lot of little novelty numbers, not all of which comes off. Restful is the word for it, I suppose. Incidentally, the origination of what might be described as the bop attitude stems way back to Bing Crosby, that very relaxed man, but it has traveled so far from its starting point that neither Mr. Crosby nor the bop addicts would recognize one another.

Just one other word about Mr. G., his philosophy and his pretensions. His hobby is automobiles. He owns five—a Jaguar, Model T, Lincoln Continental, Swallow and Rolls Royce. The Jaguar is upholstered in natural alligator, the Lincoln in Harris tweed. Mr. Garroway upholstered them himself.

Unemployed Actor
[DECEMBER 5, 1949]

HAD LUNCH with Fred Allen the other day to find out how it feels to be an unemployed actor. "I feel like God on the seventh day." He was chomping his customary lettuce leaf at his customary table at the Plaza. Allen has just had a bout of illness which has left him twenty pounds lighter. On him it looks good. (I ought to point out that this unemployment is voluntary. Fred, at the insistence of his doctors, is taking a year off.)

"It's wonderful, this freedom. You can live on the money you save on aspirin," he remarked cheerfully. "The only trouble is I keep thinking of jokes and I don't know what to do with them. I thought of one the other day. 'These days the *price* of coffee will keep you awake.' Well, that joke has been keeping me awake. I don't know what to do with it. I wish you'd take it off my hands."

He nodded pleasantly to a lady who had smiled at him from across the room. "I have to be very careful. My public has shrunk to such an extent that I have to be polite to all of them. I say hello to people in sewers. You know, I went off the air once before—back in 1944. We got three letters, deploring it. This time we're way ahead of that. I think we got fifteen. Man spends seventeen years in this business, trying to build it up, and he goes off the air and who cares? People still write me for tickets. They think I'm still on the air. I think they have me confused with Red Skelton. It makes a man bitter."

He chomped some more lettuce reflectively. "I had seventeen years. You don't even do that to land. You wouldn't plow the same land for seventeen years without giving it a rest. But radio does it to comedians.

"Anyhow, I'll be ready for the welfare state when it arrives—not working. Most of you working people will be terribly ill at ease for awhile, but I'll be used to it."

In spite of all this talk about retirement, Allen has a contract with N. B. C. which will restore him either to radio or put him on television next fall. He doesn't know which yet, but he thinks there's no point in thinking about radio any more. "They're cutting the budgets way down. With a small budget you can't put a show like mine on the air without reducing the standards you set for yourself."

Allen is one of the most rabid as well as one of the most critical of television fans. We turned to that. "You can make more money in bed than you can in television. They ought to turn the cameras on the stagehands. They make more money than the actors.

"When you see Kukla, Fran and Ollie come alive on that little screen, you realize you don't need great big things as we had in radio. They ought to get one of these African fellows over here to shrink all the actors. We're all too big for this medium.

"What gets me is why they haven't sold the Dave Garroway

show. Whoever does that show is turning out real television; he's creating something for television. Berle isn't doing anything for television. He's photographing a vaudeville act. That's what they're all doing.

"Even 'The Goldbergs,' which has been so well received, gets tiresome after you see it four or five times. You know what the uncle is going to do and you know what the kids are going to do.

"The trouble with television is, it's too graphic. In radio, even a moron could visualize things his way; an intelligent man, his way. It was a custom-made suit. Television is a ready-made suit. Every one has to wear the same one.

"Everything is for the eye these days—'Life,' 'Look,' the picture business. Nothing is for the mind. The next generation will have eyeballs as big as cantaloupes and no brain at all."

Allen has been trotting around sampling opinion on television in some effort to find out what people like. "I talked to the oysterman at Grand Central the other day," he remarked morosely. "He likes *everything* on television. Even Morey Amsterdam looks good after staring at oysters all day long.

"That's one of the reasons you don't have color television. You'd catch all the actors blushing at the things they have to say. One thing I can't understand—all this advertising of television sets *on* television. If you see the ad, you already own a television set.

"We all have a great problem—Benny, Hope, all of us. We don't know how to duplicate our success in radio. We found out how to cope with radio and, after seventeen years, you know pretty well what effect you're achieving. But those things won't work in television. Jack Benny's sound effects, Fibber's closet—they won't be funny in television. We don't know what will be funny or even whether our looks are acceptable."

He nodded to another fan across the room. "Middle-aged," he commented. "I notice all the people who come up to me are middle-aged. No kids. I've played to three generations on radio and in show business. Now I've got to grapple with a fourth."

A Promising Young Singer
[MARCH 9, 1951]

I WAS ONE of the 10,000,000 or so Americans privileged to hear the professional debut of Margaret Truman with the Detroit Symphony Orchestra March 16, 1947, which was broadcast over the American Broadcasting Company. Miss Truman was discreetly introduced then as a young American soprano from Washington who was born in Missouri.

It was the policy of the Detroit Symphony Orchestra, declared the announcer, to encourage promising young American singers and that, he implied, was why Miss Truman was there. There was no mention of the fact that Miss Truman lived at 1600 Pennsylvania Avenue or that it was a Page 1 story or that some fifty newspaper men were sent to Detroit to cover the debut of this promising young singer from Washington.

Miss Truman then stepped to the microphone and delivered herself of "Cielito Lindo" and "The Last Rose of Summer" in a voice which appeared to lack any inherent sweetness and which she had great trouble controlling. She was repeatedly off pitch and, though she was reputed to possess a range of three octaves, there was considerable uncertainty in the lower registers and decided evidences of strain in the upper ones. In general, the critics sidestepped the voice, praised Miss Truman for her poise and charm on-stage and reserved judgment.

That was four years ago. Since then, Miss Truman's voice has become a sort of national joke, a little too thoroughly exploited in "Call Me Madam"; she has been on scores of concert stages, has turned out an album of folk songs and may earn (according to "Time") pretty close to $100,000 this year. Altogether, it's quite a success story.

Meanwhile, the reticence which cloaked her first radio appearance has almost vanished. Last Sunday, on her second appearance

A Promising Young Singer

on "The Big Show," there was no effort made to conceal Miss Truman's identity and the promising young coloratura flung herself with relish into a blizzard of Truman jokes.

"You'll be making more money than the President of the United States," said Tallulah.

"A vocalist always makes more than the accompanist," riposted Miss Margaret. It's an old, old joke and she handled it with the reverence it deserves. She went on to bandy about other political jokes with Fred Allen, Frankie Laine, Herb Shriner and Ethel Merman, displaying a comedy technique which might be described as early Independence church supper.

She also sang and it's rather a pity she struck a night on which N. B. C. paraded some of the best female singers in the game. On "The Big Show" was Ethel Merman, one of the truest singers anywhere around. Later, on a televised salute to Richard Rodgers, you could hear Mary Martin and Dorothy Maynor, both real pros. In the middle came Miss Truman, filling the Center Theater with odious comparisons. The defects in the voice observed four years ago are still there and perhaps a little worse. Miss Truman still can't seem to hit a note anywhere near the center; the voice is harsh, thin and uninteresting and still gets into grave troubles in the upper registers.

I just can't help thinking Miss Truman got on "The Big Show" because she's the President's daughter, a thought which has probably never occurred to anyone else—especially the people at N. B. C. who booked her. But who, I keep asking myself, is being exploited in this deal? Miss Truman? Well, in light of that $100,000 a year, you can hardly say she's being victimized. The people of the United States? They keep flocking to her concerts, paying good hard money to get in, and, as Miss Truman herself has remarked, no one has thrown anything yet.

The critics are still being extraordinarily kind. I doubt that even Mr. Hume, who got that Famous Letter, said what was really on his mind. It's a wonderfully polite country, America, full of infinite possibilities. Any boy can grow up to be President and any girl can grow up to be his daughter. Whatever else you can say about Miss Truman, she has fulfilled that early promise rather too well.

Food, Food Everywhere and Not a Bite to Eat
[JANUARY 15, 1951]

THE OTHER NIGHT on the Stork Club Show, Sarah Churchill, Winston's daughter, was observed munching a stalk of celery. This is a clear violation of tradition on that show and the camera hurriedly turned its back as if it had caught Miss Churchill shoplifting. Every night on that program, clams, shrimps, soups, oysters, grapefruit— all swathed in ice and silverware and expensive crockery—are laid before thirty or forty people who look over it, or around it or through it and never, never touch it. I don't know what penalty Miss Churchill can expect for molesting the celery. Deportation, I expect.

The greatest star on television these days, if anyone should ask you, is not Milton Berle or Hopalong Cassidy or Howdy Doody. It is food. The food programs start very early in the morning with Kitchen Kapers and go on all day long—Dione Lucas' cooking course, W.N.B.T.'s Cooking Show, Betty Crocker, Susan Adams' Kitchen, Shop, Look and Cook and about a million others scattered from New York to San Francisco. When the homemakers aren't preparing Turtles à la Rimbaud for the benefit of a lot of owl-eyed housewives who wouldn't cook a turtle if it committed suicide in their own frying pans, then we all move over to the restaurants for Luncheon at Sardi's, Dinner at Sardi's, the Stork Club and the other high-class joints.

But no one ever eats anything. The homemakers occasionally taste a truffle; they don't eat it. At Luncheon or Dinner at Sardi's, they dispense with the silly stuff entirely; they don't even set the table at Sardi's. On television food is something to be purchased, cooked, admired and displayed in the most elaborate settings. It is only eating that has been dispensed with as a waste of time.

Eating has been eschewed—eschew your food thoroughly, junior—in favor of conversation. Or what passes for conversation. The best eschewing, for my money, is done at the Stork Club where Sherman Billingsley, "the world's most fabulous host," has already acquired renown as the world's most fabulous interviewer. Mr. Billingsley's equipment as an interviewer consists of great ignorance of most of the subjects he's talking about, an immense thirst for knowledge—especially on how much everyone earns—and a surprising lack of tact for so noted a restaurant-keeper.

Since a man's income is generally considered a private matter, most of the victims squirm as if they were on the witness stand when Mr. Billingsley gets prying into their affairs. He has at various times asked a couple of models how much money they earned in a good week, a magazine editor the highest price he paid for a story and a very social lady how much the debutantes paid to get into a charity ball for the New York Infirmary. It's difficult to determine which of these was the most reluctant to divulge this financial information. My nod goes to the magazine editor who will now have to explain to all his other magazine writers why they don't get paid equally well.

The art of interviewing people has been unskillfully practiced on television from the very first, the emphasis being on the looks rather than the brains of the interviewer. Mr. Billingsley appears to be innocent of all knowledge of the people he talks to. Talking to Celeste Holm one night, he asked her when "Affairs of State" could be expected to open. "It's been running for six weeks," Miss Holm informed him. Miss Holm then fell to discussing her long-running vehicle, "Oklahoma!" "Oklahoma!" exclaimed Mr. B. "I came from there, too." Miss Holm told him she was talking about a musical comedy. I'm afraid Mr. Billingsley doesn't listen very carefully to the answers to his own questions. And, if he doesn't care, why should you and I?

If this is the best conversation that can be wrung from the glittering array of writers, prizefighters, politicians and actresses that pass through the Stork Club, then I'm for turning the whole idea upside down. Let's cut out all the talk and fall to. There might be a good deal of entertainment value in watching Virginia Mayo tackle a stonecrab. I'd like to observe her technique with those animals and see if she gets as wet as I do. I'd like to see Jim Farley wrestle with a squab and Gladys Swarthout up to her elbows in an artichoke.

Let's, in short, restore eating to restaurant life. I thought that was the reason for going into them in the first place.

"This Is Woollcott Speaking" . . .
[FEBRUARY 3, 1950]

FOR NO REASON WHATEVER, except that I had nothing else to do, I fell to musing today about that waspish, sentimental, corpulent enthusiast, Alexander Woollcott, whose spinsterish and extraordinarily self-confident voice has been missing from the air since his death just seven years ago. I keep wondering what he's up to in the wherever. Lunching with the more august Seraphim, I expect. Ignoring the humbler folk, the Cherubim. Spinning his improbable tales about some celestial dog who found his way clear across heaven to the master who once housed him on earth.

"And before I forget, let me pass on something I've just heard—the sequel to a story I told in one of these fireside chats back in April. Maybe I could best recall that story if I first reported something told me by my friend and neighbor, Katherine Cornell—something she witnessed this time a year ago with her own eyes—eyes filled with unshed tears."

That fragment, from Woollcott's broadcast of June 24, 1937, is typical of the Woollcott style—untidy, archaic, rambling but strangely musical. It's also typical of the Woollcott content. You get the hint of wonder to come, the casual mention of a "friend and neighbor" who happens to bear a very famous name, and—above all, above all—those unshed tears.

There isn't any one approaching Woollcott on the air today. If there were I doubt that he'd survive. Woollcott became entrenched in the earlier days when radio was more receptive to individualists. He went his own way without fear of sponsors or Hooper. And, of course, you can't do that any more. Even at this late date, his scripts are conspicuously individualist, sometimes enchanting, frequently infuriating but always Woollcott.

"Albert was a costly and preposterous Airedale who had been laboriously taught to assault all suspicious-looking strangers. In fact, at the kennels where he was born and bred, one of the underprivileged was engaged for a small weekly wage just for Albert to practice on."

I'm a little mistrustful of that statement but it is the sort of thing that would fascinate Woollcott. He was helplessly addicted to the practice of endowing dogs with the frailties and temperament of mankind. Of his own dog, Duchess, for example: "Considered as a one-man dog, she's a flop. In her fidelity to me, she's a little too much like that girl in France who was true to the 26th Infantry."

His recollections of himself and of others were tempered by an incurably romantic mind and came forth, as it were, lamplit and in pastel shades, with the facts scrupulously rearranged to meet the requirements of style rather than, as most of us do, the other way around. "Personally, I was the teacher's pet type," he would say, "and couldn't pass a school without pausing to matriculate. I went to one academy or another for seventeen mortal years. And never late once.

"One day last summer, I rather boasted of that record. There were three of us swimming slowly across the lake and I just happened to mention that in seventeen years I was never once late at school. I shall always remember how this simple statement of fact affected my companions. They tried to drown me."

Woollcott had the essayist's gift of wandering from hell to breakfast in a single script and still of giving the illusion he was sticking to a single anecdote. His broadcast of July 1, 1937, for example, was ostensibly about the leper colony at Molokai, another of his aggressive enthusiasms. It started, of all places, in Vermont. Somewhere along the route of this story about lepers in the distant Pacific, Woollcott worked in the information that Vermont had declared its independence of the British fourteen years before the rest of the country got around to it, that the Vikings had a custom of tossing an arrow in the air and the way it fell upon the ground pointed the direction their younger sons were to set sail to seek their fortune, and that a memorial to Brigham Young—how he got in there, I'll never know—bears the rather wonderful inscription: "Brigham Young. Born on this spot 1801. A man of much courage and superb equipment."

The personality—fierce, witty, petty, pretentious, unquenchably curious—still hovers over all these old scripts, these old Woollcottian anecdotes. There is no commentator on the air today who has such a rich, personal flavor. It's a pity, too.

CHAPTER 3

Here Come the Clowns

On Not Listening to the Radio
[JULY 19, 1946]

HAVE YOU EVER tried not listening to a radio? You can't do that simply by keeping the darn thing quiet all day. The type of non-listening I refer to is a conscious, deliberate, active experience. The pleasure you can get from turning off a radio doesn't approach the bliss of not turning it on in the first place.

In fact, to wander a little, a taste for not doing things is a sophisticated, though perverse, form of enjoyment which everyone should cultivate in this age of mass production. There are too many books, too many movies, and many, many too many radio programs. You can't keep up with them all but you can derive a very real satisfaction from missing some of them.

There are dozens of movies I enjoy not seeing. Some authors, notably Taylor Caldwell, affect me the same way. I am so fond of not reading Miss Caldwell's novels that I buy all of them and prominently display them in my apartment. I doubt if any of Miss Caldwell's fans ever enjoyed her books quite so much as I have enjoyed not reading them. If they weren't around the apartment, I might forget not to read them.

You see, enjoyment of not doing things takes a certain amount of effort and considerable arranging. For instance, the best way to enjoy not playing tennis is to lie on a bit of greensward and watch a couple of other people tear around a tennis court. Not all negative pleasures are that restful. Enjoyment in not staying sober, for example, is a very strenuous pastime.

Of all the things I enjoy not doing, not listening to the radio is my favorite. By the nature of this job I have to do a great deal of listening, much of which is plain hard work. Now and then, to regain my sanity and to recapture the point of view of the ordinary listener, I take a day off.

Yesterday was one of those azure days which your true non-listener waits for in order to extract the fullest measure of enjoyment from his non-listening. There are several different ways not to listen to a radio. One of the most violent non-listeners I know, an eccentric fellow in lots of ways, carries a portable radio around with him all day long and never turns it on. I find this cumbersome. My own method is to carry around the radio listings in my side pocket. Occasionally, when I find myself forgetting, I glance down the list to see what program I'm missing at that moment.

Some programs are more fun not to listen to than others. For your non-listening pleasure I recommend "Stella Dallas," "Portia Faces Life" and my old friend Gabriel Heatter. I imagine no two persons would have the same list of favorites, but I think everyone should have his collection of radio programs he takes pleasure in avoiding.

There are dozens of nice spots in New York to spend your non-listening day. The Stork Club, the Metropolitan Museum of Art, Central Park—I've tried them all and found them all stimulating in their different ways. Stay out of Third Avenue saloons because they keep the radio on all day long. Incidentally, if you go to the Metropolitan Museum, you might try not looking at "Death Stays the Hand of the Sculptor," a piece of statuary the avoidance of which is high on my assortment of negative pleasures.

Yesterday I passed most of my non-listening day in Central Park with my nephew and niece, Cork and Cricket Crosby, aged six and four respectively, who are already very expert at not listening to the radio. The kids fed a squirrel and I read the radio listings. Cork and Cricket, by the way, patronize a squirrel who is related on his mother's side to the one Heywood Broun once flipped a nickel to and then told to go buy his own peanuts.

"Did you ever listen to John J. Anthony?" I asked Cork.

" ? ," said Cork.

"Well, never mind. He's on the air right now, probably telling some woman to go back to her husband and stop playing around with other men."

"What's the squirrel's name?" inquired Cricket.

"Art Linkletter," I said. "Call him Artie for short."

Unexpectedly, the squirrel raced away. Whether he was affronted by the name or had his fill of peanuts I cannot say.

Breakfast with Freddie and Tallulah
[MAY 10, 1946]

LAST SUNDAY, Fred Allen, who has eyes like Venetian blinds and a tongue like an adder, teamed up with Miss Tallulah Bankhead, a scorpion in her own right, in a parody on the "husband and wife" breakfast programs so coruscating that, according to "Variety," it has brought loud complaints from the husband and wife performers. These programs have been parodied before, but never with the explosive violence that radio's greatest wit applied to them. So cutting was Mr. Allen's satire that many of the injured parties have requested permission of N. B. C. to hear a transcription of the program, under the theory they couldn't have heard aright the first time.

To give you a specimen of Mr. Allen's sharp mind and also as a commentary on the breakfast programs themselves, I present below a condensed version of the Allen-Bankhead parody, which seems destined to become something of a radio classic. Take it away, Freddie and Tallulah!

FRED: Ahhhh! What coffee! What aromatic fragrance! It must be. . . .

TALLULAH: You're right, lovey! It's McKeester's Vita-Fresh Coffee. The coffee with that locked-up goodness for everybody —grind or drip. . . . Peach fuzz, you've spilled some on your vest.

FRED: Goody. Now I can try some of that Little Panther Spot Remover. No rubbing.

TALLULAH: And, imagine, a big two-ounce bottle for only 35 cents.

FRED: Or, if you are a messy eater, you can get the handy, economical forty gallon vat. . . . Your hair is breath-taking. That sheen! That brilliance! What did you do to it?

TALLULAH: I just did what so many society women are doing these days. I went to Madame Yvonne's Hair-Do Heaven at 424 Madison Avenue—in the loft.

FRED: It's divine, bunny fluff.

TALLULAH: Madame Yvonne uses a sensational hair-dressing. It contains that new mystery ingredient—chicken fat.

FRED: I hear it's on sale at all the cut-rate cigar stores. (Jasha, the canary, twitters.)

TALLULAH: Ah, little Jasha is so happy, so carefree. And why shouldn't he be happy.

FRED: Yes, he knows that the newspaper on the bottom of his bird cage is New York's leading daily, "The Morning Record"— thirty-two columnists, eighteen pages of comics, and all the news no other newspaper sees fit to print.

TALLULAH: Excuse me, apple honey. I have a letter here from Mrs. T. S. Button, of Molehole, Idaho. Mrs. Button had a splitting headache for forty years until she heard about Pepso-Bepto on our program.

FRED: Only Pepso is guaranteed to fizz twice. Once before you drink it and once after.

TALLULAH: Here's another interesting letter—from a kleptomaniac. She writes. . . .

CHILD'S VOICE: Good morning, mumsy and daddy.

FRED: Why, it's our little three-year-old daughter, Amber.

TALLULAH: Isn't she cute? Amber, I just love the way your tooth is shining this morning.

AMBER: Yes, I brushed it with Dr. Pratt's Homogenized Toothpaste.

FRED: Ha. Ha. Ha.

TALLULAH: What are you laughing at, love duck?

FRED: I just thought how witty Oscar Levant was last night when he poured that bottle of catsup over Jim Farley's head.

TALLULAH: And wasn't Mr. Farley a good sport? He just sat there grinning and smacking his lips.

FRED: You, too, will smack your lips if you taste Klotnick's concentrated catsup—the only catsup that bears "The Hobo News" seal of approval.

After a bit more of this cheerful patter Fred and Tallulah decided to put a little realism into their early-morning conversation. On one of their grouchy mornings the program sounds like this:

TALLULAH: Hey, knucklehead, get out of that bed! We've got a program to do.

FRED: Six o'clock in the morning. Who's up to listen to us—a couple of garbage collectors and some burglars?

TALLULAH: If you want to go back to hustling gardenias in front of Childs, go right ahead. (Jasha twitters.)

FRED: Shut up! I thought I told you to give that canary some of Dr. Groober's Bird Seed.

TALLULAH: I did. Now Jasha is the only canary in the country with an ulcer.... What's in the mail today, chowderhead?

FRED: A summons. Someone took that Pepso-Bepto and dropped dead. Where do you find these sponsors—at a police line up?

AMBER: Good morning, mummy and daddy! (Allen slaps her and she howls.)

FRED: Sneaking up on your parents with that one tooth like an old elk. Little Amber!

TALLULAH: I told you we should have finished reading the book before we named her.

I'm afraid our time is up, as they say on the air. There was lots more of it and it was all hilarious. It was also perhaps a little too unkind to the husbands and wives who slave away at these programs morning after morning for only $2,500 a week. Some time soon, I shall discuss the breakfast programs in milder tones.

Duffy Ain't Here
[OCTOBER 13, 1948]

ED GARDNER, of "Duffy's Tavern" has restored to honorable estate the comedy of insult, a sadistic form of amusement which has enjoyed great favor since the days of Elizabeth. Not that insult does not flourish elsewhere on the air; it's just that Archie and the rest of the crew at that wonderful saloon insult one another with more authority, with greater sweep and with infinitely more imagination than anyone else in the business.

Take the opening show of "Duffy's Tavern," for example. Archie, returning from a vacation at Frenchie Mandelbaum's Irish Inn in the Catskills, brought with him some momentous news, romantic news. "I met a girl this summer," he confided to Eddie, the weary and cynical waiter of the saloon, "and I'll tell you something. I'm an expectant millionaire."

Eddie expressed polite skepticism and Archie drew out a picture of the girl. However, he seemed reluctant to let Eddie look at it without prior explanation and apology. "Please bear in mind," said Arch with a deprecatory cough, "she's got a couple of million bucks. She's awfully good to her mother. Whaddaya think of her?"

Eddie stared at the picture silently for quite a while. "Who you got in the World Series?" he said finally.

"That's no answer. Whaddaya think?"

"I'll take Cleveland."

"Well," said Archie defensively, "anyone can fall in love with a beautiful girl, but to fall in love with a girl like this takes a certain avariciousness. I'll never forget the night we met. Our eyes met and then I knew."

"You knew what?" asked Eddie.

"She was the ugliest human being I ever met."

Finnegan, a stupid but lovable habitué of Duffy's, stepped in at this point. He had spent the summer working at Coney Island, his head stuck through a canvas, dodging baseballs. "It was a little unusual this summer," he explained. "Behind me they threw darts."

Finnegan and Miss Duffy, the sex-starved daughter of the proprietor, both inspected the picture of Arch's lady love and expressed a low opinion. "Fine thought," snorted Arch to Miss D., "from a dame that hangs around draft boards waiting for rejects."

"What's the matter with a guy with flat feet?" inquired Miss Duffy loftily.

"Nothing. Except our country's standards are higher than yours."

Then there entered a man whose personality is diametrically opposite to that of Arch but who is just as adroit with insults. Clifton Webb, it was. "Look at them clothes," said Arch in admiration. "The height of sartorialism. Not a stitch out of place. Clifton, you could drop dead and they wouldn't have a thing to do." He introduced Webb to the permanent staff of hangers-on.

"I've seen him before," exclaimed Finnegan. "Wasn't he in the window at Fourteenth Street?"

Webb didn't think much of Finnegan either. "What did this person have on his parents to make them bring him up?" he asked icily.

As for Miss Duffy, Webb refused to believe such a thing existed, in spite of the evidence of his own eyes. Miss Duffy, who has easily the toughest hide in radio, was flattered by this scientific observation and regretted she couldn't stick around longer.

"I'm off to the beauty parlor," she explained.

"Don't take no for an answer," said Webb politely. "Where'd they dig her up?" he asked when she disappeared. "Navy surplus," said Arch, dismissing her. "Look, Clifton. . . ." Rather fearfully he handed the actor the picture of his betrothed.

Webb's reaction again was frank incredulity. "Well," said Arch apologetically, "up there in the moose country she didn't look so bad. She's got two million dollars."

Webb handed the picture back. "It's not enough."

Third Avenue in Puerto Rico
[OCTOBER 14, 1949]

"DUFFY'S TAVERN" is, according to the opening announcement, "brought to you by the Blatz Brewing Company, of Milwaukee." It concerns, as if you didn't know, a saloon on Third Avenue in Manhattan. It is written by a number of characters who normally eke out their pitiful existences in the vicinity of Hollywood and Vine Street. And it is transcribed in Puerto Rico.

This geographical confusion sprang from the immense reluctance of Ed Gardner, the proprietor of Duffy's, to pay any more taxes than he has to. Gardner has gathered in more than his share of the world's wealth in the last couple of years and handed most of it over to the Federal government. In Puerto Rico he enjoys a twelve-year tax holiday which was declared by the government in order to attract industry to the island. Instead of industry, the island got Ed Gardner, which isn't precisely what it had in mind. I don't entirely understand the twelve-year tax holiday, which exempts Gardner from some but not all Federal taxes, and I don't think anyone else does except Gardner. In the matter of money Gardner is very, very sharp as well as very, very acquisitive.

Gardner's Puerto Rican adventure has already drawn a bleat of anguish from at least one Congressman, Representative Noah M. Mason (Rep., Ill.), who included Gardner among a number of "tax-dodgers who are continuing their raids on the Treasury" and asked Congress to close these loopholes in the tax laws. Meanwhile, Gardner continues to bask in the warm sun of his particular loophole and to turn out a show that is in a class by itself.

I was fearful Mr. Gardner's characters, a weird assemblage of humanity if ever there was one, might mellow under the Caribbean sun. They haven't, though. The denizens of Duffy's still resemble Third Avenue characters as much as they ever did, which isn't very much. Gardner is a sort of Charles Addams of his particular medium. He has invented a little underworld—or perhaps subworld is more expressive—which resembles nothing in human experience very closely. On the whole, it's just as well.

The exchanges between Gardner, or Arch, as he is known, and Finnegan are still among the most wonderful specimens of sheer nonsense on the air. Here is a sample:

ARCH: What are you doing with them two candles stuck in your ears?

FINNEGAN: Eh? I'm sorry, Arch, I can't hear yah. I got two candles stuck in my ears.

ARCH: Well, take 'em out.

FINNEGAN: Eh?

ARCH: Take 'em out.

FINNEGAN: I'm sorry, Arch. I can't hear yah. I got two candles stuck in my . . .

ARCH: Well, read my lips.

FINNEGAN: Okay, go ahead.

ARCH: Take-those-two-candles-out-of-your-ears.

FINNEGAN: I'm sorry, Arch. I just remembered. I can't read.

(Arch removes the candles himself.)

ARCH: How come you had two candles stuck in your ears?

FINNEGAN: Well, I was standin' waist deep in water. Where else could I put 'em?

Don't ask me why Finnegan was standing waist deep in water. You get to arguing with Finnegan and you find yourself in a trackless forest. There is a new Miss Duffy, the tenth, I believe, in a role that, it sometimes seems, goes all the way back to the McKinley Administration. The new Miss Duffy, Gloria Erlanger, who took over from Florence Halop, needs seasoning. The rest of the show is as highly seasoned as ever.

The Aces Are Back
[MARCH 29, 1948]

GOODMAN ACE, one of the few genuine wits in radio and one of the veterans, is back in business again with a new show called "mr. ace and JANE," an arrangement of capital and lower case letters which spells out pretty well who ranks whom in the Ace family. The new program differs from the old Easy Aces in about the same manner as the new and old "Amos 'n' Andy" programs. It's once a week, half hour, streamlined up to date, and very, very funny.

Jane Ace is another Dulcy, another Irma, another Gracie Allen, another Mrs. Malaprop, though in her defense it ought to be added she got there ahead of most of them. She is a woman of sunny amiability who takes an extremely literal and subjective view of everything around her. This makes life very easy for her and extremely difficult for everyone else. When, for example, she is told she is to be a member of a jury, she declares heatedly, "I'll say he's not guilty, whoever he is. If he's nice enough to pay me three dollars a day to be his jury, the least I can do is recuperate, doesn't it to you?"

There are a lot of Malaprops in radio but none of them scrambles a cliché quite so skillfully as Jane. In fact, many of Jane's expressions are great improvements on the originals. "He shot out of here like a bat out of a belfry," "The coffee will be ready in a jitney," "I'm really in a quarry," "this hang-nail expression," "the crank of dawn"—those are a few of her improvements.

In most other respects Jane is a rather difficult conversationalist because she is either three jumps ahead or three long strides behind the person she is conversing with.

"Hi, Jane," an acquaintance will call out. "What have you been doing?"

"Just fine, thanks," says Jane.

Goodman Ace, the brains of this team, tags along behind his wife acting as narrator for her mishaps in a dry, resigned voice (one of the few intelligent voices on the air) and interjecting witty comment. The couple's conversations are usually masterpieces of cross-purpose.

"Dear, I've just done the most terrible thing I've ever done in all the years we've been married and seven months," his wife is likely to tell him. "I was talked into it by someone I should have known better. In other words yes."

While most of the action revolves around the scrapes Jane gets into, Ace, who writes the scripts, uses his program to take a few pokes at radio, the newspapers and the world in general. He's particularly sharp on the subject of radio, a field he knows intimately. Once, playing the role of an advertising man, he asked a prospective sponsor what sort of radio program he had in mind. "How about music?" asked Ace.

"Music? That's been done, hasn't it?" said the sponsor.

In addition to the Aces there are a number of other strange people hanging around, each with his special obsession. Bobby, a young newsboy, has stopped handling "The Sun" because he disagrees with its editorial policy and refuses a career in radio because he doesn't want to boost a competing advertising medium. (Bobby, I suspect, pretty well sums up Ace's ideas on all newspaper men.) Jane's brother, Paul, hasn't worked for twelve years "because he's waiting for the dollar to settle down," and primly objects to the use of four-letter words in front of his sister, especially "work."

There's also an announcer named Ken Roberts whose function is to kid all the commercials on the air. Here's a sample of a Roberts commercial: "Fifty years ago Blycose began selling the public its high-quality products and today, just as it was fifty years ago, it is March 20."

The real sponsor for the Ace show is the United States Army recruiting service and after President Truman's message to Congress urging re-enactment of the draft, Ace remarked blithely that he was the only comedian in radio for whom the President did the commercials.

The Comedian and the Cause
[DECEMBER 18, 1950]

THERE WAS a scurrilous rumor going around the corridors that Milton Berle has become sufferable. This was belatedly investigated and can now be pronounced a base canard. Uncle Miltie—the man, not the horse—has made spirited attempts the last year or so to become lovable, which would involve a personality change almost as profound as that of Dr. Jekyll. He hasn't quite made it, though beads of perspiration stand out all over him in the attempt.

This essay at lovableness has been made in various ways. For one thing, Mr. Berle has even gone so far as to keep himself out of other people's acts from time to time, something I never thought I'd live to see. Don't pay any attention to the gossip that four men have to thrust him into a straitjacket to keep him off the stage. I understand it only takes two men. More importantly, though, Uncle Miltie has adopted the children of America as his special province. What the G. I. is to Bob Hope, what charity drives are to Eddie Cantor, childhood is to Uncle Miltie.

That makes Uncle Miltie a target almost as difficult to hit as the Germans around Cassino. Artillerymen couldn't hit the Germans without hitting the monastery. Children, charity and G. I.'s are all sacred subjects. By wrapping themselves in these sacrosanct vestments, the comedians become almost immune to criticism. Criticize Berle and you're against childhood. One word about Hope and you're hindering the war effort.

In the cases of Mr. Berle, Mr. Hope, and Mr. Cantor, I hasten to say they are all very likely dominated only by the highest motives. However, the public ought to be warned that *some* comedians have been pushed into embracing lofty causes of one sort or another by agents whose concern with, say, the suppression of snakebite is entirely a matter of money. Most agents are privately very much in sympathy with snakebite, being more or less in that profession themselves. Publicly, though, they're against it, knowing by instinct that this is a popular stand.

When one of their properties, as comedians are known in the trade, faces starvation through lack of employment, a livewire agent may take the property aside and say: "Look, stupid, we must embrace a cause. We must be against something. Or we must be for something." He then explains as delicately as possible what a snake is, most comedians thinking that a snake has two feet and inhabits the upper floors of the R. C. A. Building.

Presently you'll find the comedian ending his program with a one-minute attack on snakehood. And send the two dollars to the Anti-Snake League, a new organization of which the comedian is honorary chairman. The public instantly perceives that Joe Schmaltz is not only very skillful at pratfalls but is also a civic-minded individual whose pratfalls it is now a public duty to witness. It is not only a public duty to witness these pratfalls but all right-minded citizens should laugh at them or they will be suspected of being secretly in sympathy with snakebite.

Well, it's a fairly harmless, though hardly disinterested, game and it raises a couple of bucks to combat snakes. The trouble is that there are only so many causes and most of them have been gobbled up long ago by other comedians. Motherhood was pretty well retired from the lists by Al Jolson. Bob Hope owns the G. I.'s. Cancer, heart disease, Communism have all been spoken for.

That left little except childhood for Mr. Berle, who came to the feast late. It wasn't the happiest choice but it was just about the only one. Emotionally, psychologically, every way, Berle and childhood seem antipathetic. Even on my ten-inch screen, Berle regards the children and the children regard Berle with what appears to be ill-concealed distrust. Both, I think, have good reason. In our family, we use Uncle Miltie as a threat. If the little so-and-so doesn't go to bed this minute, we'll make him look at Milton Berle. That sends him, scampering.

But after Berle, what? There aren't any four-square causes left. A comedian can't take on any controversial causes. He couldn't take sides on, say, the Brannan plan, even if he could understand it, which is doubtful. It's got to be as incontestable as the Bible. And there isn't much left. No, you can't take over fatherhood, either. That belongs to Bing Crosby.

The Mechanical Joke
[JANUARY 3, 1951]

LIKE TO SAY a few words about comedy. On television as on radio, it has become mechanized and it will become increasingly unfunny as we get deeper into the topical joke, the Harry Truman or "something to write Hume about" joke.

It has always seemed to me that the essence of comedy, the best of it, was the imminence of tragedy. There was a very funny cartoon in "The New Yorker" a little while ago which showed a theater usher opening a door to the outer lobby and saying: "Curtain going up for the second act. Curtain going. . . ." There was no one there. It's only after the laughter subsides that you realize it's a rather sad situation. Another funny cartoon showed a drowning man shouting "Au secours! Au secours!" A couple of bystanders were casually watching him and one of them said: "If he's not a Frenchman he's certainly an awful snob."

Disaster almost always lurks in the center of a comic situation. Some of the wittiest and certainly the most memorable bits of comic invention have come from wars which are not essentially comic. The most famous cartoon from the first World War was Bruce Bairnsfather's drawing of two Cockneys in a water-filled shell-crater with bullets whistling all around: "If yer knows of a better 'ole, go to it." In World War II, it was Bill Mauldin who made the country laugh with the imminence of death. A cartoon, for example, of a medic lighting a match in the dark for all the world and the enemy to see, remarking: "It's all right, fellows. I'm a noncombatant." At least one of the reasons Mr. Mauldin couldn't duplicate his war success in civilian life is simply that civilian life is less hazardous, less tragic.

The greater the hazard, the more trenchant the wit. No one has ever quite equaled the Marine captain in Belleau Wood with his famous remark to his men: "Come on, you sons of bitches. You wanna live forever?" Harold Lloyd, one of the greatest of our comedians, made a profession and a fortune from skirting perils of one sort or another. But the greater perils provoked the greater laughter. The possibility of his dress suit coming apart in "The Freshman" is not nearly so funny as the possibility of falling off a building to his death in "Safety Last."

Comedy is fundamentally a serious thing, which leads me to another aspect of the case. The hero need not necessarily be circumventing destruction but he must be involved in something whose consequences are reasonably serious and you must care about him, one way or another. Your feelings should be engaged, either way, in whether the old lady slips on the banana. You should hope she does or pray she doesn't. But you can't be indifferent.

And in order to care—either way—she must be a person worth your consideration. She must be well rounded enough to be worthy of your love or hatred. One of the reasons for the great success of "South Pacific," I feel, is the fact that the characters depicted by Mary Martin and (formerly) by Ezio Pinza were sufficiently warm, human and likeable to engage your feelings. And the racial antagonism which separated them briefly is a very real problem indeed.

The greatest of the silent screen comedians—Charlie Chaplin, Buster Keaton, Harry Langdon—were, in their public appearances, poignant characters who enlisted our sympathies. The present crop of millionaire comedians—the Milton Berles, Bob Hopes, Bing Crosbys, Jack Bennys—are a different breed. You feel that nothing untoward can happen to these wealthy folk. Chaplin was richer than all of them but he kept his private personality entirely separate from his public one. The contemporary comic, with his jokes about his racehorses, his ball clubs and his bank account, doesn't.

There is no place for him to go for comedy material except into the public domain which leads to forty-five different jokes from forty-five different comedians about Mr. Truman's letter-writing proclivities. In short, the mechanical joke.

CHAPTER 4

Sitting Ducks and a Few Dead Ones

Lotsa Fun, Lotsa Laughs and Lotsa Loving
[MAY 25, 1950]

DAYTIME TELEVISION has been strenuously avoided in this space as a matter of simple sportsmanship. You shouldn't shoot sitting ducks. However, this duck has been sitting in one position so long I'm beginning to suspect he's already dead. If he is, somebody else shot him. I haven't pulled a trigger for months. Also, if he is dead, the body ought to be removed. It's a violation of the sanitation laws to leave these things around.

I have neither the space nor the inclination to go into all of daytime television. I submit only one specimen. Not a typical specimen, either. I've picked out the most terrible daytime program I've yet run across, the deadest duck on the air.

It's called "Okay, Mother." The bright, particular star of this hideous firmament is Dennis James, a man of many faces, none of them especially edifying. "Okay, Mother," as its title implies, is a salute to motherhood, and if anything will kill motherhood in this country, this is the one that will do it. Down in Washington, we have the Communists undermining the country and here in New

York we have Dennis James undermining motherhood. Nothing is safe any more.

Mr. James or his henchmen—who, I suspect, are trolls—round up two or three hundred mothers every day. I don't know how they do this. I imagine it's something like an elephant hunt. The beaters fan out in the New Jersey veld, setting fire to the bush and shouting their weird cries, and gradually they drive the poor, hunted mothers into the kraal. Then each day the mothers are shipped to New York for exhibition.

I must confess they don't seem to mind being exhibited. They take to it like a dead duck to television, to coin a phrase. Almost every single one tries to get her face into the camera and, by George, almost every single one succeeds. Most easily domesticated mothers I ever saw.

"Who's the girl with brush and broom?" shouts Mr. James.

"Mother!" cry the captives dutifully.

"Who's the girl who chases gloom?" says Mr. James.

"Mother!" is the riposte to this one. (No, they don't have to push any teak logs around, Junior. They just have to yell "Mother" at appropriate intervals.)

"Lotsa fun, lotsa laughs and lotsa loving," Mr. James declares heartily. The novitiate is likely to get the impression his ears are playing him tricks from that last word. But, no. Loving is what Mr. James said and loving is what he does. Anyway, it's a reasonably accurate euphemism for what he does. What he does is to kiss the mamas, fondle them, hug them and, in general, muss 'em up. They appear to like it. In fact, there's severe competition for the role of most mussed-up mother.

Mr. James—I throw this in as limply as possible—is tall, dark, husky and handsome, and I expect he appeals not only to the girls on the set but to the ones at home. Thousands of them probably swoon over their ironing boards every day, causing—I devoutly hope—endless casualties. Mr. James may easily have set fire to more mothers than any man since Nero.

There isn't much else to tell you about this program. Mr. James, from time to time, recites what he calls Mothergrams, a form of verse I shan't inflict on you. Occasionally, he vaults two or three rows of mothers to land squarely on the lap of a mother in the upper tiers, busses her roundly and vaults back—easily the most specialized form of exercise I ever saw. For all I know he's the only athlete in the world who can do this.

Incidentally, this is the same Dennis James who kids the bejabbers out of wrestling on TV by simulating the sound of breaking bones, torn limbs and other tortures on a series of mechanical contraptions. He's pretty funny at it, too. Just why he should get mixed up in this mother thing, I don't know. Maybe he needs the money. Maybe he never had a mother. Or maybe—this is my theory—the whole thing is a freak of transmission, a collision between a cumulus cloud and a low pressure area, which produces a picture that never took place at all.

If that last theory is true, I apologize to Mr. James and to mothers everywhere. I now propose to adjourn to my favorite saloon where I shall sing "Mother's Day Falls Once a Year but Every Day Is Mother's Day to Me" until closing time. Or until they throw me out.

Yes, Virginia, There Is an Arthur Murray

[OCTOBER 23, 1950]

ARTHUR MURRAY's determination to teach everyone the rumba, an incomprehensible ambition, has extended now to television. If you can learn the rumba by television, then the medium's capacity for evil has been infinitely underestimated. The "Arthur Murray Show" will teach you not only the rumba, but the samba, the mamba, the framba, the plamba, and ultimately, I suppose, the Lambeth Knuckleball, a dance I invented, in which the girl breaks sharply to the left and down as she crosses the plate. The man in the Lambeth Knuckleball swings from the heels and if he connects, he gets two points and a new girl.

I bring up the "Arthur Murray Show" because it is one of the most conspicuous examples of a trend in television toward the amateur spirit. My friends in the sports writing dodge are everlastingly complaining about the growth of the professional spirit in amateur sports. In our racket the situation is reversed. Television is essentially a pro's game and amateurism is something that ought to be rooted out now. Before its tendrils entwine the—you'll never get this metaphor off the ground, Crosby—living branches of the ... aah, the hell with it. Anyhow, the amateur spirit should be resisted in television. Perhaps we could arrange a trade. We'll put the Army football team on television and schedule Mrs. Arthur Murray against Michigan.

Mrs. Arthur Murray is the emcee of the Arthur Murray show. She reminds me strongly of relentless hostesses who insist that I bob apples when I have other things on my mind. Of course, on this particular show, her pitch is not apple-bobbing; it's the samba, or the rumba or whatever. She insists that everyone do these things and, on her show, everyone does.

One of the principal features of the show is a chorus of males and females, dressed to the nines, who commit the samba at every conceivable opportunity—when someone else is singing, when the juggler comes on, and just after the seal act. As I said earlier, they do a lot besides the samba. They burst into jitterbugging one night and, brothers and sisters, you have never seen such jitterbugging except in every juke joint in the nation where the dancers feed nickels into the box for the privilege.

Mrs. Murray also bursts into dance when the amateur spirit seizes her, which is often, and one night she did the bumps-a-daisy with a professional wrestler and won. (Thirteen rounds to two, according to my score card.) Recently, she scored the news beat of the year. There were two questions, she said, which had been agitating the nation for years: 1) Is there an Arthur Murray? 2) Can he dance? Well, there is. (She produced him.) And he can. (They did. No, he isn't spectacularly good at it. Just average.)

From time to time, Mrs. Murray and her guests, who sit around at tables applauding someone else's samba, play games. Dancing games, that is. They are the sort of games which you used to play at dancing school if you were unfortunate enough to go to a dancing school. (What am I saying? The Murrays *run* a dancing school.)

Then, there's the Magic Step which Mrs. Murray will demonstate for you. It has twenty variations. It so happens that the Magic Step is the only step I know in dancing and, through diligence, I have acquired 102 variations. The 102nd variation, a tricky step, is the one where you twirl the girl out the French windows and down to the swimming pool where you and she can discuss Jackie Robinson's batting average. The Murrays haven't caught up with this refinement yet.

Graduates of the Murray school are put on exhibition at intervals and tell you how much their training did for them and why they went there. One man said he went to Murray's because in his non-dancing days he had to sit around night clubs buying drinks for the girls. By dancing, presumably, he kept the girls occupied so they couldn't spend his money.

There are guests, too, some of them pretty high-priced entertainment. All of them, transfixed by the other monkeyshines on this program, leave their talent home in the upper left-hand drawer. Even Bert Lahr, that wonderful man, was appallingly bad on the Murray show.

How's Your Witchery?
[OCTOBER 20, 1950]

IF MY MEMORY is at all trustworthy, the brassiere industry is a comparatively recent American phenomenon. The things existed certainly for centuries, but the huge industry that now assaults us with its advertising in subways, buses, magazines and newspapers is fairly recent. I have always been struck forcibly by brassiere advertising simply because I never realized the nature of the engineering problem was so extraordinarily difficult. The problems of stress—if you believe the advertising implicitly—are comparable to those of the geniuses who strung up the George Washington Bridge. Matter of calculus, solid geometry and physics.

Anyhow, the brassiere people have now taken to television, where they have encountered an even more formidable problem—how to advertise the product without getting all the Parent-Teacher Associations down on their ears. One typical program is "The Robbins Nest," sponsored by the Exquisite Form Brassiere Co., creators of the HI/low Witchery & Disguise Bra. In promoting this miracle of engineering resourcefulness, there was a good deal of witchery but practically no disguise.

The HI/low Witchery & Disguise Bra was displayed on a model. She is—what's the phrase for it?—the straight man for the advertising pitch. That is, she just stands there and smiles and smiles and smiles while from somewhere out of sight a voice purrs on about its youthful uplift and exquisite form, and especially about how it couldn't fail to mould me into charm and grace. I don't know about that. A lot of people have tried to mould me into charm and grace. My mother, my wife, to name only two. No one has got very far. I doubt that the HI/low Witchery & Disguise people can manage it either. Some things defy even witchcraft.

Somebody, who realized that this form of witchery is a rather delicate thing to sell on television, has carefully instructed the model who displays the HI/low etc. to stand very, very quietly during the commercial pitch. She does, too, but this just accentuates the—uh—positive, if I make myself clear, and I'm afraid that I do. Her lips twitch from time to time. Her eyes roam the ceiling; then, when they've exhausted that area, she glances roguishly at the camera, which is to say, you. Meanwhile, the sales pitch goes on and on. I don't know how the girls behave on the block of an Arabian slave mart, but it must be something like this.

Bow Down, Barnum!
[JULY 17, 1950]

SOME YEARS BACK when an electron beam was still a novelty, decent citizens deserted their homes by the millions and took to the saloons where they stood like bewitched children around primitive television sets and watched wrestlers performing their ancient tribal war dances. Many of these hitherto law-abiding folk took to drink. Others were struck blind by the wonders, or possibly the inadequacies, of early television. This period, known as the Saloon Age of Television, was altogether deplorable, sociologically speaking.

However, one man decided to do something about this terrible situation. And that man was—a little introductory music on the clavichord, mother!—Sherman Billingsley, the noted temperance worker of East Fifty-third Street. "Why should these poor misguided folk be lured out of their parlors and into saloons?" Mr. Billingsley asked himself. Or some such question. "I shall restore these people to their sanity. I shall bring the saloons into their parlors. I shall return the parents to their little neglected ones. And while I'm at it, I can teach the little ones how to order a double gin sling with the proper inflection."

Mr. Billingsley took his proposal to the Columbia Broadcasting System which enthusiastically agreed that this was the greatest advance in the temperance dodge since Carrie Nation hung up her ax. Well, the upshot—a little upshot music, mother, we're approaching the denouement—was a program called "The Stork Club," which you'll find on C. B. S. TV network.

By one of those freakish coincidences, the Stork Club happens also to be the name of Mr. Billingsley's well-known temperance saloon where the patrons are strictly forbidden from drinking more than is good for them, unless they have the money to pay for it. In addition to his zeal on the behalf of temperance, Mr. Billingsley is also extraordinarily gifted at the art of publicizing his saloon, which is a very widely renowned place indeed.

The Stork Club has been celebrated variously in a "Cosmopolitan" serial, a motion picture and more national columns than I care to count. Last winter, in case the name was growing dim in some citizen's mind in Dubuque, there was a television program entitled "Murder at the Stork Club," starring Franchot Tone and featuring Mr. Billingsley himself. Mr. Billingsley's principal task in this epic was to appear at the end of it to assure the audience that no one ever had actually been murdered at the Stork Club. After this column, I propose to stay out of the place forever. I wouldn't like to sully that record.

But of all Mr. Billingsley's publicity feats, I should say this one is the most wondrous of all. I know of no other innkeeper in all history sufficiently mellifluous to persuade a national network to build a $100,000 studio on top of his saloon and to pay him $2,000 a week for the privilege of publicizing his waterhole from coast to coast. Bow down, P. T. Barnum, you old dilettante! You're in the presence of a real pro.

As for the program itself—and it's high time—"The Stork Club" strives for informality and achieves it. Peter Lind Hayes and his wife, Mary Healy, two of the most gifted and charming young people in show business, drift about a replica of the Cub room introducing celebrities (and some folk who have only remote claim to the title). When they find a real good one—Jack Dempsey, say—they interview him. If a guest, like Yvonne Adair of "Gentlemen Prefer Blondes," happens also to be a singer, she sings. Mr. Hayes contributes a dry, sardonic chatter to the proceedings, and occasionally he and Miss Healy fill in with one of their song or patter numbers.

It's a very pleasant, though hardly notable, fifteen-minute show. And, if it succeeds in keeping people out of saloons, I should like to be the first to express my incredulity. It'll keep me out of one of them, anyhow.

Kathi Will Get It for You Retail
[JULY 3, 1950]

TELEVISION IS UNOBTRUSIVELY staging a significant change in our merchandising practices. The changes may yet reach the status of revolution. Right now, it's just an uprising. I refer to the daytime women shoppers' programs, bursting into flower on television stations all over the country.

On these programs, a woman, usually affiliated with a department store, simply demonstrates everything from potholders to seamless brassieres for hours on end. A good deal of this is straight advertising as we know it, an appeal to come to the fifth floor of Gimbels and buy the potholder. But there's another twist. Just call Gimbels. They'll mail it to you. This makes television a sort of electronic Sears-Roebuck catalogue. A small-scale experiment is now going on in Chicago to put the whole thing on a mail-order bracket or telephone-bracket basis. Project that idea far enough and you could eliminate the department store entirely—the clerks, the expensive real estate—and the housewife would never have to leave her own living room except to play bridge. I don't know if this will ever happen. I just pass it along as a novel idea.

In New York we have two or three televised women shoppers. I pick out one, Kathi Norris, because she's been at it longer than anyone else, and also because "Quick" magazine predicts she will be one of television's most important figures in a few years, a not altogether agreeable prospect. Miss Norris is the comfy or daytime or non-Faye Emerson-type personality. A house dress as opposed to a plunging neckline girl. For a solid hour over WNBT, Miss Norris beats the drums for Saks-Thirty-fourth Street—showing, demonstrating, expostulating on about thirty or forty different items of merchandise every day.

She's assisted in this chore by her husband, a man named

Sweetie. If Sweetie has any other name, I've never heard it. Sweetie's job is to hold a heavy cardboard display while Kathi explains what it contains and how much it costs and what floor you'll find it on. The other day he was asked to model a sarong for men. It's for keeping stains off the clothing while mixing Martinis, if I understood Miss Norris correctly. A perfect Father's Day gift, guaranteed to remain unused by any father I know.

"Take your hands out of the pockets, Sweetie," said Miss Norris. "Show the handsome design. It comes in small, medium or large."

Her tone toward her husband is one of affectionate indulgence, reducing the role of husband to that of Mummie's little helper. Occasionally she tries to correct his pronunciation, and here she'd better watch her step. She's sometimes wrong. ("It isn't 'IM-pregnated,' honey; it's 'im-PREG-nated,'" just as Sweetie said first.) Once in a while, the pair engage in a little innocent love-making, pawing each other tenderly.

The merchandise runs the gamut. And what a gamut! Patio dresses. Ketchup dispensers. Satin woofie slippers (washable, $2.95). Lotion for teen-age skins. (Don't fool around with it if you're in your twenties.) One-armed eggbeaters. (For housewives with hives, I expect.) Pre-cooked canned hamburgers. (For husbands whose wives have run off with the chauffeur, is my theory.) A spiel goes along with each item, and, I imagine, much of it has to be memorized because it's an ad man's spiel and I don't think anyone can speak ad man extemporaneously in this country.

Example: "The perfect long-line strapless seamless nylon bra to make you figure-happy." (If any of you girls are figure-unhappy, there's a woman at Saks-Thirty-fourth Street who'll revise your figure for you. Tell her Kathi sent you. Don't pin it on me.)

Kathi has a guest or two at the beginning, or end, or both, of her program, but essentially the hour is one long commercial. Some intellectuals are going to break into loud wails over a program that's just an hour-long commercial. But I'm not. Women like to look at merchandise and I don't see why they should be prevented. Kathi offers another service that housewives may find useful. If you want something she doesn't have on view, write in and ask for it. She'll dig it up for you. She once procured some sweet-faced baby monkeys for someone or other who had been scouring the city for them.

I'm afraid we men will have to get used to the house slowly filling with those curious gadgets—male sarongs, ketchup dispensers and such-all. The other day, Sweetie demonstrated a picnic basket for small children with built-in knife, fork and spoon. Just the thing for a small boy who plans to run away from home.

Johnny Olsen Gets Four Years Older
[JUNE 5, 1950]

NOTHING EVER GETS LOST around here. My files, through no fault of my own, are appallingly efficient, which is why I have at hand some notes taken four years ago on Johnny Olsen's Rumpus Room. These particular notes I've tried cunningly to lose, misfiling them under Jack Benny, "Portia Faces Life" and Mary Margaret McBride. Always they are put sternly back where they belong.

Four years ago, Johnny Olsen's Rumpus Room was a radio program; today it's a television program. We have made great strides in electronics these last four years, rendering Johnny Olsen visible, but Mr. Olsen hasn't kept pace. Four years ago, I discover through these yellowing notes, Mr. Olsen plucked a girl named Esther Something-or-Other, of Boston, Mass., from the studio audience, bussed her roundly and sang "How Many Hearts Have You Broken" at her. For submitting to this she received a pair of nylons.

Four years later, on much newer notes, I discover Mr. Olsen detaching two matrons from the crowd, kissing them both and singing more songs at them. They get nylons, too. Of course, you can watch Mr. Olsen perform these gallantries now. You can get a good clear look at the ladies, too, and that may inspire a few sonnets from the more susceptible onlookers. And then again, it may not. Also, Mr. Olsen has gained in proficiency, being able now to handle two babes at a time, where he once could take care of only one. Otherwise, Mr. Olsen and the Rumpus Room have not matured a great deal, beyond getting four years older.

The TV Rumpus Room, like the audio one, is an audience-participation show, composed almost entirely of women. In the event you never saw it, you might get some idea of the nature of the audience by a recital of a few of the organizations that sent delegations the other day. They are the Perth Amboy Mah Jongg Club, the Companions of the Forest, the National Guard Ladies, the Mothers of Cub Scouts—I don't know where any of those last three are from—the Linden, N. J., Women's Bowling Team, and the Gin Rummy Club of the Bronx.

There was also one unaffiliated lady from Bensonhurst, N. J., conceivably the only female in New Jersey running under her own silks. I go into all this detail about the audience because they comprise a large part of the show. The camera keeps panning back and forth over the Mah Jongg Club, endeavoring to get each and every member into the picture at least once. This affords a splendid opportunity to study the sort of hats the girls are wearing in Perth Amboy these days, in case you're writing a thesis on the subject.

Besides kissing them and singing at them, Mr. Olsen and his assistants—one male, one female—play little games with the girls. No, not mah-jongg. Kissing games. Guessing games. Charades. The sort of games I used to play at children's parties when I was twelve years old. Win, lose or draw, the girls are awarded pots, pans and nylons.

Mr. Olsen has all the necessary qualifications for the job. He can smile at will and, on this show, that takes some doing; he can laugh indefinitely at his own jokes, and his personality reminds me strongly of those immortal words of Mr. Gillette's—"Look sharp! Feel sharp! Be sharp!"

As for his wit, I have a sample right here:

"So you want to be famous? Well, I can place your name in lights all over the country."

"You can! How?"

"Change your name to Exit."

The best feature of the Olsen show, for my money, is a parade of children at the end of it. (The mothers bring their offspring along.) They're all pretty cute kids—some of them frightened, some sullen and some exhibitionist. I've got a little file of names of the kids in that last category. Twenty-five years from now—mark my words—you'll find all of them on the Johnny Olsen show, clamoring to be kissed. I'll be waiting for them with my little list.

Nothing—as I remarked earlier—ever gets lost around here.

The Perils of Maternity

[FEBRUARY 9, 1951]

THERE ARE TWENTY-SIX soap operas on the air involving a total of thirty-two and a half hours of network time a week. This great assortment of suffering though indomitable heroines and weak heroes are variously afflicted by prosecution in court for crimes they didn't commit, sickness, accident, insanity, unrequited love, requited love to a man or woman already married, broken or about-to-be-broken marriages, and children.

The last one may surprise you, but actually the problems connected with having children or with *not* having them leads the list in point of popularity. At least eleven soap operas have children at the root of the heroine's problems, or at least at the root of some of her problems—heroines sometimes being stricken by two or three catastrophes at once.

Perhaps the most exquisite form of torment is that of women who are dying to have children and can't have them or—better yet—the women who had them and had them torn from them by death or divorce or some such thing. Several soaps are actually dedicated to bereaved or unfulfilled motherhood, notably "Stella Dallas," who took a powder because her daughter married into high society ("the story of mother love and sacrifice"); "Young Widder Brown," "the story of the age-old conflict between a mother's duty and a woman's heart," and "Hilltop House," which is a soap opera about an orphanage.

In "Hilltop House" right now, Mrs. Barnes, whose baby was just killed, has fallen in love with a new baby at the orphanage and wants to adopt it. She can't have it, due to circumstances I have no intention of explaining. Over in "Pepper Young's Family," Peggy has just had a baby whose chief purpose seems to be to torture Peggy's friend Linda, who can't have one. In "Young Dr. Malone," the sight of a nursery is enough to drive one of the girls nuts because she can't have babies either. And in "Our Gal Sunday," Dr. Julian Abbott's wife has just discovered that her husband had put young Dr. Julian Forrest, the son he wished were his because he never had one, through medical school. It's causing a serious rift between the old doctor and his wife.

Soapland is stuffed with adopted children partly because so many parents can't have them, partly because so many people die violent deaths and somebody has to take care of the kids they leave behind. It's rather difficult to explain why anyone should adopt a child or have one in soapland; they cause nothing but trouble. Over in "Just Plain Bill," Mona Kane has just about succeeded in breaking up the marriage between her stepfather, Basil Kane, and Barbara. At least Barbara has left home. On "The Brighter Day," a very misleading title, Althea Dennis is doing her best to drive the faithful old housekeeper, Ma Kennedy, out into the streets by poisoning the good Reverend Dennis's mind against her.

On "Guiding Light," Ray and Charlotte are headed for almost certain trouble by adopting Jimmy, fourteen-year-old brother of their adopted daughter Penny. Jimmy is a problem child, and I can predict with considerable confidence that he'll raise cain with that household. Incidentally, Ray and Charlotte have just been bereft of another adopted child, Chuckie, whom they adored. And

Papa David, of "Life Can Be Beautiful," was last heard from leaning over the bedside of his beloved ward Chichi, crying, "Speak to me! Speak to me!" She isn't coming out of the operation nearly as well as we'd all expected. Papa David is a one-man example of the perils of foster paternity in soapland. His eyes have been filled with tears almost uninterruptedly for about fifteen years over the terrible trials poor Chichi has undergone.

Soap opera is largely directed at the mothers of America. Yet, much of it could easily be construed as the greatest propaganda campaign against motherhood in the history of this mother-happy country. If the children don't turn against you, they get kidnaped or run over or stricken by polio (baby Wendy in the "Second Mrs. Burton"). After listening to enough of this, the young bride could easily be persuaded that maternity was a serious mistake and take up gardening instead.

Death in the Afternoon
[FEBRUARY 7, 1951]

EDNA FERBER once attributed the success of her novels at least partly to the fact that they dealt in the fundamentals of life—birth, marriage, disease, death. Soap opera deals pretty much in the same primary commodities except that the emphasis lies on their frustration or perversion. Soapland is full of women who can't have children, of marriages that have broken up or are breaking and of deaths that are anything but ordinary.

Murder, which intruded only occasionally in soap opera years ago, has become overwhelmingly fashionable. That old sleuth, Perry Mason, has Walter Bott on trial for his life for murder. My old friend Larry Noble of "Backstage Wife" just beat a murder rap for a backstage killing. It was Claudia Vincent, as you and I knew all along, who was the killer. Claudia's mind snapped under the strain and she's been put away. But not before she threw acid into the face of Mary Noble, "Backstage Wife," possibly disfiguring her forever.

Some instinct tells me she'll recover her beauty. She's done it before after even worse tribulations. As a matter of fact, poor Mary has a rather nasty habit of falling victim to the mentally deranged. Last time I listened, in February, 1946, she was recovering nicely, after having been drugged, locked in a room and left to die by someone described as "mentally not well."

Backstage and theatrical murders are rather fashionable among current soap opera. Front Page Farrell, the demon reporter, is currently trying to solve a double murder of stage folk. And Portia, the demon lady lawyer of "Portia Faces Life," also has a twin killing involving nightclub people. The freshest corpse anywhere around is that of Ralph Kirkland, who was done in by Rupert Gorham on "The Second Mrs. Burton." Rupert then proceeded to elope with his victim's mother-in-law, Grace Burton, a nice touch. Ralph is so freshly dead that his wife, Marsha, doesn't know it yet. She thinks her husband is off again with that Elizabeth Miller girl who has again escaped from the hospital.

A good many of the murders have been committed by women. The "Backstage Wife" and the "Young Widder Brown" killings were both done by women and I strongly suspect the "Front Page Farrell" murders had a woman behind them, too. In addition, there is a woman swindler, Lady Audrey Jones, now trying to get her claws on all that Peabody money in "Lorenzo Jones."

That pretty well winds up the homicide in soapland, except that Stella Dallas just escaped a couple of attempted assassinations and there has been a good deal of bloodshed in "Lorenzo Jones," which was once primarily a comedy show. Murder has been popular a long time in the evening hours, but this afternoon murder is a rather different dish of tea. In the first place there is almost no element of mystery. The listeners almost always know whodunit. Murder is committed, not so much to remove the victim from this planet—he is better off dead than living in soapland—as a means of causing suffering to the quick.

Almost always an innocent person is indicted and the trial goes on for weeks or months, keeping the housewife in a wonderful state of sustained anxiety. Sometimes murders are committed for no other reason than to implicate Nora or Caroline or whoever, the victim having been unfortunate enough to be around when a corpse was needed. Jealousy is the principal motive, but the girls, curiously enough, don't kill the other woman; they are much more likely to kill the man they both love. In that way, Nora is kept alive —after all, the Noras have to live forever—to weep her eyes out and then stand trial.

While good women are nobler in soap opera than anything in your or my experience, the bad women are more venomous than anything you'd care to encounter. In either case, the women are strong, just as men, whether good or bad, are weak or at best rather simpleminded and easily bamboozled by women. Also, while women are committing a good many of these soapland murders, these lapses from feminine grace are offset by the fact that women solve the crimes, too. It was Mary who put the finger on Claudia in "Backstage Wife"; Portia is running down the nightclub murders and even Front Page Farrell is getting a lot of help from his wife. The man's job in soapland murder is just to stand around. Or better yet, to fall down gracefully when the bullets strike.

The Inside Story of the Man on the Pogo Stick
[AUGUST 7, 1950]

FOR THE LAST ten years, Ralph Edwards, the emcee of "Truth or Consequences," has been getting people to drive golf balls across the country or to get in bed with a seal at the corner of Hollywood and Vine or to get dunked in a tank of water. Why do people submit voluntarily to these indignities? This question has baffled a lot of people, including this one, and the other day, when Mr. Edwards blew into town, he was asked to explain it in his own way.

"Our show has a keen insight into the taste of America," explained Mr. E., who at thirty-three is one of the youngest toupee wearers on the air. "It's the kind of show that could easily go off key. To use a four-bit word, it could have its empathy destroyed, if we didn't know exactly how far you can go. We have a perfect feeling between the artists—you should excuse the expression—and the audience.

"We have a husband and wife in the act, say. One pushes a pie in the other's face. But the important thing is that it all works out well in the end. The audience has to feel that the husband and wife got together again before it's over. It just can't be one of them pulling a gag on the other."

As for the man in the bed with a seal at Hollywood and Vine, Edwards telephoned his preacher, his boss, and his wife and dispatched them to that celebrated corner. In turn, they walked by, stared and asked in effect: "What on earth are you doing here?" He couldn't explain without forfeiting his money.

"We had him groveling," Edwards admitted, "but it was all right with the audience because they knew it had been explained to the preacher and the boss that it was all a gag. People worry about gags involving anyone's boss. They wouldn't like it a bit if the boss wasn't in on it.

"The contestant was ready to kill us. But afterwards we reveal all. In the handling of any contestant you get the man to a point where he can be made a fool of—but you keep on top of it by your attitude. The kidding department, for instance. We keep saying 'Aren't we devils?' or 'Aren't we angels?' which is a switch for when we do something nice. Then—the important thing—we tell 'em in the end, 'Don't worry. It's all a joke.'"

How, Mr. Edwards was asked, do you find people who have time to hit a golf ball across the country? Well, in that case, they sent tickets to golf clubs to be sure they'd get a golfer. When the audi-

The Inside Story of the Man on the Pogo Stick

ence is assembled, Edwards asks: "Who's free for a week?" If it's a strenuous assignment—such as that golfing chore—he asks: "Where's a big, rugged guy who's free for a week?"

When a likely prospect is flushed from the audience, he is interviewed and watched like a hawk in an effort to determine whether he is capable of handling the stunt, whether he *will* do it to the bitter end, whether he'll be a good sport about it. "You have to be a public relations man, a personnel man, and a psychology major which I'm not. Even then, don't let any one tell you you can pick a good contestant every time."

How do you prevent the contestant from quitting in disgust after the initial enthusiasm passes? Edwards groaned: "What goes on off the show is four times as much work and of much greater importance than the show itself. You send a man off to hit a golf ball from Los Angeles to Truth or Consequences, N. M. Well, you send him off with great fanfare. Then you have to keep it on that level. We know he's going through Phoenix so we arrange with the Phoenix Chamber of Commerce for a golf match between our contestant and eighteen C. of C. men. Our man is a good golfer—or we wouldn't have picked him in the first place—and he beats everyone and that makes him feel fine. He's accompanied by a car and trailer and he has his choice of sleeping in the trailer or in hotels. A chauffeur, who has to be a diplomat, goes along and keeps an eye on him. If he looks as if he's tiring, the chauffeur tells him to take it easy."

Edwards hasn't killed any contestant yet and he doesn't want to. One man had to race an airplane twenty miles from the Los Angeles Airport to City Hall on a pogo stick. First, Edwards had the man's heart checked to be sure he was up to it.

"He got to be so good on that pogo stick," said Edwards, "he could have gone on to New York. He did the last mile without ever getting off the thing. He'd stop at red lights and bounce up and down. He beat the airplane (which took a circuitous route) by a day and a half."

For Scholars Only
[JANUARY 26, 1951]

SCHOLARS OF TELEVISION HISTORY, a small but enormously erudite bunch of hard-drinking intellectuals, will never forget Dec. 4, 1950. It dawned clear, bright and cold, and somehow in the very air you could detect the odor of history about to be made, an acrid smell if you've never noticed. Dec. 4, 1950, is the day television's first soap opera, "The First Hundred Years," went on the air, thus instantly taking rank among historic dates somewhere between the fall of the Bastille and the death of Charlemagne.

"The First Hundred Years" is an apt title for a soap opera, each of which is designed to run at least that long, though, of course, it refers to the first hundred years of marriage as being rather more trying than the next hundred. In soap opera, marriages, though fraught with every sort of peril from mothers-in-law to flirtations, endure for centuries. The particular marriage commemorated in this epic is that of Chris and Connie Thayer, a couple of misty-eyed youngsters whose wedded life is already beset by extraordinary tensions.

For one thing, Connie's mother-in-law, a flibbertigibbet, lives across the street, which will lead to endless trouble. Chris's in-laws live near by. Across the street from *them* lives Scott Blair. Any student of soap opera will tell you that a man with a name like that is up to no good. The moment he walked on to my screen I distrusted him. Sleek good looks, curly hair and a mustache—obviously a scoundrel. He's a writer, too, and you know what those people are like.

One of the more striking characteristics of any soap opera is the pace of its plots, which is about half the speed of an aging snail. In his exhaustive treatise on the subject in "The New Yorker," James Thurber mentioned several specific examples of just how slow the action is in soap opera. In one case—if my memory is at all accurate—a man clambered into a barber chair to get shaved on Monday and hadn't even been lathered by Friday.

This tradition of slowing time almost to a halt is being nobly perpetuated in "The First Hundred Years." Two weeks ago, for example, the denizens of this opera started getting ready for a dance at the country club, a relatively simple operation anywhere except in soap opera, where tying a black tie can take quite a while. They finally got to the dance last Monday. Elapsed time: eleven days. Getting them *out* of the country club is another matter. That may take up the rest of the winter.

Last week one day's plot consisted entirely of Connie and Chris getting into a spat over a girl he once knew named Mildred. Mildred crept into the discussion because Chris said she liked a song they were dancing to. Connie took umbrage and fled to her mother's house. The next day's episode was largely devoted to Connie telling her mother what Chris had said about Mildred, just in case any one had missed it the day before.

Another soap opera tradition carried forward on this program is that of giving the listener the minimum of plot and the maximum of commercial. "The First Hundred Years" opens with an extensive paean to Tide, a detergent, set in prose and in song and including both live action and cartoons. This elaborate operation takes about three minutes. There is a reprise just before closing. Altogether, this leaves about ten minutes to investigate the marital woes of Chris and Connie.

To be quite fair to the show, there has yet been little of the mood of sustained anxiety which is both the curse and stock in trade of radio soap opera. Soap opera heroines are perpetually on the brink of losing something valuable—their careers, their husbands, their homes, their virtues—to list them more or less in the order of their soap opera importance. Chris and Connie are relatively free of worries so far, but I wouldn't bank on their continuing to be for long.

About the only other thing to tell you about this historic show is that it is set—according to a press release—in a middle-sized town "somewhere east of the Rockies and west of the Alleghenies," which takes in an awful lot of real estate. The lead on this press release, incidentally, is a classic of press agentry. "Television, the young giant, reaches maturity with the start of a new day-time dramatic serial show. . . ." Reaches *what*?

CHAPTER 5

Reasonably Serious Criticism

The Totalitarian Individual
[SEPTEMBER 21, 1948]

I NEVER GOT AROUND to seeing Lillian Hellman's "Another Part of the Forest," a companion piece to her "The Little Foxes," which I did see, and I'm grateful to Lux Theater for providing me the opportunity of hearing it. I'm also grateful to Miss Hellman for giving me indirectly the chance to say something nice for a change about Lux Theater, whose meticulous and brilliant productions are generally wasted on the most frivolous material.

Whatever else you can say about "Another Part of the Forest," it is not frivolous. It's as grim as Monday morning, as remorseless as the Comintern, with which Miss Hellman is sometimes accused of flirting. Miss Hellman is indisputably gifted in what I consider an almost unique way. The plots of all her plays, with the exception of "The Children's Hour," which she got from a newspaper clipping, are almost preposterously intricate. Nevertheless, these plots and their magnificently complicated subplots stem honestly enough from her demoniac characters—if you are willing to accept the characters in the first place.

I have a hunch about these characters I'd like to dwell on for a moment. All or most of the Hellman major characters are merciless or, to choose a more descriptive phrase, possessed of a single idea, usually an evil idea, and are not to be deflected from it by any consideration at all, especially a human consideration. They have no weaknesses, these characters, and are not brought to justice, as are most tragic characters, by their own failings. They must be outwitted by other, equally possessed characters.

The Hubbard scoundrels—Marcus, Regina, Ben—are in their separate ways implacable above all else; Miss Hellman toys occasionally with the concept of good and evil, right and wrong, but such abstractions have nothing to do with the outcome. The winner wins, the losers lose, and that's that. Her characters are to my mind totalitarian individuals whose unrelenting passions clash headlong and, I'm frank to admit, make for perfectly stunning theater.

Miss Hellman professes to loathe totalitarianism, as she made perfectly evident in "Watch on the Rhine," but she nevertheless understands the totalitarian individual better than she understands the human or malleable individual. Her humans, incidentally, are invariably idiots. She comprehends—I won't go so far as to say she sympathizes with—the undeviating man as opposed to the rational man, and since the world seems now to be divided into two camps, the one implacable, the other rational, Miss Hellman, whom I consider the first literate exponent of the future totalitarian man, occupies a position of distinctive though unenviable importance in contemporary letters.

"Another Part of the Forest," to get radio into this somewhere, is a difficult play to put on the air. Miss Hellman likes to put five or six people in a room, each spinning his separate, sinister web. It would be awfully easy to get these people hopelessly mixed up in the minds of the listeners. It's to the credit of Lux Theater's superb casting and direction that this complex play with its many characters and intricate subplots came across without any confusion whatsoever.

The cast, Walter Huston as Marcus Hubbard, Vincent Price as Ben, Ann Blyth as Regina, handled their jobs as capably as any one could, but I had the feeling they were inadequate to the task. I don't think there are any actors in this country who can play these parts to their fullest measure.

Grand Old Man of English Letters
[NOVEMBER 7, 1950]

IT WAS IN "Cakes and Ale," I believe, that Somerset Maugham observed of a character, who is generally conceded to have been patterned after Thomas Hardy, that he became the grand old man of English letters by the simple act of longevity. The writer had simply outlived all the competition. It is delicately ironic that Maugham, himself a master of irony, has now duplicated Mr. Hardy's feat, though he had quite a tussle outlasting George Bernard Shaw. Maugham now holds clear title, at least partly for the same reasons.

"My great ambition," says Mr. Maugham, who has always had a profound appreciation for popular success, "is to be read by as many persons as possible. But nobody seems to be reading books nowadays. They just look and listen. So the person who wants to get himself heard by the public just goes on television." Maugham has done just that on a new dramatic series called "Teller of Tales," a half-hour program consisting of dramatizations of some of his 100-odd short stories.

The great man himself appears at the beginning and at the end of each program, introducing and closing each story with admirable brevity. He is a very old man now, seventy-six, and, in appearance and manner, remarkably expressive of his writings—dry, skeptical, perceptive, urbane and rather limited, I should say, in emotional depths.

There have been two stories so far "The Creative Impulse" and "Winter Cruise"—both of which I'd read before. They are by no means among Maugham's best, but they are still very good stories and they could be especially recommended to younger TV writers as examples of how to resolve a situation. Maugham's stories—many of them, anyway—involve situations wherein the normal currents of life are suddenly jarred by the revelation of a totally unexpected twist in a man's nature. This throws the people around the man out of kilter for a while until the community can adjust itself to this new, surprising factor in relationship. Maugham pitches you into these contretemps and then—I can think of no other word—resolves them. But he doesn't *end* them, exactly. There are no hard and fast solutions, Maugham realizing that nothing ever quite gets solved in this life.

I wish some of the younger lads would learn that lesson in these days when a bullet or a body brings everything to such a neat, unsatisfying conclusion. As television—life having gone on to some degree since Maugham wrote them—the stories still ring of sound craftsmanship but seem, in essence, a little dim and far away. Some of the direction is extraordinarily bad and a good deal of Maugham's dialogue sounds, in this day of Raymond Chandler, as if it had been originally spelled out with great difficulty in wet cement.

"Winter Cruise" is the story of a frump of a woman, a bore, who is the only woman passenger on an English cruise ship. She drives the ship's captain and the ship's doctor so berserk with boredom that they hatch up a plot to drive her into the extremely reluctant arms of a young steward. Well, the steward finds the proposition not nearly so unattractive as he'd thought; the woman almost instantly becomes so subdued and feminine and mysterious that the doctor and the ship's captain start pursuing her.

That plot has been rather diminished by wear and tear in Hollywood. But it still retains the deftness with which Maugham once wrote it. And nothing quite gets solved. The cruise ends; the matron and the steward go their separate ways; everyone is a little wiser, and that's all. No one marries anyone; no one gets shot; no permanent alterations are made anywhere—except in the characters of the people.

Maugham once said in "The Summing Up"—I'm quoting from memory here because I can't find the passage—that the critics in his early years called him brutal, in his middle years they called him cynical, and, in his later ones, superficial. That fairly well reflects the change in literary tastes since he started writing in the '90s. Today, I shouldn't apply any of those adjectives. On television in 1950, Maugham's stories strike me chiefly as wise, as knowing, and —this would surprise the old man when he first wrote them—as curiously gentle.

Shakespeare's Romeo, U. S. Steel's Juliet
[FEBRUARY 13, 1948]

WILLIAM SHAKESPEARE and the United States Steel Corporation, two institutions of massive respectability, clasped hands last Sunday in a Theater Guild of the Air production of "Romeo and Juliet," which means, of course, that Shakespeare has finally arrived. Recognition was slow in coming—some 300 years—but, having come finally, it will mean drastic changes in Will Shakespeare's manner of life. I understand he's already discreetly withdrawn from the Mermaid Tavern, where his drinking companions were of questionable social background, and applied for membership in the Union League Club.

From a scientific point of view, this skeletonized version of "Romeo and Juliet" was interesting on a number of counts that Shakespeare never planned on. In the leading roles were Maurice Evans as Romeo and Dorothy McGuire as Juliet, a decidedly explosive mixture of temperaments and techniques. Mr. Evans, whose voice is more highly developed and versatile than an organ, approaches Shakespeare ritualistically—if that's the word I mean. He charges every speech with passion and meaning. Each word, each phrase, is given a precise modulation that makes it seem almost inevitable, as if the whole world were holding its breath waiting for that one word, that one phrase.

Actually Evans doesn't act Shakespeare; he sings it. His farewell speech as he lay dying is a little masterpiece of orchestration, starting low and ending high in the upper registers. There are some who suffer intensely when exposed to this species of acting and I can understand why. On the other hand, I think the Evans method is the only way to take the high school auditorium smell off such lines as "By yonder blessed moon, I swear." Anyone who can deliver that line without reducing me to helpless laughter is a great artist, and Mr. Evans can.

In the corner opposite this great Shakespearean organ was Miss McGuire, an actress of the naturalist school and a very good one. Together they sounded like debaters arguing opposite ideologies rather than lovers. Miss McGuire defiantly emitted her longer speeches in large undigested lumps as if she didn't fully understand them and was, as it were, putting them on the record. Perhaps I'm over-sensitive but it seemed to me Miss McGuire was wholly out of sympathy with her role. I somehow got the impression she felt Juliet was a silly goose of a girl who had got herself into a totally unnecessary jam which with the exercise of a little common sense might easily have been averted. It's an opinion with which I find myself in full agreement, but I don't think anyone should undertake the part of Juliet hampered by such blasphemous ideas.

If anything was needed to fill out this weird assortment of acting techniques it was the presence of Miss Florence Reed, an actress of ferocious pretensions and almost inconceivable lung power. Well, by yonder blessed moon, she was there all right, playing the part of the Nurse. Miss Reed believes in giving the customers their money's worth: everything becomes a lot larger than life and terribly, terribly intense. The Nurse, for example, is supposed to be old, very old; in Miss Reed's hands, she became Pleistocene. In fact, she sounded as if she had just been disinterred for the part. Also, for reasons I can't quite put a finger on, she reminded me strongly of an ancient player-piano—cracked-voiced, out of tune but indomitable.

Nevertheless, after hearing Miss Reed declaim: "Help! Help! Juliet's de-e-ead!" I felt obscurely comforted for not having been present at the fall of Jericho. The blare of the trumpets on that memorable occasion could not possibly have been more shattering or more terrifying. With those four words she made a mockery of all radio. The line would have been just as effective if they had turned off the American Broadcasting Company and opened the windows.

In spite of all these crotchety remarks, I thoroughly enjoyed the Theater Guild's "Romeo and Juliet," though possibly not quite in the spirit Shakespeare intended. I'd like to hear them attempt "Othello" some time with Bob Hope in the title role, Lionel Barrymore as Iago and Joan Davis as Desdemona. That should make a real acting festival.

University of the Air
[DECEMBER 16, 1948]

THE PLANTING OF ALDOUS HUXLEY, the intellectual ascetic from England, in the over-ripe soil of California was a daring agricultural experiment and it has produced some weird fruit, including his novel, "After Many a Summer Dies the Swan." The book, which is rich in calcium and irony and rather deficient in humanity, was dramatized last Sunday on N. B. C.'s University of the Air program. It's an excellent example of the bold optimism that characterizes that program, since I can think of few things more difficult to put on the air.

"After Many a Summer Dies the Swan" is the story of an enormously rich man named Stoyte, who fears death. His manic terror, I gather, is prompted not so much by reluctance to depart this splendid orb (which doesn't afford him much pleasure) as by a childlike fear that he is going to get his bottom paddled in the hereafter. Stoyte lives in a Gothic castle, "more medieval than any building of the thirteenth century," in California, surrounded by an appalling litter of people.

Along with his Flemish paintings and Fra Angelico murals, the fearful millionaire has collected Dr. Obispo, a sardonic, wholly unscrupulous doctor whose mission is to keep Stoyte alive forever; Jeremy Pordage, an intellectual weasel who functions as a librarian, and Virginia Maunciple, a beautiful babe with no mind to speak of, whose function . . . well, never mind. There are some other unedifying specimens, but we shall refrain from listing them.

Anyway, Pordage, the librarian, stumbles on some astonishing experiments in the field of longevity made by the Fifth Earl of Gonister in the eighteenth century and turns them over to the contemporary longevity expert, Obispo. The malevolent doctor straightaway hustles his protector to England, where they discover the Fifth Earl still alive and roaring after 200 years. Regrettably the Earl has degenerated through some process of reverse mutation into a foetal ape. I didn't understand Huxley's scientific reasoning in the book, and I didn't understand it in the radio version either, so I can't elaborate any further.

It doesn't matter. At the end of the novel and of the radio play, too, Stoyte, after only a momentary hesitation, decides it's infinitely better to become a gibbering baboon than to face his Maker. This dismal perpetuity is the cream of the jest, and the whole tale is decidedly odd to hear on the radio.

On the whole, Ernest Kinoy did a fine job of translating Huxley's semi-religious treatise into intelligible radio, marred only occasionally by such passages as:

"I did some business this morning. Made a lot of money."

"How much."

"Half a million."

"Uncle Jo, I think you're wonderful."

It was rather a colossal job making any of these characters act alive in the first place. Mr. Huxley's characters are more or less a walking set of principles, which the author demolishes at will. The author has always had a little trouble with human feeling, treating it clinically like symptoms of disease.

The Disenchanted
[JULY 7, 1951]

WHEN BUDD SCHULBERG'S NOVEL, "The Disenchanted," was first published, it was both privately and publicly assaulted on what I consider unfair grounds. The book, as everyone knows, was inspired by a single unfortunate episode in F. Scott Fitzgerald's life in which Mr. Schulberg himself figured strongly. The pair collaborated on a movie centering around the Dartmouth winter carnival where Mr. Fitzgerald took to the waters a little too strongly. I happened to have seen the movie and it was—summing it up as judiciously as possible, picking my words with the utmost care—altogether lousy.

Some of the criticisms of the book, both public and private, concentrated perhaps not unnaturally on the private lives and personal characteristics of Scott and Zelda Fitzgerald. Wasn't Mr. Schulberg a little one-sided in his appraisal of a very fine writer? Wasn't he being terribly unfair to Zelda Fitzgerald who was, I'm told, quite a girl? Did Mr. Schulberg, a much younger man than Fitzgerald, know him well enough to write about him? These questions are completely irrelevant. After all, Schulberg was writing fiction. His characters were based on real people but then, so, according to Somerset Maugham, are all characters in fiction, even in bad fiction.

Characters in novels, no matter whom they are based on, acquire their own special aromas, move off in their own private directions. The question at issue is not whether Schulberg drew a rounded portrait of the Fitzgeralds but whether Manley and Jere Halliday were sufficiently real fictional characters to merit all the attention they attracted. I don't think they were. I found Mr. Halliday a little too querulous, far too self-absorbed for comfort, Jere Halliday a little asinine in her passion for self-destruction.

Still, the book has—as Stanley Walker once remarked of Fitzgerald's own books—bones in it. There are some wonderful scenes, each pregnant with imminent disaster—the Hollywood party scene, the script conference at Dartmouth, the final collapse. Mr. Schulberg—let's face it—had a hell of a good story to tell which stood up well last Sunday on NBC's "New Theater Series."

If you can tear yourself away from the television set at that hour on Sunday, you may hear some very adult drama on this series which is narrated by Eva Le Gallienne, is generally excellently cast and is produced with a scrupulous and impressive attention to detail. After too much immersion in television drama, I'm always surprised by the polish and finish of radio drama, that ancient art form.

Schulberg's dialogue, especially that of the '20s ("I feel pale green tonight, darling! Pale green!") which seemed a little sticky in print, sounded remarkably literate on the radio, conceivably because you don't expect any degree of literacy on radio or more probably because of the thoroughly expert performances of Staats Cotsworth as Manley Halliday and Joan Alexander as Jere. Mr. Cotsworth in particular deserves a low bow for managing somehow to play a drunk for almost a solid hour and at the same time remain both expressive and moving, a terrible task to ask of an actor. I was considerably less happy with Don Buka's performance as the Schulberg character, Shep Stearns, but I suspect it wasn't Mr. Buka's fault. He was badly miscast.

"The Disenchanted" is a very good title for a book but not a very apt one for this book. Schulberg, it is my guess, is hopelessly enchanted both with the '20s and the Fitzgeralds and so, it appears, is everyone else. "The '20s," said Miss Le Gallienne in her introduction, "for all their frivolity and wildness, produced fine writers."

But the emphasis, both in this book and in others, is not on the fine writing but on the frivolity and wildness, on the waste, the despair and the self-destruction of only a few of the gifted writers of the '20s. Let's not kid ourselves.

Guidebook for Dialogue Writers
[JANUARY 1, 1951]

AFTER EXAMINING THE DRAMA AGAIN—Broadway, movies, radio, television—I've decided to issue the Crosby Pocket Handbook which will come out from time to time and will settle barroom arguments among dialogue writers.

You get a couple of dialogue writers, they're discussing a scene where the girl realizes she's got cancer. Her husband is saying, "Joanna, you look like a ghost. What . . . ?" The correct line for her, of course: "I'm tired—just tired—that's all." That's now official. Any deviation, like deviations from any ceremony, will be considered blasphemous and the penalty therefore will be court-martial or, at the very least, the tab on the next drink.

Dialogue-writing has become a matter as ceremonious as Japanese drama and we had better codify these things so that everyone knows what to expect in given situations. Following are the proper lines for given situations. I've omitted some of the situations since we all know them well:

"Doctor, you've got to pull her through. You've got to. She's all I have."

"Son . . . you'd better get some rest."

Then there's that tense moment in the detective drama. Here, depending on circumstances, and the way the plot is shaping up, there are two opposite ways of handling the problem:

"Tell him, Joe! Tell him! If *you* won't say where you were at the hour of the murder, *I* will!"

"Maisie, you don't know what you're saying!"

"Inspector—Joe was with me. In my boudoir."

Or there's the other side of the coin.

"I was with you all evening! You know I was, Maisie! I was with you. Go on! Tell 'em!"

"I never saw this man before in my life."

The scene where the girl is lost, heartbroken and broke in the bus station and Cary Grant happens through and helps her out: "Why are you—a stranger—doing all this for me?"

The problems of maternity, paternity and what might be described as the You-Were-Almost-My-Daughter gambit have to be treated fairly extensively.

"Jennifer, twenty years ago I loved a woman. She never knew. I never told her. Because—well, that woman was your mother. And it was your father that she loved. So I went away—it doesn't matter where. But tonight she lives again—in all her loveliness—in you, my child. And that is why—but this is a night for youth and gaiety and love. Back to the ball with you both! I will join you—later—later—later—"

The absent or deceased parent gambit:

(A) "How proud your mother would have been to see you in your graduation dress."

(B) "Bill, you can't quit! You've got to keep fighting this thing. Mother would have wanted it that way."

(C) "And that man was—your father."

Bereavement or imminent bereavement? Well, naturally, we have to cover that.

"Oh God, I'm just a little boy seven years old and maybe I've been bad but, God, don't let my dog Rover die. I'll be a good boy, God. Thank you, God. Good-by, God. Amen."

You want some good-by music? Here it is.

"I guess I've led a pretty hard life, Miss Molly. There ain't many laws I ain't broke. But I'd just like you to know—well, since that night I met you—well, I been *trying* to go straight, anyway. I know I ain't fit to be speaking to you like this—but I wanted you to know. So, well—I guess this is good-by."

Most of these classic lines were penned in 1933 by Nunnally Johnson. It just goes to show that nothing has changed very much in the spoken drama in seventeen years.

Chestnuts Are in Bloom Again
[AUGUST 6, 1951]

I'VE BEEN WORKING on my war film which should be ready for television release some time next year. But I know you people can't wait that long so I'm going to give you a preview right now. This scenario, I ought to explain, was undertaken only after an exhaustive study of the other war films that have belted around the TV circuit all summer; it contains only the ripest old chestnuts that money can buy; it doesn't break any new ground but it makes excellent use of the old soil.

There is what I consider a wonderful scene near the end of this film. Battersby, bearded and haggard, is in the prisoner of war enclosure, staring out at the bleak parade ground, the barbed wire, the stark barracks. And he says, as you rather suspect that he will: "I was just thinking that now the heather will be in bloom in Devon."

Earlier in the film, Battersby, accompanied by young Grimsby, enters the shell-riddled, apparently abandoned village. "Quiet around here," says young Grimsby. Battersby, the more experienced officer, glances around, chewing his underlip. "Yes—too quiet." He glances up the empty street and somehow he can't prevent himself from adding: "I don't like it. . . . I don't like it at all."

The action switches from the battlefield back to the laboratory.

Naturally, I'm not going to neglect the nuclear physicist, most brilliant scientist in the free world and the only man capable of holding all the secrets of the super-atomic ray gun in his head. They're in the laboratory—Murchison from G-2, Dr. Wellsbach, the scientist —examining the ray gun. "Devilish machine," says Murchison, awed. Then after a moment of reflection. "But—can you imagine what would happen if it fell into the wrong hands?" (Next reel: It falls into the wrong hands. So does Wellsbach. Pandemonium at GHQ. Chaos at Scotland Yard. Only the Prime Minister maintains a semblance of calm. "You did all you could, Murchison. All any one could.")

Well, naturally we have to get back the devilish machine and also, if it's not too late, Wellsbach. Comes the secret, highly dangerous mission. Murchison and Battersby flying at 35,000 feet through a hail of flak, their parachutes at the ready, the intercom chattering away.

"Two ack emma—one minute more, old boy."

"Thickish out there, what?"

"Steady the plips. Fast with the ploffs. Roger and over."

"I say, old boy . . ."

"Righto?"

"If anything happens . . ."

"Stout fella."

"Say pip-pip to Dee for me, will you, like a good lad?"

"Righto."

"Well—cheerio."

"Cheerio."

Bang! That's the end of Murchison.

Battersby gets through into the enemy country. Instantly falls in love with a girl who belongs to the other side. "We've fought this thing. My God, how we've fought it!" Great scene when Battersby, who should be skipping back to his own territory, returns to the enemy girl's farmhouse.

"Why did you come?"

"I had to."

"Don't say anything—just let me look at you."
"Tonight at least is ours."

Oh, I forgot to tell you the beginning of this film. Murchison, in civvies, and his wife at their little cottage in Surrey, having breakfast.
"Anything in the paper, dear?"
"Nothing. Some archduke's been murdered."

How to Meet a Girl, English Style
[NOVEMBER 2, 1951]

ONE OF THE THINGS that has always struck me about English literary romance is its entirely accidental character. The hero rounds a corner a little too precipitately, knocks the girl galley west and is overcome with remorse. "Oh, I'm *so* sorry. Do let me pick up the bundles." Or she's pedaling through the English countryside and pauses to ask directions. "Straight down the lane, then left at King Charles Head," he says, puffing on his pipe. "New around here, aren't you?"

That is just the beginning of a series of remarkable coincidences. Later, the girl with the bundles (or the one on the bicycle) encounters the man with the pipe or the other one, the impatient one, at Baggsby-on-the-Sea. She is there gathering clamshells for her collection. He's there to paint. "Jove," he exclaims, "it's you. Coming down rather hard, isn't it?"

It is indeed. It's raining cats and dogs, as you Americans would say, and the wind is rising. "I say, we'd better get out of here. There's a house up there. Let's run for it." The house, it develops, is entirely deserted. The English countryside, the English coast, are dotted with deserted houses for just such occasions as these and it's a fortunate thing. Otherwise, the males and the females would never get acquainted in England.

"Do let me help you off with your coat," he says, when they reach the safety of the house. "You look like a bedraggled kitten. (Laughter from both of them.) Beastly wind, isn't it?"

It is indeed. The wind has risen to gale proportions. Man couldn't live a moment out in a storm like that. "I'm afraid there's nothing for it but to spend the night here." She shivers slightly and looks at the lone bed. "I'll just sit up and tend the fire," he says reassuringly. "You curl up there like a good girl and get some rest. By the way, my name is Grigsby, Oswald Grigsby." . . . And so on.

Well, that may be all very well for England, old chap. In America it won't do. It simply won't do. In America a little more enterprise is required either of the boy or the girl or both. We can't go waiting around for convenient rainstorms. Our authors have been trained to bring about these meetings by design rather than by chance. Take that girl with the bundles. Your fictional American hero would have noticed her leaving the department store.

"Get a load of that," he says admiringly to his male chum. (American heroes, especially in the movies, are never without a male friend to confide in.) "See you later. There's work to do."

He dashes around the corner and trips her deliberately. "Gosh, I'm sorry. Let me help you up," he says.

"You clumsy oaf," she declares, the love light already gleaming in her eyes.

"What are you doing for dinner tonight? I know a little place in Greenwich Village." . . . And so on.

In neither country, I might add, does the girl ever meet the boy by simple introduction. "Bill Jones—Jane Doe."—"Glad to know you." Man would get thrown out of the Authors League for violating tradition like that.

All of which leads me in roundabout fashion to "Still Life," one of the offerings of "Playhouse of Stars." "Still Life," which was originally one of the one-act plays in "Tonight at Eight-Thirty," and later bounced around the country as a motion picture titled "Brief Encounter," is the first Noel Coward work to be seen on television, a notable occasion. Shakespeare beat him to the TV cameras by a couple of years, Eugene O'Neill by a couple of weeks. Anyhow, with Coward in the fold, there's no one of consequence left to succumb to television except Aeschylus who, I understand, is holding out for more money.

"Playhouse of Stars" is the Schlitz Company's replacement for "Pulitzer Prize Playhouse." The dramatic level remains high but the emphasis, as the title indicates, has shifted from story to star. Star of "Still Life" was Margaret Sullavan whose husky voice and special radiance have been too long absent from television. (Next week: Helen Hayes.) The story is a tender, endearing, if rather exasperatingly tenuous tale of unabashed though illicit love—a woman's story guaranteed to provoke them all to freshets of tears.

The producer-director of this one, Frank Telford, one of the brighter young men around, hewed closely to the original play rather than to the movie with one unaccountable difference. The locale was shifted to America. There's nothing especially wrong with this except in the device by which the lovers met, which remained unquestionably English. You know how they met? Miss Sullavan got a cinder in her eye.

Wendell Corey springs to the rescue: "Can I help? Please let me look. I happen to be a doctor." But for that cinder, Miss Sullavan and Mr. Corey would have been taking trains out of that station for the next twenty years without so much as a glance in one another's direction.

CHAPTER 6

Witches and Plunging Necklines

The Women
[JANUARY 3, 1950]

THE WOMEN, those extraordinarily lucrative staples of radio, are infiltrating television in growing numbers, and I think one of the few safe predictions that can be made about this medium is that the distaff program will have a large and firm niche in it.

I realize that "the women" is not very descriptive, but then it was always difficult to pin a label on radio's Mary Margaret McBride, Martha Deane, Barbara Welles, Nancy Craig, Margaret Arlen and the hundreds of other women who conduct interview programs. They are not exactly commentators, not exactly reporters, not exactly mistresses of ceremonies, not exactly anything you can put a finger on with any precision (at least, not a masculine finger). Their sole common denominator is the fact that they are women, their programs appeal almost exclusively to women, and they bring in a very tidy, timeless revenue to a great many radio stations. In fact, a lot of stations would have difficulty surviving without them.

One thing can be said for certain at this early date. Television's women are likely to be a different breed from radio's. Mary Margaret McBride, possibly the most successful of radio's women, had a fling at television and got out in a hurry. Beauty is likely to be a prerequisite for the visual woman, where in radio it didn't much matter. (Some of radio's women, though, were very handsome girls.)

Looks appear to have been a commanding consideration in the selection of all three of the television women whose work I happen to have sampled—Eloise McElhone, Wendy Barrie and Faye Emerson. All three are characterized by a fearful kinetic energy, a phenomenal gift of gab, an overwhelming femininity of movement (if I make myself clear and I think that I do), and that special female gift for total irrelevance.

Of the three, I'd like to discuss only one—Miss Barrie—not because she's the most typical but because she's—well—the most startling. She sounds like most any girl on a telephone:

"Well, how do you feel? How are you?" she begins, seated at a desk, riffling through papers. "By the way, tonight in Chicago there is a Wendy Barrie party. Thirty people all looking at me on television. (Blows the screen a kiss.) Yoicks! Yoicks was put in here by my writer. It's not a word I ordinarily use.

"Well, whaddaya know! Bob Kintner, our executive vice-president, has been made president of A. B. C. Head man. Glad we knew you when, Bob. Wonder who'll be exec. Probably me. I get all the odd jobs around here. And here (fingering through some press releases) is some news about Montgomery Clift. (Wrinkles her nose.) I don't *like* Montgomery Clift. I think he's a very snooty young man. Hello, Taylor! (Waving offstage.) Oh, we've got the cutest page boy here."

It's a mixture of gossip, backbiting and impudence delivered at breathless speed and accompanied by the most superb display of hand-wringing, hair-waving, body-wriggles and facial contortions. A pretty lass, though, Miss Barrie, and this spectacle I find vastly more entertaining than some of the dog acts on Ed Sullivan's show. There are guests, too—singers, painters, actresses and the like—all athirst for publicity and all possessed of some talent which Miss Barrie succeeds skillfully in suppressing.

"He's the most magical thing. He sings," Miss Barrie will say, introducing a male guest. "Well, dear, tell us all about yourself. Get off my dress. Isn't that interesting? Isn't that simply wonderful? (He hasn't got a word in edgewise.) Now sing something for us."

This particular singer, whose name I didn't catch, sang a Calypso song appropriately entitled: "Talking Is a Woman, Listening Is a Man." Miss Barrie listened, looking irritated. She doesn't listen often. Once, a painter, whom she'd queried on the subject, said: "Painting is a very hard thing to talk about."

"Then we shan't talk about it," said Miss Barrie crisply. That ended that.

If a guest bores her, she yawns openly. One guest she looked at incredulously for a moment and then asked suspiciously: "Did *I* invite you here?" Later, she interrupted his act by clapping her hand over his mouth and rushing him offstage, practically by the scruff of the neck. The guests take this abuse with remarkable good nature.

If they can take it, so can I. In fact, after all the outrageous hand-kissing of guests on radio, this brusque handling is refreshing to watch.

The Glamour Goes Round and Round
[FEBRUARY 21, 1950]

IN HOLLYWOOD, they call it name-dropping. Out there it's almost impossible not to drop names, everyone being so incredibly famous. On television, they have introduced a refinement of the name-dropping game which I have decided rather arbitrarily to call celebrity-dropping. You don't just drop the name; you drop the whole man.

The doorbell rings.

"Now who could that be?" cries Ilka Chase, knitting her intelligent brow.

It turns out to be Arthur Schwartz, the composer, the last man in the world she expected at that hour. Especially with all those television cameras unfortunately trained on the front door.

"You know everyone, don't you, darling?" continues Ilka, doing the rounds. "That's Abe Burrows over there next to the piano. And you must know Carol Coleman. And Durward Kirby. And Bill Nalle."

Of course, it'd be better if Rita Hayworth walked in but if Arthur Schwartz is the best you can do, well, it satisfies the requirements of the game. Anyhow, that's how it's played by Ilka Chase on her program, which is called—now don't blame me for this—"Glamour-Go-Round."

The darn thing opened with the "witty sophisticated Ilka Chase" —I'm quoting from a press release—lying flat on her back, complaining that her recent trip had worn her plumb down to the bone. She'd been to Hollywood, she said, where she'd run into Hedda Hopper, Dotty Lamour—well, name anybody. She was interrupted by the doorbell before she got out more than thirty-five names.

Miss Coleman, who sang in "High Button Shoes," was standing there. "Hello! So good to see you! How was your trip," Miss Coleman exclaimed in small mouthfuls. "What a gorgeous dress!"

"You like it?" asked Ilka. ("Each week," says this press release, "she [Miss Chase] will be gowned by one of the country's leading couturiers." Some sort of advertising dodge, I expect.)

"That red wool," declared Miss Coleman fixedly, "is yummy."

(Yummy, according to Webster's New International, is slang for yum-yum—"a child's exclamation of pleasurable satisfaction in an experience, originally of gustatory satisfaction." Everyone got that straight now? If you want to know where to buy the dress, you'll have to ask Ilka. The last time we had a yummy dress around the house, the cat ate it.)

The doorbell pealed again. This time it was a blonde who explained to Miss Chase—she's sponsored by a cosmetic outfit—"four steps to envious, beauteous complexion." I didn't listen to this very carefully. My own complexion is already so envious and beauteous that small boys shoot slingshots at me under the impression I'm a street lamp.

"Everything for beauty and beauty for everyone," concluded this blonde. Bless you, my child, it's a worthy thought, though hopelessly idealistic. Just how hopeless this "beauty for everyone" idea is was illustrated two seconds later when Abe Burrows walked in. Burrows has kept beauty at arm's length these many years now. The beauticians have made vast strides in this century but they'll never get Burrows in our lifetime.

By the time Schwartz got there, the apartment was getting crowded and everyone was having the best time. Miss Coleman sang "The Trolley Song." Miss Chase danced with Arthur Schwartz. The blonde pulled Mr. Burrows off into a corner and entreated him to teach her Canasta.

And me? I was seated crosslegged on the floor, singing:

"Oh you blow through here,
And the glamor goes down and around
Yo ho ho ho ho ho."

God Bless Us Every One
[OCTOBER 14, 1951]

"THE KATE SMITH EVENING HOUR" struck me at the outset as being marked by a certain air of desperation. It occurs on Wednesdays at 8 P.M., an hour which on N. B. C. last year was sacred to comedians. However, N. B. C., I guess, just ran out of comics and somehow the full-throated and extensive Miss Smith was thrust in there to stem the flood of Arthur Godfrey, who appears at the same hour on what is known as another network.

It's hard to tell what Miss Kate, one of the perennial glories of daytime or female radio, is doing on evening television when the men are home, presumably in search of relaxation. In fact this show is pretty hard for me to explain in any terms. Miss Kate is not a mistress of ceremonies, not even an Ed Sullivan or "What-on-Earth-Am-I-Doing-Here" type emcee; she's not, apart from her singing, an entertainer; she doesn't—as she does on radio—burden the air with profound reflections on the sanctity of matrimony (which she has never experienced).

She is above all that. She is presented as a sort of American institution, like Thanksgiving, something that doesn't require explanation. Ted Collins, her personal Svengali who has guided her destiny —if that's not too sweeping a word—for several generations, accords her a reverence which I found damned irritating. The confounded show even opens with a shot of waves breaking on our rock-encrusted shores, pans next to a shot of the American flag, concentrates briefly on the star-studded section of the flag and dwells finally on a single star—symbolizing, as I gather it, Miss Smith, America, motherhood, and the National Broadcasting Company.

"God bless everybody in no trump," I murmured as this majestic opening faded and Miss Smith herself hove into view to sing "Vampin' Till You're Ready." It's a rather odd selection to follow such a patriotic introduction—I half expected her to sing the Constitution in C sharp minor—and Miss Smith didn't improve matters much by jiggling like a kootch dancer and snapping her fingers. If Miss Kate wants to be an American institution, she ought to model herself a little more closely on the behavior of other American institutions like, say, the stone lions at the steps of the New York Public Library.

The rest of the show is a mish-mash. Olsen and Johnson, another American institution, came aboard to deliver that sketch wherein they are in a hotel room, just trying to get a little sleep, and everybody, including an N. B. C. guided tour, conspires to get in the way. I first saw Olsen and Johnson do this bit in Milwaukee—let's see now

—about 1932 and I must admit they've rounded it, improved it and polished it a lot since then. It may be the most popular sketch on television, having pretty well done the rounds of all the shows. A classic, in short, which ought to be ready in another year or so for the Library of Congress. This is a real classic show.

Three guys and two dolls followed with a song number in which they bounded about without dropping a note, an impressive but exhausting mixture of athletics and vocalism. Miss Smith reappeared to sing "Longing." This led into a big dance number in which several thousand yards of crinoline were unfurled. From time to time, Mr. Collins, dinner-jacketed and acting a little like the curator of the American wing at the Metropolitan, showed up to talk about Miss Smith. There was a brief, muddy dramatic sketch, starring Sylvia Sydney and Sidney Blackmer, which proved that crime doesn't pay. It was acted in almost total darkness without scenery.

None of this was very bad but nothing was very good either. In any case, it didn't add up to anything that resembled a television show and I can't quite figure out what Miss Smith is doing there. They're trying, I speculated, to make a female Arthur Godfrey out of her. But is there any great need for a female Arthur Godfrey or, for that matter, a male Arthur Godfrey? I just don't understand the thought processes that led to the construction of this show and I'm afraid I never will.

Plunging Neckline
[JANUARY 23, 1950]

TODAY I'D LIKE to take up Faye Emerson, a pioneer in the art and one of the most indefatigable guests on everyone else's program in the business.

Miss Emerson now has her own program on WCBS-TV in New York, a chatter-gossip-interview program, at 11 P.M. E.S.T., Mondays. In other words, safely out of reach of the children, which is just as well. (They wouldn't understand Miss Emerson's peculiar gifts.) "Television Guide," a smallish magazine, referred to Miss Emerson recently as "the plunging neckline Woollcott," a tart though not entirely accurate description.

Miss Emerson, I'd be the first to admit, fills a ten-inch screen very adequately. Very adequately. The gowns are impressive. (One of the qualifications for this line of work is a wardrobe that stretches from here to there.) Besides clothes, Miss Emerson possesses a generous and mobile mouth, a brow of noble proportions and conceivably the most eloquent eyebrows in all television.

She is no Alexander Woollcott, though, and appears to have no pretensions in that direction. Her fifteen-minute show opens, as do all the feminine TV shows, with a gush of volubility, much of it the smallest of small talk. "Hello," she says, "I have a little bit of gossip."

She had a wonderful dinner, she'll tell you, at someone-or-other's house and they discussed Tim Costello's "Where all the newspaper men hang out." (Not all of them, dear. A great many of them hang out at Bleeck's. Some of the richer ones hang out at Twenty-One. And then there's that small, conservative minority which hangs out, of all places, in its own homes.)

She saw the Katharine Cornell play and thought the critics were very unkind, very unkind. Poor Kit. She's such a wonderful person. She saw the opening of Milton Berle's movie. Mr. Berle was terribly nervous. (That, I refuse to believe.) Miss E. had also been to a party at Mrs. Martin Beck's and thought we'd be interested in how the apartment looked. Description of apartment. "She was wearing just simple chamois—just simply chamois, that's all." (That can't be right. Looks like chamois on my notes but I refuse to credit my own eyes.)

After about five minutes of this, the first guest—there are two on each show—appears and there is a display of profound surprise on the part of both parties that they ran into each other in this unlikely way. "Why Denise Darcel, of *all* people!" One of these days Faye Emerson is going to catch sight of herself in a mirror and exclaim: "Why, Faye Emerson, whatever brought you here?"

The interviews follow the usual line. How did the guest get into show business or novel writing or interior decoration or whatever? There is conspicuous mention of the guest's latest book, play, movie or recipe. If the guest happens to sing or play the saxophone, he is asked to perform and does. If he knew any card tricks I expect he'd be asked to do those too. Among the guests so far have been Joey Adams, George Jessel, Abe Burrows, Irene Rich, Earl Wrightson, Robert Q. Lewis and Mercedes McCambridge.

After grappling with the guests, Miss Emerson gets back to her desk and passes along a little more gossip. "At the party last night, we all played party games. Some are a little rough but they're really gay and they really, really warm up a party."

The Faye Emerson show, I assume, is aimed primarily at women, but I know several men, including this one, who are helplessly fascinated by it for reasons which I'm sure never occurred either to C. B. S. or to Miss Emerson. The favorite program from the male point of view was one in which Denise Darcel appeared. Miss Darcel had quite a wrestling match with a strapless evening gown which kept trying to fall off but didn't quite.

Incidentally, the Faye Emerson show was originally to have been the Diana Barrymore show. Well, I was on hand with pencil and paper to record the first show. In place of it there appeared a sign: "The program originally scheduled will not take place." "Television Guide" explains that a piece of plaster came loose from the ceiling and conked Miss Barrymore on the head. You're at liberty to believe that, if you like.

Pick on Someone Your Own Size
[MARCH 31, 1950]

SOMEWHAT PEEVISHLY, I take pen in hand today to set Miss Faye Emerson straight on her neckline. Never, never did I think any woman would consult me on where to wear her neckline. Never has any woman even consulted me about where to wear her hem line. I have, it's true, expressed some forcible opinions about both necklines and hem lines from time to time, but these opinions have never been sought by women and have, in fact, been greeted by derisive laughter from all the ladies within earshot.

The Faye Emerson controversy, which threatens to start a civil war unless firmly handled, started innocently enough when I reviewed Miss Emerson's television program, in which I used the phrase—borrowed, as it happened, from someone else—"the plunging neckline Woollcott." Miss Emerson seized upon this phrase, and that night on her program she told her rapt admirers that I disapproved low necklines. What, she asked, did the rest of the listeners think? In short, write.

Well, it was a nice stunt and brought Miss Emerson bushels of mail, much of which she read over the air and 95 per cent of which upheld the low neckline. Epithets of all nature were heaped on my innocent skull. Even my alma mater was dragged through the mire. "I never heard of any other Yale graduate," wrote one Connecticut housewife, "even ones who majored in archeology, advocating Mother Hubbard gowns."

I never did either, including this one. For your information, Connecticut housewife, Yale men have been admiring pretty shoulders since your great-great-grandfather's day. The fact is, I have been maligned, misrepresented, traduced, defamed and slandered. Not once in that column did I express or imply disapproval of Miss Emerson's revelatory costumes. I simply described them in the most graceful prose I could muster at the moment. It is one of the functions of criticism, Miss Emerson, to outline to the readers the general nature of the entertainment and the entertainers. To have avoided outlining your own spectacular—uh—outlines would have been a shameful neglect of my duties.

If there was any opinion at all expressed in that column, it was one of helpless admiration. Several of the sentences positively leered. I want to go on record right now—the rest of Yale University can speak for itself—as heartily in favor of *all* necklines—high, low and upper middlebrow. In fact, Miss Emerson, I don't care if you take the damned dress off.

I now retire hurriedly from the field of feminine fashions. If any of the rest of you girls are having troubles with your peplums, your sheath silhouettes, you'll have to consult someone else. I got enough work of my own.

The Five Faye Emersons
[MAY 12, 1950]

THERE IS A scurrilous rumor going around that there are really seven Faye Emersons, that no one girl could meet so many people, attend so many parties, be guest star on so many programs (while still not neglecting her own) and, at the same time, finger stage and and screen offers.

Well, its a dirty lie. I happen to know there are only five Faye Emersons. There is one actress Faye Emerson who handles stage, screen and television dramatic work; another Faye Emerson, the smartest of the five, who appears on quiz programs; still another Faye who handles her own program and attends all the parties; there is the weight-lifting Faye Emerson and there is one spare. The spare is carried around in a velvet lined case, like Charlie McCarthy, in case any of the others break down.

The spare is the most versatile of the crowd. There was a bad period last winter, when all the four regular Faye Emersons broke down. The spare Emerson was rushed in with only a hurried briefing, and, gads, what a job she did! In that one heroic week the spare Emerson attended twelve parties, was linked—as they say—romantically with six different men in six different columns, appeared on four different quiz programs (and got everything right), lifted a 250-pound man over her head, took the lead in an hour-long dramatic program and scored three times for C. C. N. Y. against the

University of Kentucky in the last three minutes of play at Madison Square Garden. She's now back in her velvet case, breathing heavily.

The multiplicity of Miss Emerson is not the only case of its kind, though, of course, it's the most conspicuous. Radio always fell easy prey to multiplicity. (Take your dirty hands off that word, editors. I like that word.) There was one dizzy period two years ago, when, as the leading scholar of radio multiplicity, I drew up a chart of guest appearances, the darndest thing you ever saw. Bing would appear on Fred Allen's program; Fred would appear on Jack Benny's program; Benny would appear on George Burns's program; George would appear on Bing's program and then Benny would. . . . Well, you can't explain it. You have to diagram it.

Right now, multiplicity has reached new heights, both on radio and television. The Campbell Soup people are so entranced with "Double or Nothing" they have put it on the air *ten* times a week. Time was when the avid housewife could only slake her thirst for Walter O'Keefe, the emcee of that program, from 2 to 2:30 P.M. on Mondays, Tuesdays, Wednesdays, Thursdays and Fridays. This clearly wasn't enough for your real O'Keefe addict, so the Campbell people put "Double or Nothing," a very appropriate title, on in the mornings, too. That should be enough O'Keefe for anyone except a sanatorium case. But don't count on it. They may fling "Double or Nothing" at us in the evenings, too, for the benefit of those few wretches who still work in the daytime.

The leading male exponent of multiplicity is, naturally, Arthur Godfrey, who may be the most multiplied man of our time. Godfrey —there's only one Godfrey, though I understand Peter Goldmark over at C. B. S. is working on another in four colors—can be seen or heard or both on three television shows and three radio shows. One of the radio shows, heard on Saturday, is a digest of all the morning shows. Nuggets of especial value are washed out of the five morning shows, smelted and fashioned into a necklace of great price for the Saturday-night crowd. So far as I know, Godfrey is the first radio entertainer to be condensed. He probably won't be the last.

N. B. C. has nothing like Godfrey, but it's grooming Dave Garroway as the head of its multiplication table. He's moving up fast. Garroway now has three radio shows, including two five-times-a-week programs and one television show. Keep your eye on Garroway. In fact, you'll have difficulty averting your eye, Garroway being a fairly ubiquitous character.

One of the most astonishing recent cases of multiplicity was that of Jack Barry, the master of ceremonies. One night Mr. Barry was on the N. B. C. television network as moderator of "Life Begins at Eighty" from 7:30 to 8 P.M. At the same time, same night, Mr. Barry (by transcription) was on the N. B. C. *radio* network as co-star and producer of the Joe DiMaggio show. When a man starts competing with himself, he has, I feel, carried multiplicity way out of bounds.

We Televise a Witch
[JANUARY 10, 1951]

TODAY IS THE DAY the British Broadcasting Corporation proposes to televise—or attempt to televise—a ghost, specifically the specter of Catherine Howard, fifth wife of Henry VIII. She's the girl, you'll recall, who lost her head in 1542 for alleged misdeeds in the boudoir which were never sufficiently proved to my satisfaction.

I wish the B. B. C. luck in this enterprise and I'm very sorry that I can't be there to watch the operations in Hampton Court Palace. I devoutly hope someone asks Miss Howard just what *did* go on back in 1542, whether the accusation was just or unjust. After all, a girl who has been dead for upward of 400 years has nothing to gain or lose one way or another and can be expected to tell the truth.

Over here, we have televised a lot of people who have resembled ghosts in more ways than one except that they lacked the finality and dignity of death. We have, however, televised a witch, specifically Miss Lilli Palmer, who started her own program on C. B. S. last week. Ponds, the face cream, brings—as they say—this program to you and to me, which, I believe, makes Miss Palmer the first sponsored witch in the history of sorcery.

Miss Palmer, as I suppose everyone knows, plays the role of witch in the play "Bell, Book and Candle" with such enormous authority that the critics almost uniformly mourned the fact that, at the end of the play, she loses her witchhood and assumes womanhood. The critics, if I understood them correctly, felt that this assumption of womanhood was a long step down in the social scale. It's a rather odd point of view for the critics to take and, I imagine, a rather difficult one to explain at home.

Still, after watching her initial performance, I'm inclined to agree with them. Miss Palmer is such a tempting morsel that if she isn't a witch she ought to be one. Hers is an exquisitely modeled face abounding in sharp corners at the tip of the nose, the edge of the lips, the edge of the eyes; a catlike, alert, vixenish face which instantly commands attention. In fact, everything Miss Palmer does commands attention. She endows with great, though mystifying, importance, her walk, her movements, her gestures.

As a matter of fact, a kinescope of her projected show which belted around town for a while before Miss Palmer settled on C. B. S. opened with a shot of her back. She was painting. "I paint a little," she announced, her opening line. It takes great confidence in one's personal electricity to open a new TV show with a view of one's rear. Unhappily, this was abandoned for a more conventional approach, a shot of Miss Palmer singing *"Auf Wiedersehen."* "Hello, let me introduce myself. I'm Lilli Palmer. Here's my fireplace. My window. My room."

Over the fireplace was a picture of George Bernard Shaw, and Miss Palmer fell to discussing her last meeting with G. B. S. when she obtained permission to play Cleopatra in his "Caesar and Cleopatra." From there she went on to quote Euripides, whom she described as a local G. B. S. in Greece 2,000 years ago. Right away, you get the idea that Miss Palmer is a woman whose center of intellectual gravity is of higher density than Dorothy Kilgallen's. Both mentally and physically, I should say, Miss Palmer is going to be rough competition for the Faye Emersons in the television dodge.

Presently, Miss P. introduced her guest—Miss Pamela Brown, who is accused but is innocent of witchcraft in the play "The Lady's Not for Burning." I lost the thread of their conversation because I was much too interested watching the interplay of two expert actresses trying to focus the center of attention on themselves. That's about all there is to the program. Tomorrow night the guest will be the movie director Robert Siodmak, who was born in Memphis but became famous as a movie director in Germany. And next week, Miss Palmer may conceivably produce Catherine Howard, depending on how well things work out with the B. B. C. today.

Leave My Mould Alone
[AUGUST 3, 1948]

THE OTHER DAY, impelled by a sense of duty that strikes me occasionally, I met Corliss Archer, a teen-age girl anybody can meet if he's not careful with his radio dial around 10 P.M. Tuesdays (N. B. C.). I haven't seen Corliss for some time, years in fact, and it was vaguely disquieting to find she hasn't changed a bit.

Corliss was sulking because her boy friend Dexter said she would never grow up. In her imitable voice—every teen-age girl in radio seems to talk the same way—she was squealing: "He said some girls never grow up. Can you imagine anyone saying that about me? A girl like me?"

Well, yes, I can, Corliss. It seems to me Dexter has waited long enough. Miss Archer, it ought to be explained, first saw the whites of an audience's eyes in 1943 in the play "Kiss and Tell," and she was then about fifteen. How many teen-age years are there? There used to be only seven (thirteen through nineteen, the way my mathematician figures it), but in radio these girls get becalmed at the age of fifteen and live in a perpetual Sargasso Sea of adolescence. (I'll shoot the first man that touches that metaphor.)

I'm especially disturbed about the effects of these teen-age babes on all the other teen-age babes and I'll tell you why. Just after Miss Archer had vented her displeasure at Dexter she announced her determination to make him over into something more presentable than the drip he is. The word drip is Miss Archer's, not mine. She was, in short, going to mould him. I don't know whether she succeeded in moulding him; I suspect she did, Dexter being one of the most plastic representatives of his plastic age group. Anyhow, I didn't wait around for this sordid spectacle. I turned the radio off and fell to brooding about the consequences of this loose talk on the female young of the nation. The idea that all men require moulding and that only a woman is capable of it has already become too deeply rooted in our popular literature and I think it's high time somebody started digging away at it.

Years ago, I recall with distinct pleasure, in the play "Cynara," somebody or other remarked—and I'm quoting loosely from memory—"When two people get married, the husband hopes his wife won't change and the wife hopes she can change her husband. Both are disappointed."

It's a fairly accurate though sweeping statement. Despite years of failure, the girls—stirred by this incessant propaganda on the radio and in a lot of popular magazines—keep trying to mould us and I'm depressed to find this idea seeping down into teen-age ranks. A fellow ought to be able to get through boyhood without a lot of girls moulding him all over the place. Seems to me that one of the most persistent and non-shatterable myths of American life is this idea that behind every American man is an American girl leading him by the nose from the rear, if that seems possible. The myth is endlessly repeated with slight variations in story and song and radio comedy.

Every two years or so an English author with a fixed smile and a trunkful of misconceptions comes to this country and hears the songs and reads the stories and listens to the radio. Then he goes home and writes a book explaining that Ameddica is a hag-ridden society entirely under the domination of women. From this premise, which I find wholly questionable, he draws some of the confoundedest conclusions I ever read, sets up an imaginary society of Amazons and manages to fit our whole social structure into it.

All this is quite a distance from "Meet Corliss Archer," which is a pleasant enough teen-age comedy if that's one of your enthusiasms. Miss Archer, I ought to add, has a patient, resigned mother and a father who lives in a state of perpetual exasperation. Dexter is a libel on all teen-age boys. As for Corliss, I think she should be burned as a witch. Anyone who can stay fifteen that long is obviously in league with the devil.

CHAPTER 7

Bless Their Little Hearts

The Untapped Billion Dollars
[JUNE 1, 1948]

THE RADIO RESEARCH gentlemen, the closest thing we have in this country to a Gestapo, have unearthed another fact. I was under the impression they had them all. But they didn't. This is the last fact, and, though I'm impressed by the diligence it must have taken to dig it out, I'm saddened that they got it.

There should be one thing left these people don't know about us. It would add spice. Eighty-two per cent of the wage earners, let us say, leave home between 8:30 and 9 A.M., 37 per cent of them slamming the front door. That would have been a rather nice one to have kept confidential. But it isn't any more. It was uncovered a full year ago by a research man named Robertson, who thereby won the Crosby Prize—the nearest thing in research to the Nobel Prize—for conspicuous nosiness above and beyond the dictates of common sense. That, according to my figures, was the second last fact there was about us.

The last fact is a rather forlorn fragment of information. The Gilbert Youth Research Organization, easily one of the most menacing organizations in recent history, has ferreted out the intelligence that the nation's youth in the eight-to-fourteen-year age bracket have a minimum weekly income (allowance and earnings) of $1.57.

This, the Gilbert Youth Research Organization declares gleefully, amounts to an annual purchasing power of $1,000,000,000, much of it untapped. If my hunch is anywhere near correct, it won't stay untapped long. I can just see the candy companies, the comic book profession, the motion-picture industry, rubbing their hands malevolently, preparatory to turning Junior upside down and shaking hard.

Junior has been holding out quite a lot from the halls of commerce. According to the Gilbert Youth Res—— Ah, the hell with it—— the kiddies consume only about three candy bars a week. Eighteen cents, for heaven's sake! What on earth do you do with your money, Junior—save it? Less than half of the kids brush their teeth twice a day. (Bob Hope is going to catch it for that one.) Nearly 60 per cent of the girls stop eating cereal at the age of fourteen. (Jack Armstrong, would you mind stepping into the front office a minute? We would have words with you.)

I don't know what to make of this. When I was a boy—that was a long time before advertising had hit its stride—radio hadn't been invented and research was in its infancy—I was compelled to brush my teeth three times a day. I averaged three candy bars a day and, on a real binge, four or five. Yet today, after twenty-odd years of radio's special pleading, what do we have? One toothbrushing a day. Three candy bars a week.

You know what I think, Gilbert Youth Research Organization? I think these people are over-selling. You tell a twelve-year-old boy to dash right out for that candy bar, those crisply crackly Nutties, and do it now. The effect is not much different from telling the same lad to get to bed this minute. You just arouse antagonism.

I did considerable research on the problem of selling in the eight-to-fourteen-year age group myself once and I'm happy to pass along my findings free of charge. Urgency is the one thing that has to be avoided at all costs. You sidle up to your prospect, your eyes fixed on a distant tree, casually tossing your brown and white agate from hand to hand.

"You couldn't buy this glassy from me for ten trillion dollars, Stinky," you say. Stinky is immediately consumed by mirth. "That thing!" he chortles. "I wouldn't take that off your hands if you paid me ten trillion dollars."

The deal is then consummated to the satisfaction of both parties within the next ten minutes.

Parents, Arise! You Have Nothing to Lose but Your Sanity!
[AUGUST 8, 1950]

THERE'S A CHILDREN'S program called "No School Today" emanating from Cincinnati, presided over by Jon Arthur, who is known to the kids as "Big Jon." Big Jon is a great favorite with the kiddies and exercises a sway over them that any parent would envy. The other day Big Jon invited his small fry audience to lift their hands over their heads—I forget just why—and neglected to tell them to take them down again. Within fifteen minutes A. B. C. was flooded with calls from parents asking Big Jon, for heaven's sake, do tell our children to drop their arms. Kids all over the country had their hands skyward, and no amount of parental urging would get the hands down until Big Jon said so.

That's the best example to come to my attention so far of the unquestioned obedience radio (and television, too, for that matter) exacts from the junior members of the household. You tell little Oscar to trot off to bed, and you will probably find yourself embroiled in argument. But if Milton Berle tells him to go to bed, off he goes. (On his two marathon performances for charity, Berle was the court of last resort in countless cases where the parents themselves couldn't get the kids to bed.)

I think this is the last straw. More and more during the last couple of decades, the parent has had to behave with the utmost circumspection to avoid bruising his child's psyche and thus permanently damaging him for useful activity as an adult. The more deference he paid the child, the less the child paid him. Now, it's come to the point where any clown on the radio demands and receives more respect than mummy or daddy.

You know where it's all going to lead, don't you? Ultimately, there will have to be a "Time to Get Up" program in which Uncle Don shouts out, "Seven-thirty, my little friends. Old Sol—your friend and mine—is peeping from behind the purple hills, bidding us to brush our teeth like good little boys and girls." And Uncle Don will be right with us till the kids are packed off to school, exhorting them to greater effort with their Wheaties, reminding them not to forget the English composition he dictated to them the night before, even, in spirit, kissing them all good-by.

Then the day will come when Uncle Don will drink himself to death. The cheerful voice will be missing at 7:30. The nation's children will sleep on and on and on. Did you ever hear of the Pied Piper? Well, his influence was limited to the aural range of his pipe. These electronic Pied Pipers have no limits at all.

Whatever Happened to the Bad Boy?
[NOVEMBER 19, 1948]

THE CLOSEST THING we have around to Huck Finn and Tom Sawyer —and it's pretty distant—is Henry Aldrich and Homer, which proves how boyhood has degenerated since I was a boy. Boyhood—let's face it squarely—has been going down hill for years, but it's come to a pretty pass when its archetypes are Henry and Homer and Oogie Pringle and Archie Andrews.

When I was young, roughly around the twelfth century, the blueprint of my deportment was drawn to scale by Huck and Tom and Penrod and the hero of "The Story of a Bad Boy," whose name I've forgotten. (I missed "Peck's Bad Boy" entirely. Different generation, I guess.) These three provided an outline of general hell-raising that any boy could be proud of.

Judging from the radio, the lads still get into mischief (a word we wouldn't be caught dead with), but they never get into it deliberately. The difference is one of intent, and that's where a boy's character is formed, which is why I think the education of our sons is in incapable hands. When Huck and Tom ran away from home, when the Bad Boy (what *was* that kid's name, anyway?) blew up the village cannon, they knew what they were doing.

In both cases there were unexpected consequences, but the sense of wrongdoing was present from the outset. They were active little fiends destined to be captains of industry when they grew up.

For Homer and Henry and Oogie and Archie, I see no hope whatever of future brilliance. Week after week, they get into one jam after another, always by accident, never by design. The trouble they see is a censored, respectable, passive trouble. They're the victims. In Huck's day somebody else was the victim.

Modern boys—and I'm judging by Oogie and company—are a bunch of namby-pambies. They never *try* to get into trouble. They try to stay out of it. But, with the best intentions in the world, they stick their elbows through windows, they fall flat on their faces in front of their best girls. Always they're crossed by circumstance or the idiosyncrasies of adults. What I object to is that they're trying so hard to be good. And they generally are foiled by their own stupidity.

What sort of example is that to hold up before a young boy? Penrod and Huck and Tom slipped once in a while in the mires of boyhood, but they were never stupid. They didn't put their feet in their mouths with such monotonous regularity. Their parents worried about them. Henry and Homer and Oogie and Archie worry about their parents. Also, the modern girl has got out of hand. There was a place in Penrod's life and in Tom Sawyer's life for girls, but there was also a place where girls weren't allowed. The modern boy seems to have girls on the brain all day long.

I dunno. These adenoidal infants they got on the air don't sound quite bright or quite virile. Of course, you might argue that all these kids—Archie and Henry and Homer and Oogie—belong in the category of Tarkington's "Seventeen" rather than in the company of Huck Finn, but they're the nearest thing we have to Huck.

There aren't any Huck Finns in radio, the influence probably of mothers craving respectability. I'm against it. A couple of Huck Finns would be a lot better for the kids than Captain Midnight, Superman or Tom Mix.

There wasn't any real harm in Tom and Huck. They were just harum-scarum.

Enfant Terrible
[MAY 26, 1948]

NOT LONG AGO I devoted a couple of columns to the programs inflicted on children. It's only fair to add that the children inflict a good deal on the adult listeners too. There are a couple of programs, Juvenile Jury and the Quiz Kids, given over almost entirely to children and, in addition, masters of ceremony appear to have discovered only recently that a child confronted by a microphone will blurt out something unexpected with reasonable regularity.

The childhood wisecrack is open to criticism on many, many counts. but lack of sophistication isn't one of them. Unless they're sneaking in dwarfs on us, these little so-and-sos are some of the most disillusioned, cynical tots since the Russian revolution. They have no faith in parent or beast, particularly the former.

The wittiest of the juvenile Noel Cowards at the moment is little Dickie Orlan of Juvenile Jury. His comments are so penetrating that several of my adult acquaintances—I have several—have expressed the desire to beat his little skull wide open out of sheer admiration. (They want to count his brains.) While Dickie's general attitude toward life doesn't entirely conform to my concept of a well-integrated, happy childhood, I must admit he gets off some pretty good ones, considering he's only seven. At this rate, if he applies himself with diligence, he'll grow up to be Oscar Levant, provided, of course, his admirers are kept at a safe distance. I have here a few of Dickie's smarter remarks and, if they strike you as falling somewhat short of Oscar Wilde, remember Dickie's only seven. (After all, Levant spent a lot of time with Montreal before he got into the major leagues too.)

A four-year-old girl complained that her father, an ex-G. I. studying medicine, refused to take her to school with him. "Well, you're liable to embarrass him," said this enfant terrible. "You want people to think he's been left back?"

One mother complained her child kept her awake jingling the coins in her penny bank. "Teach her to save dollar bills," advised Dickie. A little girl appeared on the program one day to turn state's evidence on her mother. Her mother, she said, insisted she brush her teeth every morning and she hated the task. "Tell her not to worry about 'em," said Dickie. "They'll fall out, anyway." Dickie, incidentally, holds the longevity record for the present panel of Juvenile Jury. He's been on a year and a half.

The Children and the Experts
[NOVEMBER 20, 1947]

CHILDREN'S PROGRAMS, I've always felt, are not nearly so interesting as the uproar they cause and particularly the enemies they have made. Most children's programs are of so routine and fundamental a nature that the hubbub they arouse seems entirely disproportionate. Yet a great many distinguished opinions, couched in scientific language of impressive volubility, have been handed down concerning a subject which, to me at least, is of only perfunctory interest.

I have here a communication from the California Congress of Parents and Teachers (Los Angeles 10th District) concerning a questionnaire sent to 344 assorted experts on the subject of children's programs. Ninety per cent of the experts—pediatricians, neuropsychologists, sociologists, psychologists and educators—said they thought children's radio programs "had a detrimental psychological effect on the minds of children."

Closer study of this report revealed that, while the experts agreed on the harmful effects, they reached totally different conclusions on how the programs did the harm. A physician declared that the intense excitement generated by these programs burnt up too much energy, interfered with the digestion and prevented sound sleep. The child's health was his only consideration.

A philosopher at the University of Southern California ignored the digestion—as philosophers mostly do—and concentrated on the poisonous effects on the child's soul. "They allow the child to be merely a passive listener. Children need to act and take part in creating something. The imagination should be stimulated by beauty and thoughtfulness." (And nuts to his sleep.)

The sociologist, peering at the problem through his own specialized myopia, ruminated—as sociologists will—on the criminal tendencies the programs might arouse. The dean of men of the University of Southern California, Dr. Neil D. Warren, spoke from the high, clear plateau of the educator. Thrillers, he said, made the child unwilling to listen to programs "of a more intellectual type."

I'm sorry there weren't any nuclear physicists present. I'd like to hear the cosmic implications resulting from too much exposure to "Terry and the Pirates." Of course, it's possible some of the more lurid kids' programs effect all these dire consequences on the child, in which case there is scant hope for American civilization. I'm not going to worry about it.

I think all these emotional and mental disturbances are a little too sharply discriminated for the children. Frankly, I don't think the kids can grasp it. Of course, by the power of suggestion and a good deal of strenuous education we might teach the children that radio thrillers interfere with their digestion, their creative powers, their social bent and their education. However, it would take about a four-year course to turn the average child into a neurotic criminal with a terrible digestion and no soul to speak of.

Treading as delicately as possible along this dangerous path, I should like to suggest here that the 344 experts were expressing a fashionable rather than a scientific opinion about children's programs. Whenever experts are plunged into something in which they have little real interest they are quite likely to emit the reponse expected of them. In this case they were following the party line of the P. T. A. It's interesting to note that quite different opinions have come from equally distinguished experts employed by the opposition. The Quaker Oats Company, sponsor of several of these programs, has as its consultant on children's programs Dr. Samuel N. Stevens, president of Grinnell College, Iowa, and former head of the psychology department of Northwestern University. I assume he approves of "Terry and the Pirates" and "Those Websters."

The American Broadcasting Company and the Mutual Broadcasting System, which broadcast most of the disputed children's programs, have at times produced profound and sweeping psychiatric testimony to the effect that the blood-and-thunder school of children's programs not only doesn't have a detrimental effect but actually provides a necessary emotional release for the child.

If they wished to take the trouble both networks, I'm sure, could dig up 344 experts who would testify that children's radio programs aid the digestion, increase social responsibility, enlarge the soul and improve the complexion. One group would cancel out the other, and we'd be right back where we started. I wouldn't pay much attention to either of them. Children's programs, say I, have a radically different effect on the mind of a child than they have on the mind of an expert.

Ministers, Psychiatrists and Children
[AUGUST 21, 1947]

IN THE LAST few months the Parent-Teachers Association in San Francisco has been kicking up a devil of a fuss over children's programs. The most recent action is a resolution urging two networks (Mutual and A. B. C.) to abandon eleven programs—Jack Armstrong, Lone Ranger, Sky King, Hop Harrigan, Superman, Captain Midnight, Tom Mix, Red Ryder, Cisco Kid, Tennessee Jed and Terry and the Pirates.

"Juvenile crime and horror programs are tending to dull the minds of children," says the resolution with great piety but not much perspicacity. The parents and teachers went on to recommend that all future children's programs be submitted to a "recognized, expert and impartial board of judges" consisting of radio representatives, psychologists, psychiatrists, ministers, educators, librarians and "listeners such as parents."

I'm not quite brash enough to defend those eleven programs, but it seems to me the kids require some defense against this sweeping and unfair indictment. It's much harder to dull the mind of a child than the P. T. A. seems to think. Dull-minded children—apart from those congenitally so—are usually the ones whose imagination has been stifled by restrictions imposed by well-meaning but grim-lipped persons such as parents.

The literary merit of children's programs is rather questionable, it's true, but, in so far as the children are concerned, the programs are far better than anything turned out by any such panel of experts. The expertness, and particularly the impartiality, of psychiatrists, ministers and educators—let's leave the librarians and psychologists out of this—can't stand very strong examination. I should have violently objected to any of them passing judgment on my childhood reading. My mind might well have been purer if they had, but my point of view would very definitely have been narrower and my appreciation of style probably totally undeveloped.

Besides, the ministers, educators and psychiatrists would have great difficulty finding any common ground of disapproval. The minister eager to adjust each word to accord with the precepts of the Christian church, the psychiatrist sniffing suspiciously at each evidence of trauma, the educator, his eyes alight with the holy fires of syntax, would be hopelessly at cross-purposes and any agreement among them would be—somewhat like the operations of Congress—a matter of generous compromises in which the script would be so excised, bowdlerized, sanctified and grammatical that it would not only dull the mind of the child but put it directly to sleep. Maybe that's the idea. There's no more virtuous child than one asleep.

The last group of judges—"listeners such as parents"—is a plain contradiction in terms. It's the kids, not the parents, who listen to these things, and if anyone should be consulted it should be they. I'm not foolish enough to recommend the children be given complete control, but right now they haven't any say-so at all.

In fact, without the addition of a single parent, minister or educator, children's programs are already more carefully edited and supervised than any other group of programs on the air.

Vulgarity and horror are strictly forbidden and law and order and fair play inevitably triumph in all of them. That—to lay it bluntly on the line—is why they have no literary merit whatsoever. Not, dear parents and teachers, because they are so free from restraint but because they are so hag-ridden with regulations.

The systematic attempts to purify children's minds have recurred for years, and in restrospect they always look ridiculous. At the time they were written, "Tom Sawyer," "Huckleberry Finn," "Treasure Island" or "Snow White" (a little horror story if ever there was one) could never have passed any such impartial board as that suggested by the San Francisco P. T. A. These works have been hallowed by time and prestige—not an increase in tolerance or common sense on the part of parents and teachers.

For years Mark Twain was plagued by attempts—many of them successful—to bowdlerize his books. As recently as 1905 a group of women with minds like the driven snow attempted successfully to have "Tom Sawyer" and "Huckleberry Finn" removed from the children's shelves of the Brooklyn Public Library. At the time Twain wrote a letter to the librarian, a little gem of irony, which I reproduce in full below:

21 Fifth Ave.
Nov. 21, '05

Dear Sir:

I am greatly troubled by what you say. I wrote Tom Sawyer and Huck Finn for adults exclusively, & it always distresses me when I find that boys and girls have been allowed access to them. The mind that becomes soiled in youth can never again be washed clean. I know this by my own experiences, & to this day I cherish an unappeased bitterness against the unfaithful guardians of my young life, who not only permitted but compelled me to read an unexpurgated Bible through before I was 15 years old. None can do that and ever draw a sweet breath again this side of the grave. Ask that young lady—she will tell you so. (Ed. note: I have no idea who is the young lady referred to by Twain.)

Most honestly do I wish that I could say a softening word or two in defense of Huck's character, since you wish it, but really it is no better than those of Solomon, David, Satan & the rest of the sacred brotherhood.

If there is an Unexpurgated in the Children's Department won't you please help that young woman remove Tom & Huck from that questionable companionship?

Sincerely yours,
S. L. CLEMENS.

CHAPTER 8

Some Low Blows

Understatement, Education and Acting
[MARCH 10, 1948]

RADIO HAS BEEN accused many times, and with great justice, of pumping synthetic excitement into sporting events which were as dull as Monday morning to spectators on the scene. In television this is impossible, so sports announcers are leaning over backward to avoid any hint of exaggeration. The other night I saw a hockey match between the Rangers and the Canadiens reported by Win Elliot, who is easily the winner of the Crosby Prize of 1948 for understatement. Mark my words, Elliot is the man to watch in this field.

The image had scarcely stopped jumping to and fro when Richard started up the ice with the puck and about mid-rink was catapulted into the boards by a husky Ranger. "Richard is being bothered," murmured Mr. Elliot. Richard in this case was so severely bothered I was afraid several of his ribs were broken. A moment later two Rangers and two Canadiens started to beat in each other's skulls with their sticks. "Little bad feeling here," said Mr. Elliot as the dead and dying were carried off.

Later open warfare involving what appeared to be all twelve players broke out in front of the Canadiens' goal. The hockey players tore into each other with sticks, skates and fists in wild fury and I couldn't wait to hear Mr. Elliot explain this one. "They seem to have lost interest in the puck," complained Mr. Elliot. For a while the players were bothered—a favorite word of Mr. Elliot's—only in routine ways, a matter of a few lost teeth and possibly a broken rib here and there. Then a Ranger started up the ice and about thirty feet later was hit simultaneously by three Canadiens. He flew upward and backward about ten yards, landing on his head.

"Lost control of the puck," announced Mr. Elliot.

"And That Man Was..."
[NOVEMBER 24, 1949]

BILL STERN HAS been on the air at the same time, on the same network (N. B. C.) for eleven years, ten of those years for the same sponsor (Colgate). Over the years he has created his own little world of sportsdom, where every man is a Frank Merriwell, every touchdown an epic feat of arms, and coincidence stretches like a rubber band to fit every conceivable situation.

In fact, N. B. C. has received so many comments concerning Mr. Stern's casual attitude toward facts on "Sports Newsreel" that the program is now prefaced with the admission that Stern's stories are partly fact, partly hearsay.

Even the word "hearsay" is a rather generous description, implying, as it does, that Stern's stories have reached the stature of legend and therefore are beyond the irksome confines of journalism. This is misleading. Many of the most lurid of Stern's "legends" originated in the teeming brains of his writers and started on their way to legend only after Stern put them on the air to his devoted audience which runs well into the millions.

You can start an argument in any saloon where sportswriters congregate by picking out any Stern story as the weirdest he has ever told. Stern has told so many fantastic yarns that it's pretty hard to pin down any one of them as deserving the superlative. However, there is one story that bobs up more often than any other, the Stern version of Abraham Lincoln's dying words. As the great emancipator lay dying, Stern related, he sent for General Abner Doubleday, the man who is supposed to have invented baseball.

"Keep baseball alive," said the dying President to Doubleday. "In the trying days ahead, the country will need it." And he fell back on the pillow and expired.

Whether or not this deserves the accolade as the most flabbergasting story Stern ever told, it is typical of all of them. It links a great name and a historic occasion with a sport. And it is totally true. (Lincoln never regained consciousness, as every school child knows.) The Lincoln tale is also illustrative of the Stern philosophy that every American worthy of the name puts sports ahead of all other considerations, including the Civil War.

There is hardly an American of renown who has not been thrust by Stern, completely unsupported by the facts, on to a football field, a baseball diamond, a prize ring or a tennis court. Thomas Alva Edison, for example, would have been greatly surprised to hear that his deafness was the result of a pitched ball that hit him in the head when he was a semi-pro ballplayer, which he never was. (Edison's deafness is pretty generally attributed to a conductor who boxed his ears when he was a candy butcher on trains as a boy.) The pitcher who threw that ball, according to Stern, was Jesse James.

Stern's method of delivering these whoppers is in many ways even more startling than the stories. He tells them in short, declarative sentences, bristling with exclamation points. After every other sentence or so, a studio organ delivers what in radio parlance is known as a "sting," a chord or series of chords which are the closest musical equivalent to an elevated eyebrow. Stern generally keeps the name of his hero a secret until the very last line and then reveals him by means of a sentence that has become a Bill Stern trademark: "And that man was ——." Then the name.

One of Stern's former writers has confessed that he frequently left the last part blank to be filled in at the last moment by whoever happened to be prominent in the news—General Eisenhower, Jackie Robinson, the late President Roosevelt, anyone at all. Stern's writers, of whom he has had many, view him with a mixture of admiration for his audacity and total cynicism. One of them summed up his feelings recently by confessing that he had written a lot of utter malarkey for Stern. Then he added belligerently:
"But look here, it ain't easy to dream those things up."

It's Nice to Have a Woman around the House, Too
[MARCH 2, 1950]

"IT'S SO NICE," sings Miss Dinah Shore out of a million jukeboxes and 80,000,000 radios, "to have a man around the house." Well, thanks, Miss Dinah. It's so nice to have a song on the radio which proposes that a man around the house is a good investment. These ancient ears hark back to "My Man," "Mad about the Boy" and other laments which pointed out that a man around the house was incredibly perilous. He beat you. He cadged money off you. He was an unmitigated cad, though, of course, exciting. It's been a long time since a man around the house—at least in the popular songs—was found to be restful, useful and, in moments of stress, comforting! I don't know what has caused this sweeping revision in Tin Pan Alley, but I find it heartening. In view of it, I'm even willing to forgive that other current favorite—"A Cow and a Plow and a Frau."

I've always been mildly astonished by the nature of fight fans, those mixtures of arrant sentimentality and bloodthirsty cynicism.

This schizophrenia, which would rend the average man in half, was illustrated rather well by a fight broadcast the other night over A. B. C. The decision on a preliminary bout met the violent disapproval of everyone in the house and was being violently booed by the local populace when the announcer intervened brightly: "We will now have one minute of silence in memory of Lavern Roach" (the fighter who died from injuries received in his bout with George Small). The booing stopped. Silence fell. Sixty seconds passed. The booing, undiminished by a decibel, started up again. This neat separation—reverence for the dead, irreverence for the living—all in the space of a minute, is something that could be accomplished without acute emotional indigestion only by a fight fan. In fact, no one but a fight announcer would have dreamed up such a unique memorial, imbedded as it was in Bronx cheers, to a dead fighter.

More of Stern's Fables
[APRIL 24, 1950]

BECAUSE OF WIDESPREAD public demand—we were inundated by two letters—I report herewith some more of Bill Stern's stories, a branch of fiction largely ignored by most critics. Draw your chairs a little closer to the fire, kiddies, and hearken.

Cast your minds back to the day when John Barrymore died. The next day, Stern, who is easily ignited by the more prominent news stories of the day, told how Barrymore had got up a baseball game between two teams of actors for publicity purposes. The pitcher of one team allowed only three hits.

After the game (according to Stern) Barrymore summoned the pitcher, name of John Vernon, to his dressing room and told him he was a better pitcher than an actor and advised him to get into baseball. The following day, Barrymore went to a San Francisco ball club and volunteered to catch in one of its games if they would employ this pitcher. Well, sir, the game was played. Barrymore caught only one inning, but his actor-pitcher stayed the whole game. And that man's real name was—sting—Vernon (Lefty) Gomez.

Apart from the fact that it never happened, it's a fine yarn. Stern has a weakness for this sort of story—a famous name of one sort or another redirecting the career of a younger man who is later to become equally well known. In one of his stories, Grantland Rice was hanging around a gymnasium watching a skinny young kid sparring with another man. Later, he heard the skinny youngster singing in the shower. Rice, said Stern, took the youngster aside and told him to get out of boxing into singing. And *that* young man, naturally, was Frank Sinatra.

The story, which isn't true, made Grantland Rice, normally the most affable of men, furiously angry, one of the few times any one has succeeded in doing that.

However, the reaction of most people about whom Stern spins his fantasies is one of open-mouthed wonder, generally succeeded by amusement. Rarely are they angry. Mrs. William O'Brien, mother of Pat O'Brien, the actor, was listening to Stern one night in Milwaukee and was astonished to hear the following tale.

It seems that in 1925 Harry Greb and Mickey Walker fought at the Polo Grounds. Greb won. Later that night they met in a restaurant, glared at each other, and after a few drinks decided to renew the fight in an alley outside. The fight was broken up by a young Irish policeman, who wanted to lug both men off to jail. Greb dissuaded him and was so grateful to the policeman for letting him off that he later staked him to $200 to go West and seek his fortune. And that man was—Pat O'Brien. The only flaw in this story was the fact that O'Brien never was a policeman in New York or anywhere else.

In spite of the malarkey Stern tells about them, athletes are only too happy to appear on his program. This is understandable because, while the truth gets badly mangled, the athletes themselves invariably are cast in heroic dimensions. On his twelfth anniversary program, in October, guests (by transcription of earlier programs) included Babe Ruth, Eleanor Roosevelt, Joe Louis, Bobby Jones, Sonja Henie, Jack Dempsey, Mickey Rooney, Jack Benny, Mrs. Knute Rockne, Eddie Cantor and Herbert Hoover.

Some of Stern's wilder flights of fancy are occasionally throttled at birth by his more sensible associates. One time Stern and one of his writers were kicking around a story about Frankie Frisch. Frisch, according to this story, was signed by the New York Giants after he was graduated from Fordham, but, like most rookies, he spent most of the first season on the bench. This so disgusted him that he went back to Fordham, determined to quit baseball.

However, a priest at Fordham took him aside and told him: "Frankie, you mustn't be so brash. You're just a youngster and you'll have to learn to respect the judgment of older men. After all, John McGraw is a pretty important person." So Frisch, chastened, went back to the Giants. And that priest was . . .

Here Stern and the writer stalled. They wanted "that priest" to be a fairly sensational name.

"I know," said Stern brightly. " 'And that priest was—the present Pope.' "

The writer, a Catholic, shuddered from bow to stern. He explained gently that the Pope had never been anywhere near Fordham, that Catholics were pretty well informed about this, and that —well—it wasn't a very good idea to bandy the Pope's name around like that. When the story was finally broadcast, the punch line read:

"And that priest was—the man who wrote the song 'And You Brought a New Kind of Love to Me.' "

The Television Brain
[DECEMBER 20, 1948]

WHILE THE MINOR baseball leagues were complaining bitterly that television was killing their attendance, something called a roller derby pulled into the 69th Regiment Armory in New York and attracted 90,000 customers, about half of whom were attributed to the pulling power of television.

Television in this case didn't repel the customers; it drew them like mesmerized flies and, after puzzling over this paradox, I think I have the answer. A roller derby—in case you've never seen one and chances are you never have—is a combination between a six-day bicycle race and a football game conducted on roller skates. I know that doesn't sound possible but that's what it is. Both men and women take part, spinning around a wooden track and bumping into one another like children at dancing school.

Well, my theory is that the people who saw this positively refused to believe the evidence of their television sets and insisted on going to the armory to see for themselves. Having watched the thing on my television set, I could have sworn that the C. B. S. television transmitter made the whole thing up as it went along. "There are more things in heaven and earth, Horatio, than are dreamt of in your philosophy" and it's not inconceivable that these wonderful electronic gadgets we have invented have a sense of humor superior to our own.

It's not, as I say, inconceivable and come right down to it, it's very possible that television, a miraculous and certainly improbable invention, has its own brain. Granting this, carrying the thing forward a bit, it would be almost inevitable that this brain had critically examined the C. B. S. television schedule and found it dissatisfying. "If I couldn't do better than that," this brain probably declared, "I'd get out of the show business and into the insurance dodge."

Consequently, the roller derby.

And that's just the beginning. This television brain, certainly a more sophisticated organism than ours, will gradually elbow the C. B. S. program department aside and revise the whole schedule, certainly the sports schedule. Baseball and football, rational and rather simple-minded contests when viewed by the superior intellect of television, will be discarded. We'll have frog-leaping derbies, lady wrestling matches and dance marathons.

It's high time that life became more like "Truth or Consequences" anyway.

"My Word, That Was a Vicious Punch!"
[JANUARY 31, 1950]

THE B. B. C.'s BROADCAST of the Joey Maxim-Freddie Mills fight in London, re-broadcast in New York by WNEW, might very well have been more comprehensible if it had been done in Greek. This wasn't altogether the fault of the two British sportscasters, Raymond Glendenning and W. Barrington Dalby. Short-wave reception, varying in intensity as it does at the most unexpected times, is likely to pluck the middle right out of sentences. This confusion is compounded by the British habit of placing the emphasis in different parts not only of words but of whole sentences.

Nevertheless, enough came across to show that British broadcasters are in some ways very like our own and in others very, very unlike. I can't, for example, imagine Don Dunphy saying, as did Glendenning, "Oh, that was a vicious blow!"

Glendenning's favorite exclamation was "My word!" "My word!" he'd exclaim. "He suddenly cut loose. Maxim, making his left hand there with a beaut—three times—it worked just like a gun—bang! bang! bang!"

Glendenning, who was noticeably and perhaps understandably partial to the English fighter Mills, kept telling us Maxim had "the most apprehensive look of the two boxahs." Glendenning, in fact, was rather fond of that word "apprehensive," pinning that expression on several ringsiders and also on the Duke of Marlborough, who was in the audience. Sometimes, Glendenning would desert the fighters right in the middle of a round to tell us just how the Duke of Marlborough was taking it all, a practice that would get him fired over here. Jimmy Powers, "The Daily News" sports columnist, who was acting as interpreter for this tremendously British broadcast, commented dryly that in the tenth round when the English fighter lay prone on the canvas, "everyone was looking apprehensive."

One thing the English sportscasters have in common with our own is the tone of vast excitement they bring to the proceedings. Glendenning shouted in moments of stress even louder than most of our own but he managed, despite his blood pressure, to maintain an astonishing literacy of expression. As a rather free-handed translation, compressing here and elaborating there, this is about how he sounded—and every one of these sentences is verbatim, though not necessarily in the proper order:

"Now Mr. Mills, working. Left to Maxim's stomach. Right to the jaw. Now Mills is looping his glove as if to say 'Come on, let's have a go at it!'

"This is absolutely great *news pick* (I can't make head nor tail out of that either). It's a jolly, wonderful fight! Maxim lands another left—well down under the shoulder. Now Mills hits Maxim with *three* punches—really good, full-blooded punches! My word, those were *good* punches. You can almost smell the impact at the ringside.

"But Maxim is moving away carefully. 'Slinking Joe' they might call him—the way he keeps out of trouble. He's as elusive as a needle in a haystack. Now, Maxim launches a right to the face. Left to the stomach." (In this country we say "left to the body." Glendenning persistently and correctly referred to it as the stomach.) "A perplexing outbreak by Mr. Maxim. He's battering his man all the time with that left."

When the knockout came in the tenth round, Mr. Glendenning passed along a version that disagreed violently with the American wire services. The knockout punch, declared Glendenning, was "a tremendous punch to the stomach." (Even from here that sounds unlikely.) "I never expected," said Glendenning, a real sportsman, "to see him crumple up to that punch to the stomach. It was most unexpected. But it was a beautiful punch." According to The Associated Press, Mills crumpled under a left jab to the face and a right to the jaw, which sounds more plausible.

However, Mr. Powers' insinuation that the English broadcasters were misleading their audience in intimating that Mills was winning the fight up to that point is somewhat open to question. Powers pointed out that the A. P. scored the fight six rounds for Maxim, one for Mills, two even—which sounds like Maxim was overwhelming the Englishman. It's only fair to point out that the English system of scoring is different from ours and that two other American wire services called the fight, respectively, even and almost even at the tenth round.

CHAPTER 9

What the Advertising Man Stands For and What We Stand For

Those Soviet Hucksters
[AUGUST 18, 1947]

WHEN THE MOSCOW radio recently agreed to countenance advertising, some instinct told me the Soviet broadcasters were headed for trouble. They were too. Now, after only a few weeks of this notable experiment, complaints are pouring in from angry housewives. The Soviet laundry trust, one of the first to advertise on the air, is not—according to the housewives—living up to its promises. The laundry does not come back in five to seven days. The laundry does not take unlimited quantities of wash. And so on.

No, comrades, no! It's the wrong approach. The first law in advertising is to avoid the concrete promise—five days, indeed!—and cultivate the delightfully vague. "The Soviet laundry trust gets your clothes 22 per cent cleaner, 33 per cent whiter, 44 per cent dryer." It will be a long, long time before any Soviet housewife begins to wonder how anything can be 33 per cent whiter or what exactly are on the other end of those comparatives. We have had far more experience with these matters than you, comrades, and no American housewife has ever asked any such embarrassing questions.

When this approach palls, you must turn on the whispered seduction. "Are your hands chapped and red? Do you have that tired feeling all day? Let us do your washing the NEW Soviet Laundry Trust way!" (Something will have to be done about that name too.) While they are still turning this soft invitation over in their minds, you hit them with the direct accusation, "Do YOUR underthings offend?" After that, there'll be no more complaints. The housewife will be much too upset over her chapped red hands, her offending undergarments to make any counter-accusations. The best defense, comrade, is a good offense.

The Soviet Union may or may not discover the secrets of the atomic bomb in five years but it will never, never learn the secrets of radio advertising in that time. It's a delicate, devious art—far more subtle and difficult than anything in physics.

Our Tragic Sense of Smell
[JULY 22, 1951]

I WAS LYING in bed the other day singing that old folk song "Dream Girl, Dream Girl, Beautiful Lustre Cream Girl" and reading N. B. C.'s new code of practices for radio and television when I fell upon a paragraph which arrested the song just before that poignant line, "You owe your crowning glory to—Lustre Cream Shampoo."

"Intimately personal products which are not acceptable conversational topics in mixed social groups; laxatives and deodorants are not accepted unless the program and commercial presentation are handled in accordance with the highest standards of good taste and business ethics," says N. B. C. in this paragraph.

I don't fully understand this paragraph. You mean, N. B. C., deodorants are not acceptable conversational topics? They are in our house. We never get over discussing the romances blighted because the girls weren't half safe. Frankly, I never thought any girl was half safe or even one quarter safe; I consider them dangerous no matter what you drench them with, but that's neither here nor there.

Anyhow, that side of the story—the fact that the course of true love is largely dependent on what deodorant a girl uses—is well known. But there is another side of the story, N. B. C., and this one had better be suppressed over the air. It is the story of a friend of mine, name of Halligan, whose life was ruined, not because he didn't read the deodorant ads and take heed, but because he did.

Halligan was on the verge of marrying one of those horse-loving girls who never get more than a brief canter from the stables. Naturally, she was a little gamey and Halligan, I think, might have endured this with equanimity but for the deodorant ads. He was over-educated in this respect, reading all of them and listening to them carefully on the air. Finally, he did what he thought was the proper thing for any normal, red-blooded, full-nostriled American. He broke it off, as he had been carefully instructed to do.

Well, sir, it was just the other day this girl inherited $20,000,000. Halligan's heart, which had survived the loss of the girl without serious damage, was broken right in half by the loss of the $20,000,000. He has, to put it mildly, lost faith in the deodorant people. In fact, if he ever meets one on the street, the deodorant man had better take cover if he wants to be anywhere near half safe.

Last time I saw Halligan, he was brooding darkly over a glass of beer, muttering: "For 20,000,000 fish a man could have his nose operated on or maybe even cut it off."

As far as television is concerned, my sympathies are on the side of the deodorant mob. They've had a terrible time trying to mix what N. B. C. calls "the highest standards of good taste" with a reasonable approximation of coherence. There is one TV commercial, for example, which shows three witches—lovely, sleek, well-groomed girls, but witches, nevertheless—their eyes alight with scandal, whispering to one another: "Mary lost her man because of that. Because of *that!* Because of THAT!" Because of what? Her brother's an embezzler? She's got maybe two heads? Speak up, man.

The most abstract of them all, a commercial which is almost as pure an art form as music in that it's hard to explain by anything so mundane as words, is one where a robed woman—half in light, half in shadow—goes down a gloomy corridor as doors close on either side of her.

Pure mysticism, that one. My explanation is that this girl is half woman, half elf and she isn't welcome either in the world of people or the world of elves because neither world can see her, touch her or—the most sinister tragedy of all—smell her.

The Girl

[APRIL 4, 1949]

ADVERTISING, AN AD man told me the other day, is the oldest profession on earth, older—according to this man—than the one generally credited with that distinction. Hastily sidestepping that controversy, I'd like to point out that television commercials already show evidence of all the more mature forms of advertising.

The Girl, for instance. When I was a boy, the most conspicuous advertising symbol was a bull, which, for reasons I don't understand to this day, summed up the advantages of a certain tobacco. Then came the Girl which, supplanting the bull, summed up the advantages of everything else. She scorned the man who hadn't learned about B. O. and was in turn scorned when She wasn't dainty with her underthings.

But her most important and most used function was simply to *be* there, grinning. The Girl grinned over icetrays, soap chips, Lincolns and mink coats. Don't think for a minute we've lost the Girl just because we got another advertising medium. In television we've got the same Girl—Luxed, de-odored, decontaminated, re-hydrated—just like the old days, except that now She moves around, though the smile remains fixed and vaguely bulbous.

She peers into the icebox, smiling as if her little heart would break; she stirs up the breakfast food and feeds it to Junior, smiling tenderly as if She knew full well She was going to get $37.50 the moment the scene ended and Junior would be restored, thank God, to his rightful parents. You will find that pretty, empty-faced Girl cluttering up dozens of television commercials just as if billboards had never been invented.

On television, though, She can flex her muscles and that opens unlimited possibilities. The most luscious use of the Girl on television to my knowledge has been that of Textron, which has a clear advantage. Textron produces, among other things, nightgowns, slips, and—I hate to use the word but I can't think of a better one—scanties. Naturally that gives Textron scope. The Girl provides the scope, and any model with a nice body has lots of scope.

Textron, an ingenious outfit, puts the Girl, dressed in a nightgown, out in the middle of the stage and turns on a wind machine and, brother, you haven't seen scope like that since Commissioner Moss cracked down on Minsky's. Meantime the announcer calls attention to the durability of the Textron, the cut of the garment, the inexpensiveness of this creation and a lot of other extraneous matters. The commercial, one of the longest on television, closes with the Girl sailing through outer space, jumping from star to star, showing off her Textron.

I'm afraid we are going to see lots of the Girl on television. She'll be crossing her legs while She's telling us how delicious that beer is. She'll be standing on street corners in a gale—the wind playing havoc with her skirts—as she tells us how to guard against coughs caused by colds, caused by high winds on street corners. She'll be telling us—full-breasted, marcelled, and looking as much as possible like Hedy Lamarr—how to get the most efficient use out of Frigidaires.

The day—and what a day!—will dawn eventually when the sponsor realizes the full potentialities of the Girl on television. She'll walk in swathed in mink, chattering gaily to her escort: "If it's lovely to wear, it's worth Ivory Flakes care."

Off comes the mink. Underneath is a filmy evening gown.

"Ivory Flakes?" asked the boy friend.

"What else?" says the girl. "But that's not all I do in Ivory Flakes. I do all my lovely things in Ivory Flakes." And She starts unbuttoning the back of that filmy evening gown.

"Tune in again next week—same time, same station," says the announcer, "and see the rest of this commercial."

Next week the program will have a Hooper rating of 112.

Whatever happened to Commissioner Moss, anyhow?

It's Amazing but It's True
[JUNE 20, 1950]

I'VE BEEN LISTENING to and looking at commercials again with my usual open-mouthed wonder. I wander around the world of advertising pretty much like Alice wanders around Wonderland, neither of us quite believing any of it but not quite disbelieving it either.

I've been struck lately by the word "mild." All the cigarette people are boasting about the mildness of their cigarettes. I don't question these claims. Being the perfect target for an ad man, I believe implicitly that *all* brands of cigarettes are milder than all other brands. But I keep wondering why the cigarette people—or the rest of us, for that matter—are so convinced mildness is a virtue in a smoke. The time was a man insisted on a good *strong* cigar. I'd like to have seen anyone sell my grandfather a mild cigar.

Grandfather used to boast that his cigars could knock a horse down at ten feet. We're becoming a nation of sissies.

Now this mildness thing has stepped into the whisky ads. Joe Doakes' whisky is milder than anyone else's whisky. Who wants to drink a mild whisky, anyhow? The dictionary defines "mild" as "gentle, soothing, bland, moderate." Does that describe any whisky you ever drank? With the price of whisky where it is, who's gonna buy the stuff if it hasn't any more effect than Coca-Cola, which is a lot cheaper? I should like to get my hands on one of the lads who write these whisky ads, present him with the mildest whisky I could find and say: "Drink up, son. It can't hurt you. Says so right here in your own words."

I also question the wisdom of another line which fascinates ad-men. "It's *amazing*, but it's true"—a line that has been shooting out of my loudspeaker for years. So many years that my boiling point in the matter of amazement has risen to a point where it's difficult for an ad man to stir me at all.

Now if an ad man really wanted to amaze me, he'd change his pace now and then and throw out something like this: "You'll be left completely unmoved, but the facts, discounting for a certain amount of bias on our part, are . . ." And then into the free trial offer. An announcement like that would bring me straight out of my chair, amazement written all over me.

Some years back, one of the soaps sponsored a commercial which went, as I recall, like this: "Blotso brings new freshness to old pores. Literally takes years off your complexion. As one satisfied customer wrote us: 'My smile is 20 per cent more radiant since I use Blotso.' Yes, Blotso actually removes those wrinkles . . ." And on and on. The one claim this soap did *not* make was that it got the dirt off.

At the time I suggested rather diffidently that this ad be reworded, not so much in the interests of accuracy but simply to exploit a brand new angle in soap salesmanship, to something like this: "Blotso removes the filth from small children, washes adults reasonably clean and unsticks stuck windows. It's also useful in washing out the mouths of profane urchins. It tastes awful." The suggestion was not followed.

Lastly I've been bewitched by the wristwatch commercials on television. One of them shows a man kissing a girl who's almost devouring him. "How does a guy rate an embrace like this?" asks one announcer. It developed that he rates it because of his embraceable watch. Or maybe her embraceable watch. Something like that. The watch—if I understand this thing correctly—acts as an aphrodisiac on any one of the opposite sex for miles around. Well, of course, it has been steadily hinted for years that various brands of toothpaste, deodorants and soaps are really love potions in disguise. But I think that ascribing these powers to a wristwatch is carrying the thing too far. If the ad men aren't careful, we customers will begin to suspect that a man, in addition to possessing all the soaps and cleansers and wristwatches, must have some innate qualities of his own to land a girl.

The same watch, incidentally, in another TV ad shows Bert Parks, the "Stop the Music" man, taking a shower, wearing his watch. "Can your watch take a shower?" inquires Mr. Parks.

My dear sir, my watch can not only take a shower; it goes for a two-mile swim in the ocean every day. This summer I plan to enter my watch in the channel competition. Can *your* watch swim the English Channel, Mr. Parks?

Nature Isn't Always Right, Isn't It?
[MARCH 28, 1951]

THE UNSWERVING FAITH in American advertising, which I learned at my mother's knee, has well swerved. Just when this came about, I couldn't say, but I suspect it started when two of America's most noted entertainers, Bing Crosby and Bob Hope, started advising me on spot announcements, scattered all over the radio, "to open a pack and give 'em a smell."

Entertainers, who a few years back would as lief have played the tent circuit as stooped to commercials, are now busily engaged in selling the product rather than in telling the jokes. My credulity, normally as elastic as a rubber band, has reached the snapping point. In fact, it has snapped and I'll tell you why. For years I believed these famous people smoked and ate and washed with the products they said they smoked and ate and washed with.

It's hard to say when doubts reared. Maybe it really began, deep down in my subconscious, years ago when the late Lou Gehrig blurted out (on the air) that he ate Wheaties rather than Corn Flakes (or something like that) and then reversed his field the next morning. Confusion reigned at the breakfast tables from coast to coast and the reason of American boyhood tottered.

Well, we boys got over it, on the surface at least, and grew to young—well, fairly young—manhood. Then in December our faith was rocked again. Arthur Godfrey advised us to drink Lipton's Tea instead of whisky over the Christmas holidays. Of course, he didn't go so far as to say that *he* was off the sauce and on a Lipton's jag, but he sort of implied that he was. Again faith crumbled, just a little bit around the edges. It was a good thing my mother's knee happened to be within reaching distance or it'd have crumbled altogether. Even then, it took a good, firm talk from mother to convince me that Godfrey was dipping his beak in Lipton's on New Year's Eve.

And it's not just Godfrey, either. Take Red Barber, who broadcasts the Dodger games and whose veracity has always been beyond question in our household. When he said he smoked Old Golds, I believed him. When he said he drank Schaefer's, I believed him. But, by the moons of Jupiter—an oath I learned listening to "Space Cadet"—I began to have grave doubts when he started telling me how much he enjoyed eating his Sugar Krisp. Barber has trouble getting the words Sugar Krisp out of his mouth without choking, much less eating the stuff.

I wouldn't go so far as to call him a liar, but I'd like to take Red on a round of the saloons some day. We'd tank up on all the Schaefer's we could hold, and the next morning I'd push a big bowl of Sugar Krisp in front of him. I'd just like to watch what would happen next. No, on second thought, maybe I wouldn't.

You don't know who to trust any more. Why, just the other day, Sherman Billingsley was asked on the Stork Club show how he knew who to let into the Stork Club. "That's easy," declared the noted host. "The people who smoke Fatimas, of course." That would be interesting information to Humphrey Bogart, who is no longer welcome at the Stork, in case he wants to get back in. Frankly, I don't think Bogie could get back in the Stork Club if he blew Fatima smoke through his ears, and I don't care who knows it.

I just don't believe these people any more. You know what I think? I think these people are paid to say these things. My faith in the probity of the screen stars, the celebrities, the debutantes who use Ponds survived a lot of severe shocks, but it couldn't survive Miss Joyce Matthews. It was Miss Matthews, the first and second wife of Milton Berle, who pointed a finger practically through my screen and said:

"This year your hat accents your Tintaired hair. Color your hair for Easter with lovely Tintair. Remember, nature isn't always right."

That did it. I've eaten the Wheaties, drunk the Schaefer's and Luxed the undies. But color my hair for Easter—no! You know what I colored for Easter, Miss Matthews? Eggs a symbol of spring's fertility for some thousands of years now. These were unendorsed eggs; they came unrecommended by Bing or by Bob or by Arthur or by Sherman. The kids didn't seem to know the difference.

Our Ingenious Ad Men
[JANUARY 22, 1948]

THE ADVERTISING FRATERNITY, a high-strung group whose brains work three ways like cold tablets, has been exhibiting unusual mental activity recently. Even at normal speed an ad man's mind operates around the genius level and when he is deeply stirred, his mind shoots out sparks like the aurora borealis—long, shimmering streamers of thought in four colors. It's an impressive and terrifying sight to see an ad man thinking hard.

Some authorities are of the belief that unusual mental activity in ad men is caused by sun spots; others, including Professor J. Halder Phelps, of Oconomowoc University, think it's the other way around. The ad men, he says, cause sun spots by thinking too hard. In fact, the professor thinks we could pretty well harness the sun by controlling the intellectual efforts of the advertising industry. But, of course, no one has ever harnessed an ad man's mind.

At any rate, whether caused by sun spots or martinis, the intellectual ferment among ad men lately has been considerable and I have here a little file of the brighter sparks generated by this high-powered activity. Here's one from Austin, Texas. When Lux Theater presented "Nobody Lives Forever," a representative of a funeral parlor in Austin hurried over to the local station to purchase spot announcements following and preceding the show.

An ad agency is preparing a radio show for a company that makes hearing aids. This presented what might be described as the ultimate problem in radio advertising. In the last twenty-seven years, the ad men have just about licked the problem of how to make a man, who can hear, listen to something he doesn't want to hear. But to make a man listen to something he can't hear, well, sir, that is a dilemma your real ad man likes to grapple with. Here's how they solved it. The commercials will be aimed at friends of the deaf who will be urged to send in the names of the afflicted. Information about the hearing aid will be mailed to these people. If you think you can escape radio commercials simply because you can't hear, you're crazy.

Here is a novel idea plucked from "Radio Daily." In South Bend, Ind., there's a program called "Wash on the Air," which features —and I quote—"a dramatization of the Bendix automatic washing machine." So far as I know, this is the first time the life of a bit of machinery has been dramatized. We have heard plenty about the lives of Lassie and Silver and even a talking Siamese cat, but up to now, we know nothing of the home life of a Bendix.

It'll be a difficult thing to dramatize. Drama, whether it's Hamlet or Jack Benny, revolves around the flaws in a man's character or personality. But a Bendix is not supposed to have any flaws in either of those departments. The gleaming perfection of a Bendix might grip an audience for the first week or so, but after that the housewives are going to become restive.

"Doesn't anything ever happen to this machine?" they are going to mutter and turn over to "Stella Dallas" to whom virtually everything happens.

If this Bendix wants to stay in radio any length of time, it'll have to develop a few imperfections. Small, lovable imperfections like Jack Benny's tight-fistedness or Dennis Day's gullibility. A bolt that persistently loosens itself (but is easily tightened, of course). Possibly a faint but perceptible cough in the motor.

A really interesting Bendix character would be one that had a mental block against purple shirts and ground them to ribbons. But I don't suppose the Bendix people would like that.

The Leisurely Class
[JANUARY 10, 1947]

BACK IN THE days of Louis XIV and of his immediate successors, a courtier was a nice thing to be. Members of the court came from the nicest families, possessed imposing titles such as Keeper of the

Royal Closets or Master of the Royal Silverware and in consequence of these titles drew outrageous salaries which permitted them to live luxuriously at Versailles. Their duties were nebulous, consisting largely of assisting the king to amuse himself. In fact the differentiation among this class between work and play was so shadowy as to seem nonexistent.

When the French Revolution happened along it was discovered that the state could no longer afford these extravagant and useless appurtenances and they were dispensed with in a rather arbitrary way or to put it in modern language, liquidated. Much, much later in the tide of human affairs—in the mid-1920s, to be exact—there came into being another class of people whose duties were as shadowy and as pleasant as the Master of the Royal Silverware.

They inhabited Wall Street and were known as customers' men. Like the French courtiers, they came from the best families, went to the best schools, were very learned in the arts of eating and drinking but little else, and were welcomed in the best homes. Though well paid, their duties were not onerous. In fact, to the disinterested observer they didn't seem to do anything much except take wealthy potential or actual stock buyers to dinner at the most expensive restaurants. The only requirement for this job was an inexhaustible affability, a speaking acquaintance with headwaiters at the tonier spots, and nice manners. It was a lovely way to earn a living and, at one time, was the goal of all right-thinking Yale men.

Along came the depression, and again society discovered that it had a class of people on its hands that it could no longer afford. The customers' man didn't lose his head, though; only his job. However, when he vanished, he took with him a whole way of life with its pleasant customs and manners and legends. These days you have to work to earn a dollar in Wall Street and survivors of the ancient regime tell me wearily you have to work very hard.

However, whenever prosperity rears its pretty head, society appears to create another of these leisurely classes. (You can hardly call them leisure classes since the members work for a living even though it's hard to define just what they do.) Today, the leisurely class has sprouted, like a mushroom in wet weather, in the advertising and publicity industry. The gentlemen in this new leisurely class don't write advertising copy or photograph the pretty ladies in the ads or do layouts. They don't write Jack Benny's dialogue or dream up Red Skelton's jokes. They're above manual or creative labor of any sort.

They go under the name of account executive, contact man and half a dozen other titles as meaningless though not as romantic as Keeper of the Royal Closets. They take important people to dinner where the conversation is warm, relaxed and pointless. They play golf with radio stars and sponsors and later accompany them to expensive night clubs where they assume the checks. They avoid office hours like the plague. So numerous has this advertising and publicity nobility become that a large part of the luxury night spots in New York are absolutely dependent on it. Take away the advertising expense account and 90 per cent of New York City's expensive restaurants would have difficulty in surviving. Today the young bloods at Yale dream, not of a partnership in Wall Street, but of a partnership in an advertising firm. Prerequisites for the job are for the most part the ability to hang on to a cocktail, hold up one's end in the realm of gossip, and look presentable. Any Ivy Leaguer can handle it with his eyes closed.

When taxes hit their war-time peak, the job became, it must be admitted, a little more strenuous. Expense accounts were so swollen it took concentrated effort to get them down. A theater critic told me wanly one night that he was awfully tired of eating at "21," but that he couldn't persuade press agents to feed him anywhere else. It's much easier to dispose of a bundle of money in "21" than anywhere else.

As the expense accounts grew to astronomical heights, the number of these contact men, account executives or whatever names they went under, grew proportionately and the work, if you can call it that, consequently diminished. Instead of one contact man for six or seven important people, you got one contact man for each columnist, radio star, sponsor or anyone else who had to be appeased, mollified or buttered up in some way. I'm told several contact men have been assigned to me whom I've never even met. I don't know how these gentlemen pass the time unless they've taken up solitary drinking.

You mustn't confuse these people with ordinary press agents who make an honest living chivvying their clients' names into the newspapers, no easy task what with the paper shortage. The contact man doesn't demand anything and doesn't sell anything except that vague commodity known as good will. The ones I've met have been charming, easy to talk to and only too ready to pay for the drinks. They also take up a lot of time which, as far as I'm concerned, might be more profitably employed in listening to the radio or writing about it.

In these opening days of the new year, when prophecies of things to come are on everyone's lips, I have one small prophecy of my own. A Republican Congress has just taken over affairs in Washington with the avowed aim of cutting taxes. Disposal of surplus profits is not going to be the pressing problem it once was. I predict that the advertising expense account is going to be sharply reduced this year and the number of well-pressed young men anxious to take people to dinner is going to dwindle sharply. The contact man won't vanish altogether just yet. But if another depression strikes, I have a feeling that the contact man will join the customers' men and the French courtiers among history's outmoded and useless professions.

CHAPTER 10

Would You Like to Try for $64?

The Jackpot Takes Up Culture
[DECEMBER 21, 1948]

THE INTRODUCTION OF $1,000 worth of books as part of the $27,000 grand prize for "Hit the Jackpot" is possibly the most significant development in recent giveaway history, easily surpassing the gift of Adolph Menjou to a Mrs. Claire Stark on the "Whiz Quiz" program.

Menjou, as a matter of fact, was only lent to Mrs. Stark for the evening; she had to return him the same night in good condition. The books, on the other hand, are a permanent gift and could easily be a prelude to disaster for the giveaways or even for radio. The supposition that giveaway contestants can read is perhaps unwarranted, but they can learn, can't they?

The printed page is a competitive medium and, while it has been consistently losing ground to the blandishments of radio, it still seems to me a risky proposition to expose a radio listener to $1,000 worth of books, the sheer bulk of which is sufficient to keep him entertained for a couple of years without any assistance from the radio.

The idea of giving away books was that of Bill Todman and Mark Goodson, producers of "Hit the Jackpot." Mr. Todman in particular has become increasingly sensitive to the charge flung by irresponsible columnists, this one included, that giveaways—he doesn't like that word either—are a form of lunacy for which giveaway producers will be held accountable on the day of judgment. The addition of books to the grand prize is intended to add tone to the giveaway industry, putting it in the same class as the Rockefeller Foundation. I expect the press releases will be designating Mr. Todman and Mr. Goodson as philanthropists as soon as the C. B. S. publicity staff learns how to spell it.

A thousand bucks' worth of books is a lot of books, 331 by my count. Rinehart & Co. were needled into donating the books, which was no easy job. It took virtually the publisher's entire active list to make up $1,000 worth and consequently there will be some strange and highly specialized titles in the lucky winner's library.

Along with "The Lost Weekend" and "Short Novels of the Masters," the winner will find ten manuals on applied electricity ("Industrial Electric Heating," "Primary Storage Batteries"). His mental health will be almost too adequately cared for ("Mental Defect," "The Substance of Mental Health" and "Psychiatry for the Curious"). His sexual knowledge will be suitably enlarged ("Sex in our Changing World"). And his nerves will be soothed by "Calm Your Nerves." If the winner really wants to buckle down and improve his mind, he'll find "Einstein's Theory of Relativity," "The Citizen and the Law" and the entire "Rivers of America" series (thirty-seven volumes). There are also about twenty-five pounds of mysteries.

Oh, yes, "The Hucksters" is on the list too, a case of radio biting the hand that feeds it. But the two volumes I consider most appropriate to award a giveaway winner are "Living Abundantly" and "Living Prayerfully."

While making this genuflection to culture, Messrs. Todman and Goodson are by no means depending on it entirely, since a grand prize composed only of books would attract about as many customers as a concert in Cleveland. Along with the books go a new

De Soto, a plot of land near Palm Beach, a two-bedroom house ready for construction, and a lot of other things more familiar and infinitely more precious to giveaway winners.

Incidentally, the book gift idea has spread to another C. B. S. show—"Winner Take All," which is offering about 100 books, also from the Rinehart stable. If strong steps aren't taken soon, this reading will take root in the homes of the multitude and, once rooted, will be as difficult to get rid of as the giveaways.

Mrs. Caniff Goes to Town
[JANUARY 23, 1947]

To THE STUDENT of human nature, audience participation shows generally reveal only that a great many citizens are hopelessly greedy and totally misinformed. However, on rare occasions, the master of ceremonies will unearth a gold mine of personality and character. I'm speaking specifically of Mrs. Caniff, who appeared recently on a program called "Give and Take."

Before we get into Mrs. Caniff's unique personality, it might be well to describe "Give and Take." It's a quiz program presided over by a good-natured gentleman named John Reed King, an ornate handle that would look better on a Supreme Court Justice than on a master of ceremonies. As I understand it, Mr. King invites members of the audience to come up and help themselves at tables full of loot. The only requirement is that they answer a few questions, most of which would insult the intelligence of your ten-year-old son. (Was Washington's birthplace in Massachusetts or Virginia?)

You can't miss on this program. Mr. King, for instance, asked one contestant whether the title page of a book was on the left or right hand side of the book. The man guessed the left side. After informing him that this was the wrong answer, Mr. King asked the second contestant whether the title page of a book was on the left or right hand side of the book. The second guy got it right. Process of elimination, you see.

Well, that's just background. The real heroine of this story is Mrs. Caniff, whose accent suggests she lives in New York City. Mr. King asked her a question which comes up on all these give-away programs. "Where are you from?" inquired Mr. King.

"De Far East," said Mrs. Caniff happily.

"The Far East!" exclaimed Mr. King.

"Foist Avenoo," explained Mrs. Caniff.

Right there, Mr. King appeared to take stock. You run into a lot of problems as emcee of an audience participation show and the worst problem of all is a participant who has more personality than you have. Mrs. Caniff was one of those problems. "Now, Mrs. Caniff, just look over those tables and tell me what you'd like to have. How about that toaster over there—chromium-plated, automatic...."

"I got three toasters at home," said Mrs. Caniff benignly. "I give you one."

Mr. King explained hopelessly that he gave things away on this program; he didn't get them. "Let's look over some of the other things. Forget the toaster. There's a wonderful assortment of ..."

"I'm expecting a baby," said Mrs. Caniff.

"You're . . . uh . . . when?"

"Tomorrow."

"Tomorrow!"

"Not tomorrow," said Mrs. Caniff briskly. "I have company coming in tomorrow."

"Look, Mrs. Caniff, time is running short. We have come to the point in this program when ..."

"Don't you ask me questions?" inquired Mrs. Caniff anxiously.

"I'm trying to ..."

"I like the bedspread."

"Good!" shouted Mr. King. "The bedspread! Now listen carefully, Mrs. Caniff. Tell me ..."

"And the layette. Right there—the layette."

"You said the bedspread. No, you can't have them both. Now listen carefully, Mrs. Caniff. Tell me what is wrong with this sentence. 'A horse divided against itself cannot stand.' What is wrong with that sentence?"

Silence fell on the program, as Mrs. Caniff wrestled with the problem. "A horse divided against itself cannot stand," repeated Mr. King. "What is wrong with that sentence?"

"I need my glasses," said Mrs. Caniff.

"She needs her glasses," muttered Mr. King. "Now why on earth . . . Well, she's GETTING her glasses." Again silence enveloped the program while Mrs. Caniff got her glasses and put them on. "A horse divided against . . ." started Mr. King.

"House," said Mrs. Caniff promptly. "House is de woid. Not horse."

"That's correct," shouted Mr. King. "And here is the bedspread. No, we haven't got a coffee-maker, Mrs. Caniff . . ."

Couple Unusual Quiz Contestants
[JUNE 16, 1948]

I SEEM TO be stuck for the moment on quiz contests. If you'll just bear with me a moment, I'd like to put on the record a small, significant anecdote concerning "Double or Nothing." One of the contestants was an Englishman, a very proper Englishman (from England, y'know), the first Englishman I've ever heard at a quiz contest. Bounder didn't know the rules of the game.

First crack out of the box, Walter O'Keefe, the quiz master, asked the fellow—perfectly natural question at a quiz program—where he met his wife. Well, sir, any decent American knows the proper answer for that. Met the old girl in a revolving door. Or jostled her at the two-dollar window at Belmont. Something like that. Adds a little spice, y'know. Audience likes a little witticism. Any man knows that.

Not this chap. Fellow drew himself up stiffly and replied: "I was introduced to her by her sister."

Audience couldn't believe its ears. Just sat there, thunderstruck. Not a peep out of them. Not a boffola. Introduced to her by her sister, indeed! What sort of way is that for a man to meet his future consort? World's going to the dogs!

That's not the half of it, old chap. Not the half of it. The bounder answered every question correctly. Had the most preposterous information stuffed away in him somewhere. Knew all about the Scotch wearing kilts, the Spanish girls wearing mantillas, the Romans wearing togas. Walked off with eight guineas, if you please. Not cricket to come to a quiz program so fully prepared. Not cricket at all, y'know. Man's obviously not an amateur. Probably been educated. Ought to be barred from the turf for life.

And that's not all. The chap had the infernal cheek to ejaculate the correct answer to the jackpot, placed there by decent, well brought up, properly misinformed folk who didn't know the name of the second President of the United States. And this cad had the incredible effrontery to know the name of the first Pope and walked off with the whole amount. Not cricket, y'know. Not cricket at all.

Who was the first Pope? My dear fellow, you don't suppose I didn't forget it as quickly as possible. My amateur standing has never been questioned at quiz contests. I've never got beyond the four-dollar question. . . .

One last mention for quiz contests, an episode that may be common to the more relentless quiz program listeners but was my first experience in this line. There's a quiz program over WOR in New York called the "Tello-Test." It's one of those telephone jobs. A man calls a housewife in Glen Ridge and asks her who wrote "Ben Hur." She stutters a moment and then dashes around the house trying to find a source book which divulges that information. Ten seconds before the deadline she's back on the phone and announces triumphantly Charles Dickens. The man says "I'm sorry, madam" and tries again over in Bound Brook.

The other day the emcee got hold of a housewife in the Bronx and started to explain that he represented the Tello-Test program. That's as far as he got. He didn't even have a chance to ask her who was the defeated candidate in the disputed election won by Rutherford B. Hayes. She didn't give him a chance. She was mad. To my knowledge she was the first housewife who ever got good and angry at a radio emcee for interrupting her housework with silly questions.

In vain, the emcee sputtered that it wasn't a wrong number, that it was a *radio* program, that he was trying, for heaven's sake, to give her some money if she just knew the name of . . . that's as far as he got. She hung up.

Maybe it's a trend. Maybe housewives aren't interested in money any more. It's just possible they're more interested in getting the dusting done than in chattering over the telephone with radio announcers. Maybe it's the millennium.

Viper in the Jackpot
[APRIL 19, 1949]

GIVEAWAY PROGRAMS, WHICH normally defy criticism, have been coming up with some pretty funny prizes lately. And by funny I don't mean funny exactly. Sit down, "Hit the Jackpot." Got a few questions. Just what did you have in mind when you awarded John J. Noone, a postal clerk, a trip to the North Pole? What are you trying to do with John J. Noone, anyhow? Get rid of him? I see listed here among $28,000 worth of prizes in Mr. Noone's jackpot another one which is pretty suspicious. "A night on the town for a year," an expression that doesn't seem to mean anything and yet has an ominous ring. You mean this man Noone, fresh back from the North Pole—*if* he gets back—is to be flung into the night clubs for a solid year?

It sounds to me as if the giveaways, drunk with their own success, are trying to commit the perfect crime. I've been listening to mystery programs too long not to know what the score is. Someone around these giveaways, some little guy who gets $100 a week for thinking up dizzy prizes, has gone quietly but criminally insane. He wants to fix all the John J. Noones—them and their $28,000 worth of prizes.

"Stop the Music" the other day gave Mrs. Freda Perry, of Donora, Pa., an eight-thousand-pound elephant, a homicidal gift if ever I heard of one. I wouldn't allow the beast in the house, Mrs. P.

Let's everyone stay away from the telephone till this thing blows over. It's a dangerous instrument.

Sixteenth-Century Lunacy on Twentieth-Century Kinescope
[SEPTEMBER 12, 1950]

IF YOU'VE NEVER heard Ralph Edwards' "Truth or Consequences," which seems inconceivable, you must at least have heard some nasty rumors about the granddaddy of giveaway shows, all of them true. The latest and nastiest rumor of all is that "Truth or Consequences" has taken to television. I'm afraid the latest rumor is true, too. I got witnesses.

In girding his loins for this latest assault on my sensibilities, Mr. Edwards declared: "From the time the show first went on the air over ten years ago, we knew we had a Number One television show, but we also knew that it could not be simulcast. On the air for ten years we have aimed our stunts at a listening audience and thrown out stunt after stunt because it was too visual. These stunts were filed against the day of television."

Altogether, that's an extraordinary statement designed to show what an astute student of show business Mr. Edwards is, and the fact that there isn't a great deal of truth in the statement could only be caviled at by people who go around caviling at everything. Me, for instance. Mr. Edwards' device for aiming a stunt at a listening, as opposed to a visual, audience consisted generally of dunking some innocent into a tank of water (splash), throwing a pie in his face (squish), or making him kiss a cow under the illusion that it is a pretty girl (moo). As any fool can readily see, these are primarily auditory stunts, not conducive to a visual or television audience.

Well, I was right there, pencil in hand, to see how well Mr. Edwards had converted himself to visibility. On his first TV show a blindfolded man was persuaded to kiss a cow under the illusion that it was a pretty girl. No, no pies in the face yet. But then this is only the first show.

The main stunt of the evening consisted of dressing a lot of outlandish contestants in outlandish costumes and perpetrating them on an audience full of dance lovers in another auditorium as a serious dance group. This must have been one of the stunts that Edwards had lying around in his files waiting for television. Probably waiting since 1942, when Edwards pulled a similar stunt on a bunch of music lovers at Town Hall in New York, introducing a housewife from New Jersey who had never touched a violin as the "distinguished European concert violinist, Yifnuff."

She scraped away at the violin while the Town Hall audience stared incredulously. Essentially, the same thing happened on the TV show. A collection of paunchy middle-aged men and women, who looked as if they had been swept out of a convention in Los Angeles, were dressed in ballet skirts, doublet and hose, and feathers and they inflicted what Mr. Edwards referred to as "The Dance of the Delirious Deer" on an audience of astonished dance lovers who were at first astonished and then embarrassed. Of course, a ballet is a little more visual than a violin, but otherwise it was the same eight-year-old stunt.

I'm afraid I can't agree that "Truth or Consequences" is a natural for television. The radio version, which is still on the air, was the ultimate in silliness, but at least it was decently veiled. Its television counterpart is a monstrosity of vulgarity. It reminded me strongly of Bedlam, the first English lunatic asylum, whose inmates provided amusement to throngs of spectators.

The shrieks of laughter from the studio audience were enough to drive the children from the room gibbering with fright. New York children, of course, are well inured to bloodshed in all its most devilish forms. They're not yet accustomed to lunacy. The quality of this laughter—if that's the word for it—is quite different from that at even the dizziest comedy show. You'll find traces in it of embarrassment, of sadism and of drooling idiocy. It's a frightening noise, and to be sure you can see it as well as hear it, the cameras are frequently turned on the audience while they are in labor.

The visible Mr. Edwards is a pop-eyed gentleman with a wolfish grin who acts and even looks a little like a maniacal Bob Hope. The participants are indescribable except to someone with the gifts and the space of Charles Dickens. Their appearances are not helped much by the fact that this horrible operation is on kinescope, which is murky enough to malign them and not quite dark enough to obscure them entirely.

The Author Meets His Doom
[JANUARY 23, 1948]

ILKA CHASE, the sharp-toothed lady who writes books, once referred to "The Author Meets the Critics" as "a major sporting event which has replaced bear baiting." The fact that literature gets no mention in this definition is significant. In many ways, "Author Meets the Critics" is more suited to prizefight fans than to bookworms.

To sum up the program as simply as possible, an author who has just emitted a book is confronted on the one hand by a friendly critic who liked his book and on the other by a decidedly unfriendly critic who loathed it. In the middle is a moderator, John K. M. McCaffrey. First, the book is briefly summarized, sometimes by the author, sometimes by a critic, sometimes by Mr. McCaffrey. Then the friendly and unfriendly critics explain why they feel as they do. After that the author defends himself and his book. That's the way the program is supposed to go, but it rarely ever does.

In the first place, the friendly critic frequently damns the book with such faint praise that the unfriendly critic leaps to its defense. Sometimes nobody defends the book except the author. In the second place, Mr. McCaffrey violates all the rules of the moderator profession by taking a violently partisan stand on each book and by inflaming the controversy rather than holding it in check. Since the relationship between an author and his book is at least as delicate as that between parent and child, this is extremely hard on authors. One author, Contran de Pochin, author of "Kabloona," became so enraged he walked out in the middle of the broadcast. Others have sounded as if they were on the verge of tears.

The critics vary from week to week, but you're likely to find Merle Miller, former "Yank" writer and now an editor at Harper's, and Eugene O'Neill, Jr., a Princeton professor, at opposite ends of the table. Mr. Miller, who was a rather intense young man in the Army, has been mellowed by civilian life, but not much. Mr. O'Neill is a classical scholar of frightening erudition, who likes virtually nothing written since the birth of Christ.

Last Sunday, the book on the operating table was Marcia Davenport's "East Side, West Side." I don't know what happened over there before the broadcast, but Mrs. Davenport was fighting mad before anyone had dropped a single derogatory remark. Though the rules say she is supposed to sit there, hands in lap, quietly awaiting her turn at insult while the critics do their devilish work, Mr. McCaffrey had great difficulty keeping her quiet right from the outset.

It's impossible to reproduce the air of chilly grandeur which Mrs. Davenport brought to this program. Just imagine, if you can, a lady author (a phrase Mrs. D. detests) who is both outraged and, at the same time, magnificently condescending and you get the idea. When Mr. Miller complained that Mrs. Davenport's heroine seemed to be taking a bath all the time, Mrs. Davenport replied frostily: "So is practically every other woman, y'know." There was just the faintest implication that Mr. Miller's female acquaintances had very likely never heard of bathtubs.

At another point, when Mr. McCaffrey was attempting to soothe her, she enunciated—I know that isn't the proper word but it somehow suggests the way Mrs. Davenport speaks: "I'm having a very good time."

"But that isn't allowed," objected Mr. McCaffrey. "You're supposed to be suffering."

"I do my suffering in private. Not over the air," said Mrs. Davenport with superb hauteur.

The part of the defending critic was taken on this occasion by Elissa Landi, the actress and sometimes author who is not one of the great critics of our time. Miss Landi's criticisms were cast at about the cocktail party level. "But didn't you feel everything was so RIGHT?" was one of her more coherent remarks.

It's misleading to suggest that "Author Meets the Critics" is only a hair-pulling contest. Only about half of it is, which is possibly a little too much. Nevertheless, it is frequently literate, almost always entertaining, invariably informative. It helps arouse interest in books (though some of the books aren't worth the trouble), and it certainly deserves a sponsor which would give it a far wider audience. As a literary discussion it lacks the urbanity usually associated with books and the detachment that ought to accompany criticism. But if it had these qualities it probably wouldn't be such a good show.

Hollywood Celebrates a New York Anniversary
[FEBRUARY 2, 1948]

PERHAPS THE MOST revealing portion of a broadcast commemorating the fiftieth anniversary of the establishment of Greater New York was the introduction by James Cagney, a native New Yorker and master of ceremonies, of Henry Morgan. Mr. Cagney was broadcasting from Hollywood, which isn't one of the five boroughs. Mr. Morgan was in Manhattan, which is.

"This guy," said Mr. Cagney in aggrieved tones, "is so crazy about New York he won't even come out here. So we're going to switch you to New York City. New York City itself!"

Mr. Morgan then took over from New York City itself. It was one of the few portions of the broadcast that came from New York. All the rest of it emanated from Hollywood, where a distinguished cast of former New Yorkers had been assembled and where they all now live. It's extraordinary how sentimental a Hollywood resident can be about the city he no longer inhabits.

Cagney and William Bendix, who contrary to popular legend was born in Manhattan and not in Brooklyn, fondly recalled Dorfmeyer's Meat Market and particularly Margie Dorfmeyer who spelled out "I love you" in wieners. Dennis Day, of the Bronx, spoke of his early encounters with the opposite sex in New York City, which were as inept as his present ones in Hollywood. Hedda Hopper, another former Manhattan resident, rhapsodized about New York in the fall. There was champagne in the air, she said, and the trees donned their autumn tresses. The trees seemed to have stuck vividly in the minds of all the Hollywood group of ex-New Yorkers. Earlier, Robert Montgomery had spoken of the trees in spring, observing that they bud at that time.

Possibly because he spends more time in New York or possibly because he is that sort of person, Henry Morgan struck a note of sober realism. He spoke mistily of the hole in the street in front of his apartment which had been there practically forever. He dwelt briefly on the loud, unsentimental noises made by the garbage collectors when they empty the cans at 5 in the morning. "New York's a wonderful city," he said. "Look at the remarkable way they remove the snow. They push it off Fifth Avenue onto the side streets so the people can't get out of their houses. Well, I wasn't going anywhere anyhow."

I guess you have to be way out in Hollywood to get decently sentimental about New York. The Hollywood New Yorkers remind me strongly of the Third Avenue Irishmen who live contentedly under the elevated and dream without discomfort of the green sod of the ould country. "I love m'native land from a distance," one of the hard-headed members of this group told me once. "It's only when I get up close I begin to wonder."

CHAPTER 11

Whomsoever God and The General Electric Company Hath Joined Together

The Better Half
[OCTOBER 17, 1947]

"The Better Half" has one curious distinction: it was selected for immortality in the "March of Time" film short on radio as one of the horrible examples of contemporary broadcasting. All things considered, it was an excellent choice. As a matter of fact, I suggest they bury this part of the film in the Time Capsule in Flushing as a sort of permanent record of at least one phase of our life and times. The program contains most of the ingredients of all the other audience participation shows—quizzes, wild practical jokes, gags and, of course, uproarious laughter. No record of our time would be complete without something of this kind.

"The Better Half" is a sort of quiz contest between husbands and wives in which the loser is forced to pay a penalty. At least I think that's the idea. There is such bedlam on the show it's hard to tell what is going on. In the "March of Time" the losing husband was placed in a box with holes in it. Every time he stuck his neck out his wife beat him over the ears with what I gathered was an upholstered stick of some kind. A great many other punishments are inflicted on the program, all of them showing a certain weird and horrible ingenuity. The other day a husband was blindfolded and then asked to kiss a pretty girl who turned out to be his wife. A dirty trick.

The punishment—the husband beaten over the head, the man kissing his own wife—is, of course, the nub of the show. It appears to satisfy the audience, but it doesn't satisfy me. What, I ask myself, are the consequences of these marital jousts after the show? What exactly does a husband who has been lammed over the head with a stick do to his wife when he gets her home? Get a stout board from the woodshed and retaliate, do you suppose?

What thoughts pass through the mind of a woman on the way home in the cab as she coldly gazes on the husband who had agreed blindfolded to kiss some pretty lass? Even though they dealt him the wrong queen at the last moment, his moral guilt is established; the suspicions which lie so close to the surface of every wifely mind could easily bubble to the top to poison a relationship which is at best delicate.

On second thought, in place of burying a motion picture of the show, they had better bury the whole show.

Homicidal Wives
[NOVEMBER 18, 1949]

THE WIVES ON TWO successive television programs last Monday night—"Lights Out" on N. B. C. and "Studio One" on C. B. S.—slew their husbands in very ingenious ways. In the former, the pretty thing, fully aware that the storm warnings were posted from Hatteras to Halifax, persuaded her fisherman husband to take his small craft beyond the breakwater where, she said, the big ones were. A perfect crime.

On "Studio One," a fragile and wide-eyed lady took part in a plot to undo her husband of such monstrously complicated nature that she couldn't conceivably get away with it. And she didn't. Still, just as an intellectual exercise, it was remarkably mature for such a delicate creature. Meanwhile, on Broadway, Regina, the poisonous heroine of Lillian Hellman's "The Little Foxes"—now wired for sound—nightly watches her husband, whom she might easily preserve, die of heart trouble. Takes a keen relish in it, too.

Up the street aways, there prances one of the most fiendish wives of all literature in August Strindberg's "The Father." This terrible female drives her husband out of his wits and finally to death by apoplexy by insinuating that his daughter is someone else's child.

That's just a few of the homicidal wives who have been, or are being, exhibited here and there. I don't know what it portends, this current literary passion for obliterating husbands in such devious and clever ways. An ax used to do well enough. Perhaps, a little strychnine. Now they attack through the mind, the nerves, or —when everything else fails—a man's love for his rod and reel.

My advice is: keep a sharp eye, men. A tightening of the lips, an unusual fixity of gaze is all the warning you'll get. It isn't enough to test the coffee on the dog any more. That sort of child's play they put behind them years ago.

The Bickering Bickersons
[MAY 25, 1948]

THE AIR LANES are aquiver with the cooings of contented husbands and wives (Ozzie and Harriet, Phil and Alice, Ethel and Albert, to mention only a few) but there is one young couple who couldn't have been more thoroughly mismated and who make no bones about it. They are John and Blanche Bickerson, who are heard at the tail end of the Old Gold show, and who are a sort of contemporary Jiggs and Maggie. On second thought I withdraw the reference. Jiggs and Maggie aren't in the same league with the Bickersons.

Blanche, played very capably by Frances Langford, is one of the monstrous shrews of all time. She makes her husband Don Ameche take two jobs, a total of sixteen working hours, in order to bring in more money which she squanders on minks and the stock market. Meanwhile he can't afford a pair of shoes and goes around with his feet painted black. In the few hours he has to sleep, she heckles him all night with the accusation that he doesn't love her. Her aim appears to be to drive her husband crazy and she succeeds very nicely. The harassed John's only weapon is insult, at which he's pretty good. I have here a sample of John and Blanche's conversation culled from a couple of scripts. Bear in mind that this is 2 A.M. and John is trying throughout to get to sleep.

BLANCHE: You used to be so considerate. Since you got married to me you haven't got any sympathy at all.

JOHN: I have too. I've got everybody's sympathy.

BLANCHE: Believe me there's better fish in the ocean than the one I caught.

JOHN: There's better bait too.

BLANCHE: I don't see how you can go to bed without kissing me good night.

JOHN: I can do it.

BLANCHE: You'd better say you're sorry for that, John.

JOHN: Okay, I'm sorry. I'm sorry. I'm sorry.

BLANCHE: You are not.

JOHN: I am too. I'm the sorriest man that ever was born.

BLANCHE: Did you take care of the cat?

JOHN: No.

BLANCHE: Why not?

JOHN: Cat can take care of himself.

BLANCHE: Don't be funny. What about the goldfish and the canary? Were they hungry?

JOHN: Starving.

BLANCHE: What are they eating?

JOHN: Each other. Why don't you let me sleep, Blanche?

BLANCHE: All you have to do is give me a civil answer. Just tell me what you gave the goldfish to eat.

JOHN: Eggs! Fifteen poached eggs. And the cat had the same.

BLANCHE: Where did all those eggs come from?
JOHN: The canary laid 'em. Please, Blanche, I've got to get some sleep.
BLANCHE: Male canaries don't lay eggs and . . . How is the canary?
JOHN: I haven't seen him since I vacuumed his cage.
BLANCHE: John Bickerson!
JOHN: Oh, don't blow your top. The canary's fine!
BLANCHE: Did you give him his bath?
JOHN: I gave him his bath. I powdered his tail and I plucked his eyebrows. What do you want from me, Blanche?
BLANCHE: I'll bet you didn't let the cat out tonight.
JOHN: I'm sick of playing nursemaid to a broken-down alley cat!
BLANCHE: He's a beautiful cat and I love him.
JOHN: I hate him.
BLANCHE: You wouldn't feel that way if you got a little friendly with him. Why don't you bring him something to play with?
JOHN: I'll bring him a dog in the morning. Good night.
BLANCHE: Is there any milk for breakfast?
JOHN: No.
BLANCHE: Then you'll have to eat out.
JOHN: I don't care. I've been doing it all week.
BLANCHE: What for? I left you enough food for six days. I cooked a whole bathtubful of rice. What happened to it?
JOHN: I took a bath in it.
BLANCHE: Why didn't you eat it?
JOHN: I've told you a million times I can't stand the sight of rice.
BLANCHE: Why not?
JOHN: Because it's connected with the saddest mistake of my life.

Just how pretty Miss Langford contrives to transform herself so convincingly into this venomous witch is her own little secret. She nags with the whining persistence of a buzzsaw, a quality that can barely be suggested in print. Mr. Ameche responds in accents of tired loathing which could hardly be improved on, though they may well cost him the women's vote.

At the risk of losing the women's vote myself I'd like to go on record as saying I think the Bickersons very funny. In a medium which strives so desperately to spread sweetness and light, in which every wife is an angel of tolerant understanding and every husband dumb but lovable, the bickering Bickersons are a very refreshing venture in the opposite direction.

"This Is Madness! Sheer Madness!"
[MAY 4, 1951]

MY WIFE AND I are as derivative as lizards, changing the color of our thoughts and our speech habits according to our environment. Since we have been exposed to television, it has left a deep mark on our conversation. It was just the other night, speeding the departing guests, that I found myself exclaiming:

"Goodbye for now. You've been a perfectly *wonderful* audience."

The guests, a non-TV crowd, turned a little pale, I thought. Uneducated people.

My wife, who knows her lines as well as Wendy or Faye or any of the girls, threw in that classic, almost unavoidable line: "You must come back again—real soon."

The guests fled. Haven't seen them since. It's just possible they didn't have a good time. My wife and I were discussing it just the other day, employing only the very best clichés.

"John, you don't think . . ."

"I don't know *what* to think."

If you follow the well-established precedents laid down by television's emcees and quizmasters, "the wonderful audience" and "come back again real soon" are the only respectable formulas for getting the guests out of the house. Getting them *into* the house is another matter. Our favorite, a line that must be declaimed with the utmost joviality, is:

"Almost anything can happen in this house—and it usually does."

I think this is a perfectly wonderful opening gambit but it does seem to unsettle the guests. Not nearly so much, though, as our new form of introduction, something we also picked up from TV: "I want you to meet the most wonderful girl in the world AND HERE SHE IS—MARY CROSBY!" The cheers and wolf whistles and tumultuous applause are provided by my small son, another devotee of television, who can imitate an audience of 500 persons with the utmost ease.

My wife's opening line here is: "We have some perfectly marvelous drinks coming up. But first, a word about something that I'm sure will be of interest to *everyone*."

She has another line, this one for use when we are doing the visiting in other people's houses. She says brightly: "I feel as though I'm sitting right in your living room." The last time she used it, the host snapped back: "You *are* sitting right in my living room." I ought to explain that he is a non-television churl, a man unacquainted with the ordinary civilities of life, especially televised life.

It was a stiffish and, in the end, disastrous visit we had that night, though we tried everything to put them at their ease. "Here we are again, folks," I exclaimed, "with a half hour of fun and frolic all for *you*." They didn't seem to think it was all for them and they didn't take very kindly to the fun and frolic, even the custard-pie throwing which has always been a surefire bit in our repertoire.

In fact, it was just about then that we got thrown out of the house. My wife got in a good line, though, just before she was tossed out: "This is madness! Sheer madness! I should never have come."

I got in an even better one. Just as I hurtled out the front door,

I fixed my host with a steely glance—difficult thing to do in midair —and declared, ringingly: "I'm seeing you now—for the first time— as you really are!"

We don't see them any more either. As a matter of fact, we don't seem to *have* any friends any more.

"The Sponsored Marriage"
[JULY 15, 1946]

ON FRIDAY NIGHT Art Linkletter, one of the busiest as well as one of the noisiest masters of ceremony in radio, told a young couple on the threshold of wedlock that the chances of their marriage being a success were only fifty-fifty, according to current statistics, whereas the chances would have been much greater than that 100 years ago. He then proceeded to outline a stunt that would win this couple $1,000, courtesy of the General Electric Company, if everything went well.

Before we get into the stunt, which is a honey, I should like to interject a plaintive query. Are there any statistics on what Henry Morgan refers to as "The sponsored marriage"? What are the chances of success of a marriage arranged, or at least paid for, by the General Electric Company? G. E. proudly boasts that its refrigerators last a lifetime, but do its marriages last that long? A G. E. phonograph is easy to manage and a wonderful companion in the home—but what about a G. E. wife? Has she the latest single-action disposition impervious to heat, cold and hard times? Is her complexion guaranteed stainless? Is she an automatic self-starting housekeeper? Is she dew freshened? Well, no matter.

The stunt Mr. Linkletter outlined was this: A new movie, whose name I didn't catch, has as its setting an Oregon valley 100 years ago. Since marriages were so successful 100 years ago and since the motion-picture company is paying good money to Mr. Linkletter to publicize its product, Mr. Linkletter decided that it would be a fine idea if this young couple had their honeymoon in the same Oregon valley.

The couple would be outfitted just like the pioneers of 100 years ago, the bridegroom in a coonskin cap, buckskin jacket and moccasins, the girl in a sunbonnet, gingham dress and high button shoes. They would drive to the valley in a covered wagon drawn by oxen and pitch their tent beside a bubbling stream.

"Do you know how to bake bread?" Mr. Linkletter asked the bride-to-be.

"Oh, no," gasped the girl.

"Well, you'll find it much easier over an open fire," observed Mr. Linkletter, and turned to the prospective bridegroom. "Do you know how to milk a cow?"

"Oh, no."

"Well, try the overhand double-crostic method," said the master of ceremonies, and presented the young man with a 100-year-old flint-action squirrel gun with which to shoot game.

Incidentally, the $1,000 prize is not theirs just for taking part in this adventure. They must find it. The first clew to its whereabouts was a fishhook. The bridegroom must catch a fish with the hook, find the nearest forest ranger and give it to him, and the forest ranger would give him the second clew. The couple must find the $1,000 before Wednesday. After that it will diminish $50 daily.

The couple were married at 7 P.M. on Friday and whisked by plane to Oregon, where they were feted at a banquet in their honor by the Governor of Oregon, and then pushed off to their honeymoon valley aboard the covered wagon.

Best wishes to you both, folks, and I devoutly hope you find the $1,000 before Wednesday. When you do, tear off $50 of it and mail it to me and I shall send you by return mail three sample radio columns and my own free booklet entitled "How to Be Happy Though Unsponsored."

Romance has always been a highly profitable enterprise, and it seems to me that this sort of radio program is the latest phase in the long history of the romance industry. Many, many years ago Alexandre Dumas *père* ran an immensely successful romance factory in Paris. Dumas outlined his plots and then turned them over to the hired hands to fill out the dull details. The products of this factory, notably "The Count of Monte Cristo" and "The Three Musketeers," are still widely sold.

Then Hollywood stepped in to improvise a far more efficient means of romance manufacture, and the authors turned to anger in place of love for their plots. But in these realistic times, it is increasingly difficult to identify oneself with Clark Gable or Loretta Young.

Hence, the sponsored marriage program, which brings you a skillful blend of romance, lavish gifts and adventure. It's easy enough to identify oneself with this young married couple who are people just like you and me. Vicariously, we go along on the Oregon honeymoon. Vicariously, we are making bread over an open fire, milking the cow overhand and double crostic, and looking for that thousand clams. Today the press agent has supplanted the author and the script writer as the purveyor of dreams.

Incidentally, the name of the program on which you can follow the married couple's quest for gold is "People Are Funny." The program emanates appropriately from Hollywood, which is inhabited by some of the funniest people on earth.

The Wonder of Electronics
[FEBRUARY 25, 1951]

CONCEIVABLY THE GREATEST contribution radio ever made to society was the sponsored marriage. In the old days, it was the relatives and friends who kicked in the pots, the bedroom lamp and the kitchen clock. Then the sponsor came along and provided all that and more. Sponsored matrimony as practiced on "Bride and Groom" and other radio programs, was actually a more sensible deal all around since the gifts were generally all-electric (AC or

DC), lifetime-guaranteed, earthquake-resistant and stainless. Aunt Emma never kicked in with stuff like that.

No one has ever proved that a sponsored marriage lasts any longer than the old-fashioned, or sustaining-type, marriage, but the gifts last forever. Sponsored matrimony, you'll be happy to learn, has been taken over and elaborated on in television, too. Just the other day on the TV version of "Bride and Groom," Samuel Jamieson, of Granger, Ind., and Myrtle Thomey, of Laredo, Tex., were married after a courtship conducted over 1,500 miles by short-wave radio. After the ceremony, Mrs. Jamieson happily summed up the new order of things with the statement: "We owe a great deal to amateur radio and good operating conditions."

That's going to be the rub in the new order of courtship—operating conditions. How's a girl to know whether that's true love in his short-wave voice? Or just an ionic disturbance in the upper stratosphere? How's he to know whether she, so young and lovely in the living room, will survive the pitiless glare of the TV cameras? The all-electronic marriage brings in a lot of handsome loot. But you'd better consult a few experts—a couple of engineers, a makeup man, a good TV director—before plunging into something you may live to regret.

The electronic age has had a baleful effect on the activities of animals, too. On "Blind Date" a chimpanzee named Bonzo expressed a vehement opinion on this newest branch of show business by biting the mistress of ceremonies, Miss Arlene Francis, so severely in the third finger that she sat down hard while the chimp's trainer pulled the beast away. Miss Francis, a trouper, bounced right up again and went straight into a plug for Bulova watches, a shining example of that old show business adage: The commercial must go on.

In East Orange, N. J., a four-month-old Siamese cat was dozing by the TV set when her owner, Mrs. Norman Wolfson, snapped the set on and brought a pack of prize terriers from the Westminster Kennel Club show right into the living room. It was an invasion of privacy no Siamese will put up with, though humans will. The cat leaped at the set, clawed at the dial, sent the terriers right back to Madison Square Garden.

Meanwhile, all the way from Hollywood, Bing Crosby Enterprises announced a new children's program now in production. It's a mystery series done entirely with trained chimpanzees.

One last note, this one from the Old Southland: Tom Fesperman reports in "The Charlotte (N. C.) News" that a six-year-old citizen named Chuck Barton had his parents mighty worried when he started talking like a Yankee from Perth Amboy. It developed he'd picked up the dreadful accent straight off the coaxial cable.

It's quite a problem all right, but we're working on it. My spies tell me R. C. A. is developing a new-type coaxial cable which will convert Arthur Godfrey's accent into pure undistilled Dixie the second it passes the Mason-Dixon line. Howdy Doody will sound as if he were raised on hominy grits and corn liquor. As for Milton Berle, this new cable will not only make him sound like Al Jolson but also look like Larry Parks.

Well, just one more then. Laughs Unlimited, which peddles jokes to comics and disc jockeys and such people, has issued a new price list. A comedy monologue on Dr. Kinsey will cost you $1. But if you want to get funny about "television in the home," it'll set you back $2.

Royal Wedding
[NOVEMBER 27, 1947]

THERE'S SOMETHING OVERPOWERING about any wedding, and the royal affair concluded last Thursday, which anyone in the world might sit in on via radio if he chose to get up that early, was a good deal more than that. Even over the radio—in fact, especially over the radio—it was awe-inspiring. The sheer majesty of the occasion infected the radio reporters, who in turn infected the listeners.

Since the listeners couldn't see, since they could only imagine the medieval banners, the ancient ceremonial costumes aglitter with history, the procession of kings and princes and dukes, it all sounded curiously remote and unlikely, as if we had been precipitated unexpectedly into the Middle Ages.

God knows the five American reporters on the scene—Edward R. Murrow, Howard K. Smith, Frederick Opper, Merrill Mueller and Arthur Mann—tried hard enough to inject a little normal daylight into the scene, but they couldn't manage it. The shrilling of the trumpets, the glass coach, the sword and shield of the ancient kings of England, the silver breastplates of the Guards—details of that sort they spoke of a little gingerly, as if they expected them to vanish or turn into pumpkins before their eyes. The Americans are all seasoned, hard-boiled reporters who had gone to London to cover a news story of considerable importance and found themselves in the middle of a fairy story which they didn't quite believe and for which they had no precedent to guide them.

They tried, poor democratic souls, to bring in the common touch which works so well in any news story except royal weddings. "Through the entrance of the chapel, I can see Elizabeth adjusting her gown," said Edward R. Murrow, inside the Abbey. "The Duke of Edinburgh is glancing anxiously back to see how his wife's train is making out. (It had caught earlier and caused some confusion.) But the two pages seem to have things well in hand." This is the sort of human anxiety and human mishap that occurs at weddings in Salt Lake City, but it somehow seems improbable in Westminster and I choose not to believe it.

Outside the Abbey Merrill Mueller tried to explain that the glass coach wasn't really a glass coach, but his listeners were too far gone for such nonsense. The glass coach, they knew, was solid glass —glass wheels, glass turnbuckles, glass livery, glass horses, driven by a glass coachman.

A moment later Mueller was back into the familiar, the prosaic, where he was more at home. "The crowd is suffering severely from the crush. The ambulance men are carrying away a woman or a man every thirty seconds to a minute." That's the sort of detail an American reporter can understand. It happens all the time in New York when a Lindbergh or an Eisenhower parades up Fifth Avenue.

Outside Buckingham Palace, the most forlorn of the American contingent, Frederick Opper, told how some people in the crowd had brought along little stoves and cooked their lunch on them just like Americans standing in line for the World Series bleachers. One of the chimneys in Buckingham Palace was smoking rather badly, he noted. There was little else for him to report since he was outside and the wedding party was inside. He tried to make up for his disadvantageous position by imagining what was afoot inside.

"I suppose at this moment the Princess is being kissed by all her female relatives just like the brides back home." Not at an affair like this, Opper. The female relatives at these things tap her lightly with their wands and endow her with Wisdom, Grace, Humility and—something of which she'll need a good deal—Luck.

The British reporters on the B. B. C., steeped as all Englishmen are in their own immemorial history, living simultaneously as only the British can in the glorious and ancient past as well as the sordid present, were untroubled by the feeling of anachronism that seemed to afflict the Americans. Where the American reporters had a shrewd eye for detail, the British had an almost mystic appreciation of pageantry. They spoke reverently of the costumes and of their significance, of the Dean of Westminster's ancient right to escort the bride and bridegroom to the west door, of the colorful pennants and symbols of empire.

At the Admiralty Arch, Audrey Russell, of the B. B. C., reported of the Princess: "She looks very dignified and serene. Something quite magic comes alive in the crowd as she passes. This is OUR Princess and the crowd is giving her its affectionate acclaim."

The words "dignified" and "serene" sounded on several lips that day. I suppose it would be out of keeping with royalty to use the word "happy," and, come to think of it, no one did. However, in one respect Elizabeth was like any other bride. Her faint, tremulous, hurried "I will," which echoed around the world, revealed that she was frightened nearly to death.

CHAPTER 12

Some General Observations

The Girls Should Protest
[NOVEMBER 1, 1949]

I HAVE ALWAYS been an indefatigable collector of small, disturbing trends—the smaller the better. Lately a good many small, upsetting trends have been brought to my attention. Carrie Munn, for example, a girl who designs clothes, has included in her Fall line a dress called "Before Reno," a demure thing in white-collared velvet, and a companion piece, "After Reno," a brazen outfit in checked taffeta with one bare shoulder.

I think the girls ought to rise in revolt here. This custom—this costuming of females so that their marital status and even their marital plans are emblazoned for all to see—has been widely practiced for some centuries by South African tribes where the virgins wear one color, the new brides another, the widows still another. It had dropped into disfavor in most civilized countries until Mrs. Munn restored it. I'm against it. Every time I see a girl in checked taffeta with one bare shoulder, I fall to speculating: "When you suppose she got back? How much alimony she clip him for?"

There's another thing you girls, especially the younger ones, better do something about before it spreads around. Up at Syracuse University, College of Liberal Arts, Mrs. Ada Allison has enrolled as a freshman. Her daughter Peggy is a junior, same college. Now, if there was one person in the world I wanted least to be hanging around college, borrowing my anthropology books, it was mother. She's a wonderful girl, mother, but I didn't want her around college, tidying up the room, asking silly questions about why I cut English class and why didn't I get home earlier and where could she borrow a Latin trot. Colleges have two or three excellent reasons for their existence. Foremost among them, I should say, is that they teach a girl how to get along *without* the assistance of her mother. If mother insists on going to college at the same time, the least she can do is enroll in one 2,000 miles away.

Up at Columbia University recently, a bunch of deep-thinkers got together to discuss control mechanisms or thinking machines, and worried about whether mankind was smart enough to control himself in a world full of memory machines, guided missiles, chess-playing machines and one thing and another. One of the scientists, Dr. Karl Deutsch, of the Massachusetts Institute of Technology, made bold to say that mankind wasn't yet entirely obsolete because no one had yet invented a machine that could fall in love or crack jokes.

I don't know as that proves anything. I bet they will invent a machine that falls in love. One massive mathematical calculator at Harvard already has shown all the symptoms of a nervous breakdown. It wouldn't surprise me at all, when these machines get a little farther along, to see one of these calculators at Harvard making passes at a near-by cyclotron. Giving it a box of atoms. Showing off by multiplying two sixteen-figure numbers in its head.

As for making jokes, why, sakes alive, a good many of Milton Berle's jokes sound as if they were turned out by machinery right now. Last year a joke-writer wrote a book explaining how to write jokes for radio. He reduced the whole problem to a mathematical equation. It'd be no trick at all to invent a machine that would turn out jokes just as bad as those you hear on the radio. (I knew I'd get radio in here some place.)

The way I look at it, the question isn't whether humans are obsolete—I didn't know there was any argument about that—but whether these machines aren't already obsolete. Won't be long now before they develop the all-round cussedness of the rest of us.

The day will come when the machines gather together at their own university and someone will speak up and say: "You know, I think we're obsolete. They have developed humans that can do anything we can do. They can even play chess."

The "New York Herald Tribune Book Review" section asked about half a hundred writers to talk about themselves, which produced twenty-three pages of diffident autobiography last Sunday. In all this outpouring of personal history, what struck me most forcibly was the working hours. They're appalling. "I wake always at first light and start working," reports Ernest Hemingway. "At sixty-one," says Arnold Toynbee, "I find I have to work far shorter hours, 9:15 to 6:45, than at thirty-one to fifty-one, when I worked from 9:15 to 7:30." "I'm up early," declares John Mason Brown. "I like to get going by 9:30 and keep going until just before dinner." Says Erskine Caldwell of his writing schedule: "9 to 5, six days a week, ten months a year, twenty-six years of my life." Thomas B. Costain: "I am at my desk in a shaded, second-story library at eight o'clock in the morning, and I stay there four or five hours a day, every day, Saturdays, Sundays, holidays." There were a lot of other working schedules on record, all grim.

I hate to call such a distinguished collection of writers a bunch of dreamy-eyed prevaricators. So I won't. I'll say instead they are victims of mass delusion. I know a lot of writers, not one of whom gets to work at first light, not one of whom works from 9 to 5 Saturdays, Sundays, and holidays. The difficult thing here is to put your finger on the exact moment when a writer is working and when he isn't. "A writer," says W. Somerset Maugham in this same series, "works all his waking hours, for all he sees, all he does, all that happens to him, every thought that passes through his head, is the material out of which he develops his personality and so learns to give, within the limitations of his nature, whatever it is in him to give."

That's a fine definition of something, but whether it defines *work* is—well—questionable. At any rate, I can see a lot of writers triumphantly quoting this wonderful dictum from so eminent a source to their wives. "I was at Bleeck's until 4 A.M." the writer will say. "Saw a great many things. (He saw a drunk trying to balance a penny on the lip of a glass.) Lot of things happened to me. (He lost forty bucks at the match game.) Good many thoughts passed through (Right through.) Developed my personality materially." Working hours, 11 A.M. to 4 A.M.

It was Christopher Morley, I believe, who said that a writer's wife will never, no matter if she has been married to him for twenty years, understand that he is working when he is staring out the window. For years, writers used this one on wives who refused to believe any work had been committed unless there was a pile of completed manuscript at his elbow. Or, better yet, a check in the mail. The Maugham Doctrine is a vast improvement. A writer is working if he has his eyes open. If you can get your wife to believe this, then one of you hasn't been in the game very long.

Speaking for myself, I think these terrible working schedules are an organized conspiracy on the part of the writing fraternity to scare the younger writers away. Reading how arduous it all is, a lot of young men who had aspired to the writing dodge are going to throw up their hands and enter the banking dodge, where, at least, the hours are no longer. Then they'll delude themselves that their two-hour lunch dates were all devoted to furious work.

No Crime Today, Lady
[NOVEMBER 13, 1946]

FORMER POLICE COMMISSIONER Lewis J. Valentine, whose influence toward law and order is now distributed nationally on the

"Gangbusters" program over the American Broadcasting Company, appealed over the air the other day to President Truman, law-enforcement agencies and others in Washington to institute a national Crime Prevention Week to be celebrated by suitable observances from Boston to Carmel. The Week, any kind of Week, is an institution firmly stitched into the national fabric and not to be taken lightly either by press agent or ordinary citizen.

My friends, the Whittleseys, are the greatest observers of Weeks I know. They are plain, conscientious folk, deeply stirred by proclamations of any sort, and since most Weeks are proclaimed by President, Governor or Mayor, the Whittleseys are usually abroad early Monday morning of any particular Week taking an active part in whatever is expected of them. During Accident Prevention Week, for instance, Jim Whittlesey looked both ways even longer than usual, while Inez came to a dead stop at every intersection and tooted the horn. Kindness toward Animals Week was easy for them, too. They were both extremely nice to Bottle, their dachshund, though, of course, they're pretty decent to him anyway.

Then came Fire Prevention Week, which confused them. Jim and Inez had never set any fires and they didn't quite know how to take part in an active campaign against setting them. Before they had come to any decision, the Week was over and they felt rather bad about it. They didn't set any fires, of course, but they didn't prevent any either.

Crime Prevention Week has upset them even more seriously. How did the Commissioner expect them to observe Crime Prevention Week, Jim asked me. He and Inez felt they could postpone any crimes they had in mind for one more week. But what else were they supposed to do—prevent one? The amount of gunplay you run into up there in Scarsdale during any one week is severely limited, he explained apologetically, though it might be hard to explain that to an ex-cop who takes gunfire for granted. The murder situation has been quiet ever since they moved into the neighborhood, and that was ten years ago. The Whittleseys are wondering if they could just sit out Crime Prevention Week and save all their strength for Adopt-a-Democrat Week, which, they feel, will take all the strength they have.

The Last Secret Thought
[JANUARY 28, 1948]

THIS IS THE great age of confession. We are required now to tell everything. We tell the quiz master how we proposed to our wives. We tell the Inquiring Reporter whether we have ever kissed anyone who was not our wife. We tell Dr. Gallup how we are going to vote and Mr. Hooper what we propose to listen to on the radio. Our psychiatrist delves into our dreams and Dr. Kinsey into our actual performance.

Candor is the hallmark of our time, as was reticence in the day of Queen Victoria. A man who withholds any of his inmost secrets is considered slightly suspicious, certainly neurotic and possibly dangerous. Spain had her Inquisition; we have our suffering under a Reign of Creeping Inquisitiveness, less horrifying than the former, but more intrusive. Like the rest of you, my mind has been thoroughly explored right down to the last crevice. Or what They thought was the last crevice. But, They missed one small, disreputable thought I keep tucked under my frontal lobe. It isn't much of a thought, but They didn't find it. Hooper missed it by a mile. Kinsey was warm, but he didn't reach quite far enough. Gallup hasn't been in that corner of the attic lately.

Late at night when They've all gone away, by the light of a guttering candle, I take it out and fondle it, this forlorn, slightly disreputable thought. Sooner or later, They'll get it. They have methods, you know. Scientific methods. If you lie to Them the first time, They catch you at it the second time. You can fool all of the inquisitors some of the time and some of the inquisitors all of the time but you can't fool all the inquisitors all of the time. There are too many of them. If Kinsey doesn't get you, Gallup will, and if he misses, the psychiatrist will be in there with his long, scientific fingers beckoning.

That's the way They do it now. They beckon in their silky way. In the old days They used torture but now They are very gentle and scientific and much more efficient. What worries me particularly is what is going to happen to this last, sickly thought when They get it. Poor thing, it'll be thrown into a sort of statistical Auschwitz with a lot of strangers which resemble it but aren't quite the same. It'll be indexed, cross-filed and tabulated. One more for Jack Benny. One more for Eisenhower. A vote against the New Look. Another sexual reactionary or possibly a sexual liberal.

The trouble is that this thought doesn't fit into any exact category. It isn't all the way for or against the New Look or the Soviet Union. It's a little gray thought with a number of jagged, unpredictable edges which will have to be filed off before it'll fit into any card catalogue. If They try to machine tool this thought into a statistic, it'll die.

All the foregoing rather agonized reflections were prompted by a fairly new radio program called "Child's World" which you'll find on A. B. C. right opposite Jack Benny, who isn't a child at all but a case of arrested development. "Child's World" is a sincere, reasonably expert attempt to probe the mind of a child right in front of your eyes. It's a pretty good program too—I'd planned to review it here but I got sidetracked—but it is also a rather alarming one. The mind of a child is the last citadel of the secret, delicious heretic thought and if They get in there, there won't be any mystery left anywhere.

The Embittered Liberal
[NOVEMBER 24, 1948]

I HAVE RAILED occasionally, hopelessly, against stereotypes who get imbedded in radio literature (*Radio what!*) and stay there forever.

The apoplectic boss, for example. The dumb, gum-chewing, man-crazy Brooklyn blonde. The squealing teen-age girl. The nasal, left-footed teen-age boy. The lovable, four-thumbed stupid young husband and his consort, the all-wise, tolerant, beautiful, magnificently capable young wife. (I've never understood how those idiot girls grew into such paragons of virtue and wisdom through the simple act of matrimony.)

These are just a handful of radio stereotypes and that's enough for today. Today, to get what is known in advertising circles as the full picture and also to speak a word or two in defense of radio, I'd like to point out that radio is by no means the only one guilty of stereotypes. The current issue of "Fortune" contains a wonderful study by John Chamberlain of the business man in fiction. Mr. Chamberlain deserves a bonus for this piece if only for the fact that he has had to wade through some of the sloppiest fiction ever written to pluck out his case histories. There are dozens of case histories of fictional business men, ranging from Dreiser and Upton Close to Norman Mailer and—well, who wrote the last novel?

Chamberlain traces the origins of this character, admitting there was justification for his creation, and his development into the fossilized caricature he now is. At some point—probably in the '30s—writers stopped looking at business men and began copying from each other. The business man of fiction became through a process of literary determinism (or what my grandfather used to call plain ordinary laziness) a profit-driven reactionary, whose better instincts are overwhelmed by economic determinism (writer's myopia).

I won't dip any further into Mr. Chamberlain's article except to urge writers to read it for themselves. Publishers might look into it, too. At any rate, it has seemed to me for a long time that the novelists have wandered pretty far from their source material.

Years ago, George Bernard Shaw, who made better sense then, issued a petulant complaint about the quality of fictional cockney. Writers, said Shaw, hadn't listened to any Cockneys for a generation. They had learned Cockney at the knee of Charles Dickens and simply carried on from there. In an attempt to rectify this literary error, Shaw designed his own literary Cockney straight out of the Cockney's mouth. It was almost unreadable but it's quite speakable. So far as I know it didn't start a new trend.

The other night I attended "Goodbye, My Fancy," a play which contains Madeleine Carroll, Shirley Booth, Sam Wanamaker, a very funny first act curtain line and not much else. It went along smoothly enough until the beginning of the second act when this character walked in, a man I somehow expected. The play couldn't have continued much longer without him. He puffed fitfully at a cigarette, fingering it incessantly. He slouched—a walk is not quite the word for the way this character gets about—across stage, in a sort of permanent, panther-like crouch.

His face was impassive, hard-bitten. He spoke mostly in monosyllables. What he said was elliptic, cryptic, styptic. He had just come back from Manchuria, Mongolia, Spain, Yugoslavia, Pakistan, South China, Indonesia, Moravia, East Jodhpur, Bulgaria and Rhodesia. What he had seen there had stripped him of his remaining illusions (though you have the feeling he never had many to start with) and, at the same time, had filled him with the determination to throw himself into the fight to save humanity while there was yet time.

He gets around, this character, not only geographically but fictionally, too, having spoken with quiet bitterness for S. N. Behrman, Lillian Hellman, Robert E. Sherwood, Erich Maria Remarque, Arthur Koestler and several hundred lesser writers. His convictions are in the main sound; his mannerisms I find trying and his clothes appalling. In all these years he has worn one set of garments—a sports jacket, dark pants, a dark shirt and a tie that looks like a string. He has made a number of authors quite wealthy and—speaking as one embittered liberal on behalf of another—I think it's high time they bought him a suit with matching trousers. Maybe two pairs of trousers.

Two Dying Arts
[JUNE 9, 1948]

THE IMPACT OF television on our culture is one of the liveliest little topics of discussion to come along in some time, much of it conducted between clenched teeth. The most obvious and dire effect, one that strikes everyone who has seen more than two television broadcasts, is on conversation. There isn't any. The moment the set goes on, conversation dies. I don't mean it languishes. It dies. Messages are transmitted back and forth by means of eye-rolling, eyebrow lifting and frantic wigwagging of the hands. (Only high priority messages are permitted: You're wanted on the telephone. Could I have another drink? That sort of thing.) People who will venture an occasional whisper in church remain awed and silent in front of a television set.

There are two points of view concerning the death of conversation. One group—an aging, moss-backed crowd—finds it altogether deplorable. Conversation, these people say, is one of the highest exercises of the civilized mind and its end means the end of civilization. Another group, composed largely of silent, irritable, restless folk, is convinced that the death of conversation is the greatest boon to mankind since polygamy fell into disfavor.

The other day I ran into Jim Mainwaring, a member of the last-named group and he explained his point of view. "Television," he said happily, "is the only thing that has ever managed to suppress Joe Pratt and his damned stories about Bermuda. He was over at the house the other night with a bunch of people and every time he opened his mouth, every one said 'sssh' at once. We'd been trying to shut him up for weeks but this was the first time we succeeded. There's something about television that intimidates people. Even Joe Pratt.

"He just sat there, storing up his stories, figuring he'd get a chance later. I didn't give him the opportunity. After the fights ended, I switched over to a fashion show at Grand Central Palace. Went on for hours, dullest darn thing I ever saw, but better than those stories. I tell you, television is the greatest invention since the wheel."

Jim Mainwaring isn't the only one who has found this out. I know another man who has an Aunt Priscilla he's been trying to head off for twenty years. He bought a television set recently and already he has assumed that air of furtive happiness which distinguishes Jim Mainwaring these days. She can't get a word in edgewise.

Of course, that's only one point of view. The opposite point of view is held with equal firmness by quite a lot of people, notably Joe Pratt and Aunt Priscilla.

That's one social aspect of television. There are many others, not the least of which is its effect on hostesses. Grace Mainwaring, Jim's wife, looks on television not nearly so kindly as does her husband and with good reason. The other night the Mainwarings had one of those small dinner parties which women dash off with as little as four days' concentrated effort. The dinner table gleamed with damask. The silver candlesticks—the ones they got from Pete Thristle for a wedding present—were justifiably radiant, Grace having spent a large measure of the afternoon polishing them. Grace had also pulled out of the camphor those little silver nut dishes which appear only on state occasions. They were polished and replete with nuts. The centerpiece glittered with flowers, representing a good half-hour's work on Grace's part.

Altogether the table was a splendid spectacle, the sort that provokes cries of admiration from the ladies and an exhibition of superb depreciation from the hostess. Nobody ever got to the table at all. That was the night of the Ryan-Puccini fight and it was a honey. Grace couldn't drag anyone away from the television set and ultimately everyone ate in the living room, the plates balanced on their laps. Someone spilled salad dressing all over her petit point chairs and little piles of crumbs appeared here and there on the carpet, where eventually they were ground in as the menfolk argued as to whether Puccini was robbed.

The art of conversation, the art of dining, they're both on the way out. Take care of your eyesight, brother. It's all you'll have left.

Small Trends
[NOVEMBER 2, 1948]

TODAY IS OUR DAY for small trends, the smaller and better, for little happenings in radio of minute consequence and virtually no significance. A man gets tired of handing down sweeping judgments every day; every man should have a day of rest devoted exclusively to any minutiae he happens to have lying around. I have a whole bagful at my elbow. Here are just a few.

The announcer on "We, the People," last week summed up the apathy characteristic of this election with magnificent though unconscious irony in a routine announcement which went: "Next Tuesday, election night, 'We the People' will not be heard."

A few weeks ago in the soap opera "When a Girl Marries," the tangle of misunderstanding which characterizes that as well as all other soap operas suddenly cleared. Nobody was at cross purposes with anyone else. No one was frustrated about anything. No one was struck with hysterical blindness or, more importantly, with even the fear of approaching blindness. For one day, every blessed soul on "When a Girl Marries" was blissfully happy.

As if that wasn't enough to shake my faith in the established order of things, there was the case on "Suspense" of Ray Milland playing the part of one of those tough, extraordinarily competent detectives who is tracking down a murderer. He thought he had his man, a very suspicious character, but the guy wouldn't answer questions. In a moment of anger, the cop slugged the murder suspect, who instantly dropped dead. The rest of the story was devoted to Milland's efforts to beat a murder rap himself. I can't think what drove the writer of that program to shatter an ancient tradition in such an uncouth manner, to make a cop behave in a way that no cop has ever behaved on the radio. Iconoclasm? Desperation? Or simply the belief that radio hasn't long to live anyway and we might just as well start breaking up the joint right now?

On "Ladies Be Seated" the other day, a woman was presented with a question which would tax the intellect of a three-week-old child. "What state," asked Tom Moore, the emcee, "is distinguished by orange groves, mineral deposits and gold?"

"Illinois," said the lady.

Mr. Moore sighed and threw in a few more clews. The state he had in mind, said Moore, was known for its cinema and sunshine; the capital was Sacramento and the theme song was, in garbled version: "Da da da da here I come." In the end Moore had to tell her the right answer was California.

"I'm from Florida," the lady informed him grimly," and I don't want to publicize that state on the radio."

The Two Biggest Networks
[APRIL 27, 1950]

I HAVE ALWAYS been helplessly captivated by research organizations. They can prove almost any proposition you care to present them—that two and two equals four, that two and two doesn't equal four, or, if pressed hard, that there are no such figures as either two or four.

Lately, I've been bewitched by a couple of full-page ads run in newspapers on successive days by N. B. C. and C. B. S., each proving beyond mortal doubt that it has the largest audience in radio. N. B. C.—according to N. B. C.—has 3,000,000 more families listening to it than the "second network" in the daytime, 4,870,000 more families at night. My own rather suspect arithmetic figures this as roughly 12 per cent more listeners than C. B. S. daytime, 14 per cent more at night.

The day after this claim, C. B. S., trumpeting like an enraged elephant, charged forth with its figures. C. B. S.—says C. B. S.—has an audience 29 per cent higher than the "second-place network" in the daytime, 32 per cent higher at night. N. B. C. quotes Broadcast Measurement Bureau as the source of its figures; C. B. S. doesn't quote any source but, since it is one of the most research-happy organizations in America, I'm sure the network is up to its hips in surveys, polls and statistics—all of them unassailable.

Because I have the fullest confidence in both N. B. C. and C. B. S., I spent the whole week end trying, by theoretical physics, to prove that *both* were right, that C. B. S. is bigger than N. B. C., that N. B. C. is bigger than C. B. S.—both at the same time. Well, I finally figured it out, and I'm now ready to tackle the H-Bomb if anyone wants any help.

The way I figure it is this. N. B. C. has more *families* listening to it. That is, the whole family gather around, say, Phil Harris and Alice Faye. Directly after that program is over, they scatter like mice to other parts of the house—father to the kitchen, mother to the bedroom, the kids in the living room, grandma in the cellar, and listen as *individuals*. Father, mother and grandma listen to Edgar Bergen on C. B. S. Junior and Sis listen to Sam Spade on N. B. C. I realize that gives C. B. S. only a 20 per cent edge, instead of the 32 per cent it claims, but after a little thought I worked that one out, too. Sis, a restive child, scampers back and forth between the kitchen and the living room, catching just a little bit more of Bergen than she does of Spade and representing that extra 12 per cent of an audience.

You both happy now, N. B. C., C. B. S.? You're both the *biggest* network. Next week end, I propose to work out a statistical survey which proves I have a larger audience than Walter Winchell. That'll be quite a task, all right, but if I don't run out of pencils, I'll manage it somehow.

Speaking of columnists, Earl Wilson has just begun a show on WJZ in New York where he is represented (by someone else) as

"America's Number 1 columnist." (According to my haphazard estimate, there are now 112 columnists competing for that Number 1 position. Very craftily, I've stayed aloof. I've staked out a claim as America's Number 5 columnist, a position for which there is no competition whatsoever. Still, I think I have a good post position there. Whoever heard of Channel Number 1?)

Anyhow, Mr. Wilson has more or less disguised himself as the biggest hayseed in New York, "a Mid-West boy"—according to the announcer—"who came to the big city and made good." This feat of necromancy is accomplished primarily by using the word "shucks," which Mr. W. throws in on all conceivable occasions. ("Shucks, fellows, we're just trying to give you a few smiles. No guest is allowed to speak better English than I do.")

He then introduced his first guest, Fred Allen, and that exclamations "shucks" flew around like popcorn until Mr. Allen remarked somewhat testily: "It must be easy to get a reputation as a wit in Ohio." (Mr. Wilson sprang from the loins of Ohio roughly around the time of the Louisiana Purchase.) "You just say 'shucks' in the morning and people go around all day quoting you."

Well, I hate to blow the whistle on such a nice guy as Earl Wilson, but I have just been to "Who's Who" and confirmed my worst suspicions. "Who's Who" reveals—I've already forwarded this information to Senator McCarthy—that Earl Wilson was graduated from Ohio State University in 1931. He's no more illiterate than James Thurber who attended (though he didn't manage to graduate from) the same university.

You take off those overalls and put your shoes back on, Earl Wilson. You can speak English as well as I can, which isn't saying much. In fact, I have secret information, which I'll turn over to anyone who subpoenas me, that the Wilsons in the privacy of their own homes converse secretly in Latin.

Goldfish, Dickens and "The Daily Worker"
[MARCH 30, 1949]

JUST A FEW odds and ends today.

At the recent exhibit of the Institute of Radio Engineers, General Electric displayed a record player completely submerged in a fish tank with eight goldfish swimming about in it. It played continuous phonograph music for hours, proving to the satisfaction of everyone that a G. E. record player can stand excessive humidity practically indefinitely. The experiment also proved, more importantly, that goldfish can endure Frank Sinatra for an indefinite period. They came through the ordeal fit as disk jockeys.

The Dickens Inn in Greenwich Village, very English, very Dickensian, has a wrought-iron sign hanging outside, very English, very Dickensian, on which is emblazoned the single word: Television.

"The Daily Worker" decided television is a social menace. "Its deteriorating effect on child upbringing is a hazard that must be met quickly," says "The Worker." The paper complained specifically about "Howdy Doody," the children's puppet program which, "The Worker" stated sternly, aroused in children the illicit, capitalistic, bourgeois, syndicalist desire to own a television set.

There has been some controversy on how much greater is the impact of television than of radio. Four times? Five times? Fifty times? It's a hard question simply because it's difficult to measure degrees of impact on the human soul. My own standard of measurement is Johnny, the little man who screeches "Call faw Philip Mawriss." I find him five and three-quarters times as obnoxious on television as he was on radio, an equation I pass along free of charge to anyone who cares for it. John Chapman, of "The

Daily News," informed me that his annoyance at Johnny costs him twice as much effort for television as for radio. He used to turn the volume down to zero when Johnny came to the radio. Now, on television, he turns down the sound with one hand, thumbs his nose at the image with the other. Takes both hands.

Turn It Off
[AUGUST 4, 1948]

I READ IN "The New York Times" that show business has reached a nadir—well, one of its nadirs, show business being one of those professions where ultimates are attained every other day. Radio stars are fighting salary cuts. Guest stars will be eliminated or bought at bargain rates next season. Top stars are unsigned and programs are reducing their prices $3,000 to $4,000.

The profit margins on movies are down in some cases by as much as 50 per cent. Sheet music sales are down 40 per cent. Records are down 10 to 35 per cent. On Broadway, Brock Pemberton, who has been prophesying disaster for the theater ever since I was a little boy, declared: "The financial slump is greater than anything since the pre-war depression."

Exhilarated by these portents of doom, I had lunch with a publisher. "The book business," he announced with unwonted zest, "is through. Nobody reads books any more and I've an idea that reading of any sort is on the way out. You want a brandy? Might as well make an afternoon of it. Nothing to do at the office."

After digesting this information slowly, I rang the secret number of my spy in the picture magazine game, a character who lives on the Street with No Name: "We're advertising in all the newspapers but the circulation is going down anyhow," he declared bitterly. "People just don't seem to *want* to look at pictures any more. Makes a man think, doesn't it?"

It certainly does. The Hooper ratings are as close to zero as they ever get. If people aren't looking at the picture magazines, listening to a radio, reading the books or going to the movies, what on earth are they doing? My researchers are up in the Adirondacks fishing, so I paid a visit to Jim and Grace Mainwaring up in Bronxville. Jim and Grace, I ought to explain, are to statistics what guinea pigs are to science. If Gallup consulted them first, he'd save himself a lot of trouble. Whenever there's a 30 per cent slump in anything, you'll find Jim and Grace involved in it somehow.

I found Jim, tanned and healthy, spraying copper and rotenone on the tomato plants. "The radio?" he said vaguely. "Well, I don't know. Grace and I get pretty tired at night. We go to bed. No, we haven't seen a movie in months. Books? Well . . ."

I looked up Grace and found her splashing waterproof paint on the bottom of the catboat. "The hell with the amusement industry," she declared heartily. "Have you seen the new puppies? They're out back."

I withdrew and scrutinized the puppies, who had the unearthly sweetness of all puppies, reflecting that the amusement industry was up against some stiff competition.

This is the season when the joke about Harry Truman's piano begins to pall. The simulated thrills of "Suspense" are nothing next to the bursting gladiolus in the backyard, the distant sails on the bay. "The Saturday Evening Post" romance has no charms comparable to the new girl who moved in four doors down the street, and neither has Judy Garland. The sports commentator chattering about the Dodgers can't outtalk the tennis racket in the front hall closet.

This is not the time for vicarious thrills; this is the time for one's own. In this curious age when the tendency is to sit passively and watch the professionals at work, this is one season when the amateurs avoid the movies, cast aside the book, turn off the radio, and —just for a change—participate. On these fragrant summer evenings, when conversation blooms shyly on the front porch, who wants to listen to the radio?

Or read a radio column?

Or write one?

CHAPTER 13

My Attention Wanders to Other Matters

Who He?
[DECEMBER 12, 1951]

HAROLD ROSS'S CONTRIBUTIONS to modern journalism are so far-reaching and pervasive that they are as hard to explain as the air around you. We take them for granted. To understand properly the impact Ross had on all of us, you have to go back a bit and examine the journalism of the pre-"New Yorker" era.

I should like to reprint one reporter's lead on one of the greatest of news stories, the end of the fighting in World War I.

"They stopped the fighting at 11 o'clock this morning. In a twinkling of the eye four years' killing and massacre stopped, as if God had swept His omnipotent finger across the scene of world carnage and cried, 'Enough!'"

Such a sentence would hardly be tolerated today; the reporters have got God out of their prose and got down to the facts. Not only has the style of journalism been drastically revised but a far healthier point of view toward the responsibilities and the purpose of journalism has been established.

Journalism—pre-Ross journalism—didn't reflect very accurately the people who were being written about or the people who were doing the writing, generally a hard-bitten crew whose conversation bore no resemblance at all to its prose style. Ross's stable of very talented writers introduced a style that was far more colloquial and—since style is largely determined and conditioned by content—they got a lot closer to the essential facts.

"'The New Yorker,'" said Ross, "was founded to make sense and to make money." It made a lot of both but, much more importantly, it shamed practically every American who writes into making—or trying to make—sense, too. It's rather odd that a man whose own rather untidy life was hardly dictated by common sense should have imprinted common sense into the journalism and a large part of the fiction of the nation.

But then Ross was full of contradictions. Robert Benchley swore that Ross once said to him: "Don't think I'm not incoherent." And he was. Yet, he expected and demanded of his writers a degree of coherence that has rarely been equaled. "The New Yorker" is surrounded by an aura of elegance but Ross's great preoccupation was not elegance; it was clarity. He drove his writers crazy with a host of explosive, frequently profane and often hilarious marginal notes —"Who he?" "What mean?" sometimes just a wild curlicue indicative of hopeless desperation. A. J. Liebling once got back a manuscript containing 160 of Ross's peppery, petulant marginal notes, the world's record at "The New Yorker." This immense thirst for clarification, amplification and accuracy spread far beyond the covers of "The New Yorker"; it touched and deeply influenced everyone who read "The New Yorker"; ultimately, it influenced writers who hadn't read the magazine but who were under the spell of writers who had.

Ross, of course, had much more in him as editor than a simple thirst for accuracy; he was an intuitive genius who knew when writing was right and when it was wrong (though frequently he didn't know why it was wrong). But the intuition died with the man; it could hardly be imitated. The hatred of bunk, of which "The New Yorker" and especially Ross was a personification, left its mark on everyone who writes or edits or publishes. An awful lot of malarkey disappeared from journalism in the twenty-five-year history of "The New Yorker."

Who's Dreaming of a White Christmas?
[JANUARY 2, 1948]

A RADIO IS a great comfort when you're snowbound. We were isolated by snow for twenty-four hours and in that time I developed a new feeling toward the broadcasting industry. Isolation is nothing new to us country dwellers but snowboundness, it ought to be explained, is a special form of isolation, a circumstance that is both frightening and in an obscure way comforting because you can't do anything about it. The emotion changes hands frequently during the course of the day, depending on whether you're worrying about the state of the Pablum supply (low) or the enforced and luxurious suspension of activity.

Into this comforting and frightening isolation, undeterred by two feet of snow or sleet or rain or dark of night, came the radio bringing contact, comfort and a strange form of cheer which, I'm sure, wasn't planned exactly that way. For hours on end the Andrews Sisters (by transcription) were caroling something about a winter wonderland, the gist of which is that it's fun to get your feet in the pretty snow. There was something so grimly inappropriate about this song that it was funny. At least to me, it was. Not to my wife. She had been to get the mail—it's a quarter mile down a steep hill through drifts waist high and there wasn't any mail anyway since the mailman has more sense than to go out in weather like this in spite of any postal propaganda to the contrary—and consequently her feelings about snow were, to put it mildly, unpoetic.

"A beautiful sight. We're happy tonight
"Walking through the winter wonderland," declared the Andrews girls spiritedly.

"I think your point of view is a little detached," my wife remarked with just a hint of exasperation. Arguing with a radio is a habit you get into out in the country. Since I don't like hard feelings to creep into the relations between my wife and the radio, I switched to another station where a disk jockey, hour after hour, spins records.

"I'm dreaming of a White Christmas," rumbled Bing Crosby. Outside the snow, now driven by a brisk west wind, was encroaching slowly but menacingly on my car, which was beginning to disappear under a mantle of winter wonderland. "Jingle bells. Jingle bells. Jingle all the way." Mr. Crosby was now teamed up with the Andrews Sisters.

"There's something indecent about the way those girls go in for winter sports," remarked my wife.

"I think these disk jockeys are a little out of touch with the customers," I said. "They've heard about the storm but they haven't seen it yet. There'll be a change of attitude."

The change came about noon when the beauties of snow were replaced by its terrors, an aspect that never creeps into popular songs, though it should. "The snow shows no sign of abating," said a newsman with that grim relish which radio newsmen reserve for catastrophes. "It's the worst snowfall since the turn of the century. New York is buried under fourteen inches and all the city's snow removal equipment has been mobilized."

There was no more nonsense about jingle bells or winter wonderlands; there were just bulletins. The Long Island Rail Road was hours behind schedule. The New York, New Haven & Hartford was stalled completely. Commuters everywhere struggled to get home and failed. Hotels were overflowing. My wife's exasperation vanished and, I'm afraid, I too felt an unseemly elation. The strangulation of a city the size of New York is a terrible thing but it has a certain fascination, if you look at it in a detached way. (We're seventy miles from New York and we were, at the moment, feeling extraordinarily detached.)

Outside the snow crept past the fenders of the car and headed for the windshield. The Merritt Parkway was closed, said the radio, the East River Drive was not closed but it was in such terrible shape that it was inadvisable to proceed along it. The We Don't Tell Girls basket picnic in Central Park was canceled till further notice. Just at that point, from my lawn there arose such a clatter I sprang to the window to see what was the matter. It wasn't Santa Claus; it was Frank Bennett, who lives on the next farm, and his snowplow, which had just swept clear my driveway. He came in snorting and steaming and pounding his palms together.

"Cold," said Mr. Bennett, a man not given to loquacity. I warmed him with bourbon, a Christmas gift, I explained, from the National Broadcasting Company. "Good," exclaimed Mr. Bennett, bestowing upon my radio a glance of appreciation which would have gladdened the heart of every vice-president of N. B. C.

The radio was advising its listeners to stay home, for heaven's sake, and not put any extra burden on the railroads, the roads, the buses, anything. "I'm going to town," announced my wife—to the radio, not to me. "Jingle bells, jingle bells, jingle all the way," she was singing as she left.

A radio, as I remarked earlier, is a great comfort when you're snowbound but an even greater comfort when someone else is.

There's a Corey Ford in Your Future
[MAY 29, 1950]

COREY FORD will be 114 years old next Tuesday. This is especially remarkable in Corey's case because of his misadventures in the Civil War. (War between the States for papers below the Mason-Dixon line.) Well, Corey is the sentry who kept falling asleep while patrolling in front of General Grant's tent or General Beauregard's tent or somebody's tent. After each offense they shot him. It didn't cure him. He kept falling asleep. The sight of a tent would make him drowsy. The more important the person inside, the sleepier he got. He fell asleep while guarding President Lincoln's tent one night, and it took three M. P.'s and fourteen pails of water to wake him up.

Well, naturally, he was severely disciplined for this one. Six different firing squads worked over him. It didn't help. He's lazier than ever. He just turned out a book called "How to Guess Your Age," which, I'm afraid, is on sale at all book stores, drug stores, shoe-shine parlors, saloons and bookmaking establishments. Costs $1. It's a very funny book. It's also a very short one, Corey never extending himself any further than is strictly necessary. It's 1,050 words, or forty-one pages, long.

Well, holy jeepers, I turn out 1,050 words every DAY (or almost that much). They wrap fish with these essays. Now and then I get severe complaints from housewives. They say I don't work hard enough, that my pieces are not long enough to give a decent cover to a lemon sole much less a haddock. Ford's 1,050 words are put into a book, selling for $1. Is this justice?

Let's get to the book. Ford complains that stairs are growing steeper these days. Everything is much farther away, especially shoelaces. Young people are much younger, and people his own age are much older. There's quite a lot more in the same vein, but you won't get it out of me. Run around to the nearest saloon and buy it for yourself.

Well, I suppose these are valid complaints. I'm 100 or so years younger than Corey Ford, and I haven't encountered his particular difficulties yet. But I have a few of my own, if this will make him any happier. MY complaint—in this atomic or cold-war age—is that the assault on one's nerves these days surpasseth endurance. The voices of children are more strident than they were twenty years ago. Taxis miss buses by a much narrower margin. Taxis miss ME by a much narrower margin.

The most striking phenomenon of all is in the construction of dishes. Time was when a dish, falling to the floor and breaking, made a not too unpleasant tinkle. Today—I don't know what they're putting into dishes these days—a breaking dish makes a shattering roar, enough to frighten a man out of his skin. The sounds in the night are different—louder and infinitely more terrifying. I remember back when I would lie awake, on the brink of slumber, and listen to the distant honking of the cabs on Park Avenue and to that most wonderful of all sounds, the deep-throated roar of the "Ile de France" moving down the Hudson on its way to the open sea.

They were comforting sounds, reassurances that one was in his own bed, in one's own county (Manhattan) and that nocturnal life was proceeding at its normal hectic (Manhattan) pace. Not any more, though. Not any more. These nights there are coyotes outside my window. I don't know how coyotes got into the middle of Manhattan, but I hear them night after night. And they're getting closer. Once in a while they pounce on an unfortunate woman, and her screams tear me from my bed. My wife keeps telling me it's only a taxi with faulty brakes, stopping belatedly for a red light. But I know better than that.

Mr. Ford says that suits get tighter every day. The nerves do, too.

Henry Morgan Views the Press
[MAY 23, 1950]

HENRY MORGAN, a sardonic, sometimes misguided but always honest man, lumbered to his feet before reporters, columnists, editors and publishers at the annual dinner of the New York chapter of Sigma Delta Chi, the national journalistic fraternity, and delivered a speech. It lasted all of a minute and a half, a fine length for a speech, and it was a fine speech.

In that minute and a half, Mr. Morgan, one of the more thoughtful radio comedians, summarized his opinion of the American press. This is a difficult assignment for a radio comedian. His listeners—reporters, columnists, editors and publishers—could crucify the man in print if they didn't like what he said. A radio comedian needs the support of the press. He'd have great difficulty existing without it. Still, Henry spoke his mind about us freely and, while there were some barbs in this small essay, it was on the whole a flattering and (I hope) intelligent estimate. I'd like to pass it along.

"I was asked here this evening," said Mr. Morgan, "mainly because it's common knowledge that I am an authority on this stuff. A number of people here work on newspapers. That isn't nearly as bad as what I do. I have to read them. Some people produce radio programs. I have it much worse than they do. I work for them—newspapers and radio—the two greatest influences of our time, I figure. You see before you the creature you have made. I am the average warped man.

"Because of you people in this room I believe Owen Lattimore is a Communist. I also believe he is not a Communist. Because of you people I believe F. D. R. was a genius and also that he ruined the country. I believe that there is more crime in this country than ever before and that our police are the best in the world. I believe that Eisenhower would make a great President except that I have read that military men don't make good Presidents and besides he will run if enough pressure is brought, he will not run, he can't run, he refuses to run, he doesn't want the job, you can talk him into it, he's trying very hard to make it look as though he doesn't want it, he's happy at Columbia, he's miserable, he's got a cold, he feels great.

"You have made it possible for me to take five cents and buy, in one package, a new picture of President Truman, my horoscope for the day, fifteen comic strips and the stock market reports. And I've read some terrible things about you. You work for money. Advertising dictates your policy. The department stores dictate your editorials. Don't you think you'd be happier with some other system? Wouldn't it be nicer to have a bureau of some kind supervise your work? Then, if the bureau didn't like it, you could adjust or get killed.

"Still in all, it's better than having people point at you and say: 'There's a man who works for money.' Somehow it's getting to be very un-American to work for money. It's also un-American not to work and to live on unemployment insurance. It's un-American to have social security and it's un-American to have such a small amount of social security. I strongly suspect that this is all your fault.

"In short, you people in this room have put me, the average man, in a peculiar position. I now have to make up my mind for myself. As long as you keep doing that, as long as you keep forcing the man in the street to make up his mind for himself, that's as long as we'll have the only working definition of democracy that's worth a damn.

"Thank you."

Man Has a Right to Listen to a Radio If He Feels Like It

[FEBRUARY 15, 1949]

ROBERT S. BYFIELD, a member of the New York Stock Exchange, recently defended the American profit system with great eloquence on America's Town Meeting of the Air, an experience that almost landed him in jail. (Ah there, Comrade!) Mr. Byfield, it appears, decided to catch the program a week in advance of his appearance to find out just how they ran things over there. Trouble was he had promised to take his two children to "As the Girls Go" at the Winter Garden the same night.

Mr. Byfield, a man of ingenuity and no little courage, boldly cut through this dilemma by taking his wife, two children, and a small portable radio to the theater. He deposited his family in their seats at 8:25—the program starts at 8:30—and went hunting for the lounge, planning to catch the program and join his family at the second act of the musical comedy.

Well, there isn't any lounge at the Winter Garden. The only conceivable places to catch a radio program in that theater are a telephone booth in the lobby and a small, inadequate lavatory downstairs. Mr. Byfield chose the phone booth, closed the door and settled down to listen to a man who was bitterly opposed to another round of wage increases.

In a matter of minutes, a cop was at his elbow. "What you doing?" asked the cop.

"Listening to the radio," said Mr. Byfield.

The cop, one of those cops who are easily nonplussed, scowled. "You gotta ticket for the show?" he asked. Mr. Byfield showed him his stub. "Well, why don't you go in and watch it?" demanded the cop, his voice beginning to rise. If there's anything a cop hates, it's being ribbed and this certainly looked like a rib of some sort. Tickets to the Bobby Clark show cost $6.60 apiece and the radio you can hear any night, free.

"Sssh," said Mr. Byfield.

Now, if there's anything a cop hates worse than being ribbed, it's being ssshed. "You gotta get out of here. We can't tie up these phones," he announced truculently.

Mr. Byfield sighed and took his portable down to the lavatory. Twenty minutes later he had the cop on his hands again. "You still here?" shouted the cop.

"I'm listening to a radio program," declared Mr. Byfield, summoning his dignity. "I have a perfect right to listen to a radio program. I'm not bothering anyone, am I? I wish to be left alone."

That stopped the cop momentarily. "What's the program?" he asked.

"Town Meeting of the Air. Ever listen to it?"

"No. What is it—one of them quiz programs?"

Mr. Byfield decided that "Town Meeting" was a little hard to explain and let the question pass. This was a mistake. No cop likes to be ignored any more than he likes to be ribbed or ssshed. Slowly and with a distinct air of menace, the cop took out the little black book.

"What's ya name?"

"You arresting me?" asked Mr. Byfield, alarmed. "What for?"

"Vagrancy," said the cop. "What's ya name?"

The radio program was nearing its end. Questions about wages and prices were being fired at the speakers by members of the radio audience, while in the lavatory in the basement of the Winter Garden Mr. Byfield tried desperately to explain what "Town Meeting" was and why he was listening to it.

"It's a discussion program. Prominent authorities discuss controversial issues—two of them taking one side, two of them the other. Next week I'm going to be a speaker on the program. The question is: 'Are Corporate Profits Too High?' My name is Robert S. Byfield and . . ."

The whole thing, as Mr. Byfield realized, sounded arrant nonsense. The cop's expression, one of exasperated patience, showed clearly he didn't believe there was such a ridiculous radio program and, if there were, a man who listened to a radio in a theater while a $6.60 seat went to waste upstairs obviously wouldn't be invited to appear on it.

"How ya spell Byfield?" he asked.

Just then the program came to a close and George V. Denny, its moderator, was heard over the small portable: "Tune in again next week, when our subject will be 'Are Corporate Profits Too High?' Our speakers will be Robert S. Byfield, financial writer and member of the New York Stock Exchange, Henry J. Taylor . . ."

The cop closed his black book, restored it to his pocket and walked out of the lavatory, looking extraordinarily foolish. And if there's anything a cop hates. . . .

CHAPTER 14

The Animal Kingdom

The Most Versatile Actor
[MARCH 27, 1950]

THE MOST VERSATILE actor in radio by all odds is that phenomenal dog, Lassie, who, as every one knows, is a he-dog, not a she-dog. In addition to playing the opposite sex, Lassie has been about every breed of dog there is.

Not long ago, on his radio program, Lassie, by nature a collie, was an Irish setter, the property of a young married couple who, while very much in love, quarreled violently. The marriage would have gone to smash but for the dog, whose gentle nature so shamed them they became the most sweetly dispositioned couple in town.

That's one of the least of Lassie's feats. Generally, he is required to do far more difficult things. Just last week Lassie was called in on a case of psychosomatic medicine, a rather new branch of the medical profession about which much is still unknown (except to Lassie). This one featured a crippled boy whose ailment was all in his mind. Lassie's owner, a physician, had despaired of getting the lad out of his wheel chair and called in the dog as a last resort. Lassie turned on his charm, of which he has a great deal, and had the boy up and around within seven minutes. (Lassie has to work fast.

It's only a fifteen-minute show, much of it devoted to the sale of dog food.)

That particular program was rather unusual in that Lassie played his own breed, a collie. He generally scorns the collie role as being much too easy. He has played a German shepherd, a Doberman pinscher, a boxer, a great Dane, a cocker spaniel, a St. Bernard, a coon dog and a French poodle. He has been cast as a young puppy and as an aged dog, barely able to walk, and he has been both a male and a female.

His acting style, it must be admitted, doesn't change a great deal, no matter what he is. His bark is pretty much the same whether he's a Doberman or a cocker. Still, as dogs go, he runs the full gamut of expression. He has one bark for simple animal spirits, another to inform the stupid humans around him: "Take it slow and easy, kids; the murderer is right over there, hiding behind a tree." He can sound heartbroken, deeply hurt or—when the commercial comes on—just plain hungry. He also whines very expressively, indicating to his masters that if they'd just pay attention to him he'd point out where the loot is hidden.

He has solved some remarkable crimes. A week or so ago he broke a million-dollar bank robbery. This was a particularly difficult case for Lassie because the robbers made their foray by speedboat, and even Lassie's nose is not sensitive enough to track a scent in a river. He has solved almost as many murders as The Fat Man.

Unlike The Fat Man, Lassie is frequently accused of committing the murders. No dog, possibly no human, has been unjustly accused of so many crimes. Once, while playing a Doberman pinscher, he was accused of killing his wealthy mistress, conceivably for her money, an unfair charge to level at a pooch whose material wants have never extended much farther than Red Heart Dog Food. He had to break the case to beat the rap.

On another occasion Lassie was accused of killing lambs in his owner's sheep herd in Montana. Once, playing a particularly benevolent St. Bernard in the Swiss Alps, who'd devoted his life to the rescue of fallen travelers, he was indicted for killing baby goats. He was cleared of both charges, largely through his own sleuthing.

One thing about Lassie that marks him off from all other radio entertainers. You never know what he's going to do next. With Jack Benny or Arthur Godfrey or Boston Blackie, you know pretty well what's coming—jokes or murders or whatnot. But Lassie will solve a $1,000,000 holdup one week; the next he's an expectant mother who adopts a motherless baby coon.

Could Clark Gable, another M-G-M star, do that?

Some Animal Stories
[AUGUST 1, 1950]

I'VE GOT A COUPLE of items here on animals. Down in Baltimore, a baboon named Coquette died unexpectedly the morning before she was to have made her television debut on WAAM-TV. This is the second simian tragedy within a month or so. A spider monkey expired after rehearsing with Bert Parks, the "Stop the Music" man, conceivably of despair at the small strides evolution has taken thus far.

The Baltimore case was rather different. The baboon, according to Arthur Watson, the zoo director, was killed by an acute gastric disorder. Up in Radio City country, Mr. Watson, we generally refer to it as an ulcer. Ulcers usually strike nothing less eminent than vice-presidents. In fact, office boys in the broadcasting dodge who contract ulcers are fired for overweening presumption. Very unusual for either a baboon or a vice-president to *die* of ulcers, though. According to our experience, the best treatment—in case any other baboons are stricken—is to promote the victim to president. That cures his ulcers and gives him hypertension, in which case he switches from a milk diet to a salt-free diet. Hypertension kills him even more quickly, but he's happier and, above all, richer. All straight on that now, Baltimore?

My other animal story, which comes straight from "The Brattleboro (Vt.) Daily Reformer," concerns a cat which has contracted a strange passion for John Gambling, the early morning music, weather and time maestro on WOR, New York.

"As the gray dawn approaches," reports "The Reformer," "the cat meows, at first graciously and politely, then plaintively and finally peevishly if the radio is not turned on. If the owner persists in sleeping late, the cat gets up on the table, clawing the dials and our scout says he has seen the marks. When the longed-for voice and the sound of the music fill the room, the cat purrs and assumes an air of great comfort and joy, and a beatific look covers her face." Also, according to "The Reformer," the cat gets enraged and tries to shut off the radio when Gambling's programs are handled by anyone else.

All I can say is I'm glad it's not my cat. My cat loathes John Gambling and everyone else who starts broadcasting at 6 A.M. Like any sensible cat, he sleeps till ten. Then he turns on Arthur Godfrey, sips a can of Hi-V orange juice and practices his ukulele lesson. In the afternoon, he watches the Dodger games on television, meowing at first graciously, then plaintively and finally peevishly over the lamentable lapses of the Dodger pitching staff.

The Chalk and the Hunch

[APRIL 11, 1951]

JOHN MCNULTY, the Third Avenue historian, has a new book out, "A Man Gets Around," and a very nice little series of essays it is. The reviews were universally favorable since no one in his right mind would ever give McNulty a bad notice if for no other reason than that he would be exiled from all the saloons on Third Avenue for life.

One thing that struck me about these reviews is that most of them contained references to McNulty's horse-playing proclivities, which are extensive, though horse playing doesn't figure in this book very much. McNulty is strictly a chalk player, a student and scholar of the form sheets. Chalk players scorn and, I think, misunderstand hunch players, of which I am one. I don't think anyone has ever stood up and explained the hunch player and his problems, so, if no one minds, I thought I would.

A hunch player is one who bets on a horse because its name reminds him of his aunt or some such thing. There are probably as many hunch players as there are chalk players and, though it'd be a pretty hard thing to prove, I think they do just as well as the chalk players and maybe a little better. Your true hunch player won't touch a form sheet because it'll interfere with his instincts. He'd get to thinking about past performances, the condition of the track and other nonsense when he should be looking for portents.

A portent—one type of portent, anyway—is something in the name of the horse or his sire or his dam which relates to your own life or recent experience. I remember once my small son got himself locked in the bathroom and couldn't contrive to unlock himself. We had a terrible time getting him out of there. Well, that afternoon at the track, there was this horse whose sire was Shut Out. A clear portent and a rather easy one. He won easily, too.

Some hunches are a good deal more complicated than that. At Santa Anita one time, I was introduced to Mickey Rooney, who is not only a horse player but also a horse owner. Well, Rooney is locally renowned in Hollywood as the alimony kid. By the age of twenty-five he had already paid out several hundred thousand dollars in alimony which, considering his age and weight, is probably a world's record. In the next race there was a horse named Larceny (or Grand Larceny or some such thing). That was enough for me. It won at 7 to 1.

Now follow closely here. A couple of years elapsed and I was at Saratoga. In the last race of the day a horse named Alimony was running. I remembered the Santa Anita incident and acted accordingly. Alimony paid $18.20 for a $2 ticket which is all I had on him. This is known as playing a hunch based on a prior hunch, a very delicate operation and one that doesn't happen often.

One thing that differentiates a hunch player from a chalk player, most of them anyway, is a sense of guilt. A chalk player who stays up all night figuring performance, blood lines and other abstruse matters feels he's earned the money if he wins any. A hunch player feels he's stealing the stuff and tries to return it to where it came from. Mostly he succeeds. But not always. I know one hunch player who's in a terrible predicament.

"I had $10 on this horse," he explained, "and it wins and I get paid $54. Well, the man behind the window gives me a $50 bill and four singles. It's maybe the second time in my life I've had a $50 bill. I carried it around for weeks, not wanting to spend it, of course. I felt a moral obligation to return this $50 bill to the proper authorities.

"Well, I'm out at the track again one day and I get a strong hunch on a horse called Asterisk for one reason or another. On the tote board this horse is 20 to 1, for heaven's sake. I figure this is a splendid opportunity to restore this $50 bill to its rightful owners. First $50 ticket I ever own." His face took on a stricken look. "Asterisk comes in by eight lengths. And you know what they do—they pay me in *$100* bills. I'm walking around with ten $100 bills that don't belong to me."

"Well, you could always go bet the hundreds," I suggested.

"I tell you why I don't, what's keeping me awake nights. Suppose I land one of these here $100 bills on a long shot and they pay me in $1,000 bills. There ain't a horse park in the world got a $1,000 window. I'd have to *spend* the stuff."

I understood him perfectly. He's in a terrible fix.

The Flea Position
[MARCH 16, 1951]

THE MAIL PACKET is in with intelligence from overseas. I like to keep abreast of the more important news from Britain, and I'm sure you do, too. You want to know what's happening in England? I'll tell you what's happening in England. There's a shortage of fleas.

So severe a shortage—let's not mince words—that there probably won't be a flea circus at the Festival of Britain this year. Billy Rayner, who was to have staged the flea circus, reviewed the flea situation to "The Daily Telegraph," and, believe me, it's grim. Trained fleas, as any fool knows, have to come from human beings. Fleas from animals die when they are parted from the animal. Well, sir, no one seems to *have* fleas any more. Mr. Rayner has advertised for them without success. (He wants twelve.)

"Since the war the flea position has been getting steadily worse," explained Mr. Rayner. "I blame the vacuum cleaners and the newfangled disinfectants. The average flea lives only for about three months, and they do not breed in captivity. Toward the end of the three months they become stiff-jointed, just like humans in their old age. And then they cannot ride the cycles, pull chariots or do sword fighting. All the old fleas can manage is an occasional dance. The public won't pay to see that. It is just what they expect from fleas, anyway.

"We usually find that the more educated people are, the more interest they take in our fleas. At Oxford we bring the house down."

Horrifying situation, no doubt about it. Flea circuses are a much older and, in many ways, more respected form of show business than radio or television. We can't let it fall victim to vacuum cleaners and newfangled disinfectants. Seems to me, if we can ship a load of coal to Yorkshire, one of the leading coal-producing areas in the world (as we recently did), we ought to be able to rustle up twelve fleas for the British.

I've been looking around on my own. Inspected my four-year-old son from head to toe to see if he was harboring any talent. His fleas *used* to be able to do sword fighting with the authority of Errol Flynn. But not any more. Not any more. I blame it on the progressive school my son is attending. Nowadays, my son's fleas just lie around reading books. And the public won't pay to see that. It's just what they expect from fleas, anyway. They can't even muster up an occasional dance, these fleas.

It's all very well for Mr. Rayner to say that the more educated the people are, the greater their interest in fleas. But the more educated the *fleas* get, the more trouble they are. Our fleas are still young enough to ride the cycles, pull chariots or do sword fighting. They just won't. They've been educated to the point where they consider it beneath their dignity. And they don't think the money is right. These young American fleas all want to be Ed Sullivan; their aim is to *introduce* people and let *them* ride the cycles. The great ambition of one of our fleas is to introduce Ed Sullivan and make him pull the chariot for a change.

You can hardly blame them, the way the talent situation is these days. A girl can rehearse for three weeks, memorize sixty pages of dialogue and give a whale of a performance on, say "Studio One." She'll make maybe $200, if she's lucky. It's much more rewarding to be Eva Gabor, tell the guests where to sit down and say "What's new?"—an easy line. If you ask me, these fleas just wised up a little quicker than the humans. There'll come a time—you mark my words—when the actors, the singers, the dancers are going to get damned tired of doing even an occasional dance for Mr. Sullivan. Let him do his own occasional dance.

CHAPTER 15

Charms That Don't Necessarily Soothe the Savage Breast

The Compulsive Drinker
[OCTOBER 25, 1948]

A BUNCH of the boys were whooping it up in Bleeck's saloon the other night drinking more than was good for them and singing old folk songs and some of the more recent ones. About midnight the quartet, a seedy but determined bunch of singers, began, as is their custom at that hour, that old English chantey which goes:

> "It's delicious yum yum yum.
> "It's delightful. Order some.
> "Now demand it. What's the name?
> "Piel's light beer of Broadway fame."

After they finished, Fogarty, the red-headed bass of this outfit, said mournfully: "They don't write songs like in the old days." It's a complaint familiar to most of the drinkers there, especially after midnight. "Now," he continued pugnaciously, "you take a grand old number like 'Pepsi-Cola Hits the Spot.' Nobody is writing songs like that any more." He began singing a snatch:

> "Nickel, nickel, nickel, nickel."

"They took that out," Roberts, the tenor, reminded him. "It isn't a nickel any more. It's six cents."

"Inflation," said Fogarty sadly. "It's even ruining the old songs. And the new songs you can't sing at all. Now you take a song like this song I heard yesterday." He sang in his watery bass:

> "When the values go up, up, up
> "And the prices come down, down, down
> "Robert Hall this season
> "Will tell you the reason.
> "Low overhead, low overhead."

He broke off in disgust. "What sort of song is that, I ask you? 'Low overhead, low overhead.' Sir William Gilbert would turn over in his grave. Man can't open his mouth on these new lyrics."

Roberts, a dreamy and timid little drunk, spoke up. "There's another one going the rounds that's even harder." He sang it.

> "Don't be afraid to look at your hands
> "When you get through scouring pots and pans.
> "Use Ajax, new miracle cleanser
> "With exclusive foaming action."

Everyone agreed that last line foamed in the wrong places. I watched Roberts closely after that one because he is a strange little guy, what the psychiatrists call a compulsive drinker. In fact, he suffers from a lot of funny compulsions, a pushover for an advertising man. Sure enough, he started looking at his hands guiltily. He probably never scoured a pot or pan in his life but the thought had been put in his mind that he was afraid to look at his hands. I bet anything he scurried around to the grocery store the next day and bought some of that miracle cleanser.

Every one of those songs that demanded you do something, Roberts went and did it, simply because he didn't believe in taking any chances. "Don't be half safe. Don't be half safe. Don't be half safe," was his philosophy, sung to the tune of "The Volga Boatman."

I feel sorry for this little guy because I think singing commercials have wrecked his life. I remember the night we were all sitting around the back room at Bleeck's, singing. Roberts had this girl with him and Roberts, for no special reason, began singing—all by himself because no one else knew the words—that splendid old ballad:

> "You can say yes to romance.
> "Be dainty and don't take a chance.
> "Soft as a lover's caress
> "Vote for happiness."

Well, sir, this girl followed instructions to the letter; the following week she said yes to romance, married poor Roberts and has made his life miserable ever since. There's only one of these songs that ever did Roberts any good. That's the one that goes:

> "Today is Tuesday. Today is Tuesday.
> "Time for Adam, candy coated gum."

Up until the time that one got on the air, Roberts used to wander around all day Tuesday thinking in his confused way that it was Thursday. Now he's hep to the day of the week but, come to think of it, I don't know what good that does him either.

Just then the subject of these speculations spoke up: "I got to get home. Just one more, fellows." And he began and we all joined in on that rollicking little number:

> "Kasco! Kasco! Dogs all love it so.
> "What a meaty treat is Kasco
> "K-A-S-C-O.
> "Oh where, oh where has my little dog gone?
> "He's heading for the kitchen and his
> "K-A-S-C-O."

Baby-Talking Baby

[APRIL 9, 1951]

SOMEWHAT RELUCTANTLY, I tackle the popular song profession, a field I don't understand at all, simply because there's a program

Baby-Talking Baby

around called "Songs for Sale." My interest in the popular song dodge flagged after someone wrote "Save Your Confederate Money, Boys. The South Will Rise Again." You've all heard it, of course. It contains that immortal line, "When we whup them Yanks, we'll open them banks and declare a dividend." The songwriting art reached a peak right there that will never come again.

At least, that's what I think. It's only fair to point out that other scholars in this specialized field disagree. Mitchell Rawson, a world-recognized authority, favors that great World War I song, "If He Can Fight Like He Can Love, Then It's Goodby Germany."

> "I know he'll be a hero when he's over there,
> "Because he's a bear
> "In any Morris chair."

But let's not start singing the old songs. We'll be here all night. "Songs for Sale" is, according to the opening announcement, "the big chance for unknown songwriters to have their songs played by Ray Bloch and sung by Rosemary Clooney"—if that is any inducement to you young unknown songwriters. None of the unknown songwriters has yet touched the pinnacle of genius of those two songs I've mentioned or got anywhere near it. But they're trying awfully hard.

Not long ago, "Songs for Sale" introduced for the first, and just possibly the last, time on the air a song called "Baby-Talkin' Baby." Its lyric was almost exclusively devoted to baby talk. Not quite so much baby talk as you find in "I Taw a Puddy Tat" but, if my insensitive ears are to be trusted, a bit more expert baby talk than that of "Bouncy Bouncy Ball-y." I could be wrong about this. My experience is limited.

The program possesses a panel of experts who hand down indictments on these songs, and one of these experts, Russ Morgan, the bandleader, spoke up vehemently on this one. "Personally, I don't like baby-talk lyrics," said Mr. Morgan. "Personally, baby talk failed in my first marriage." I consider this opinion biased, immaterial, irrelevant, incompetent and un-American, and I think Morgan ought to be disbarred for uttering it.

Just because Mr. Morgan's first marriage foundered in a sea of baby talk is no reason Tin Pan Alley should abandon baby talk and learn English. One of the comforts of my middle years is the mental picture I conjure up, in periods of stress, of a couple of balding, paunchy songwriters trying to find a rhyme for "snookums." Just between you and me, I, too, am working on a baby-talk song, "Let's 'Oo and Me Play Pattycake but Not Here, for God's Sake!" I'd hate to think that the baby-talk lyric had been ruled unconstitutional before I got my song ready for "Songs for Sale."

The program, which seems to have got elbowed aside in this column, is presided over by Jan Murray, a sort of thin Morey Amsterdam. He tells jokes. "A good husband is hard to find," says one contestant. "You're telling me," ripostes Mr. Murray. "My aunt has been trying to find her husband for ten years." Want to hear some more of Mr. Murray's jokes? No? You're sure? Positive? Well, all right.

Along with the songs by unknowns you'll hear a good many songs by well knowns and the difference, I must confess, is sometimes slight. Still, the unknown songwriters whose work is bandied about on "Songs for Sale" have remained without exception spectacularly unknown. Tough racket to break into, songwriting. I haven't even been able to find a publisher for my other baby-talk song, "How Can Itty Bitty You Be Such a Great Big Lousy Tramp?"

Sneak to Nightmare
[AUGUST 25, 1950]

A MUSICAL BRIDGE, as if everyone didn't know, consists of a few bars of music interspersed between: "All right, Spade, reach!" and the girl at the corner wondering why Mr. Spade hasn't kept his date with her. There's an enormous library of this stuff, much of it ominous, and WOR in New York once devoted a whole program to bridge music.

The commentator on that program explained: "Bridge music—that's what they call the things that are played between the scenes on dramatic programs. They bridge you from—well, from breakfast at a lunch counter to murder in the haunted laundry. Or from the whispering in the pine trees to the discovery that the man she thought was a burglar is really her uncle."

WOR has 6,000 of these highly descriptive musical bridges in its library and, believe me, it runs the gamut. I've been browsing through some of the 6,000 titles, which are even more descriptive than the music. Here's one of the longer ones: "Wistful Yearning, Love Is Born and Surges and Surges and Surges: Then in a Pastoral Setting." One of my pets is: "Ye Old English Countryside but Something Is Amiss." Then there's "Mother, I Feel Lonesome in This Big City," which is followed directly by "A Romp through the Botanical Gardens" where presumably she has found someone to play with.

WOR specializes in murder, so naturally it has a lusty collection of these bridges. Among the murder bridges are: "There's a Face in the Window," "Quick! Follow That Car," "Macabre, Running Motor," "Sneak to Nightmare," " 'Twas a Long Dark Night and the Wind . . . etc." and—for the really gruesome one—"Out of the Dark Valley Came Slimy Crawling Things . . . etc." I love that etc. What sort of et cetera do you suppose the composer had in mind?

Naturally, love is dwelt on extensively. The love bridges include: "Girl Doesn't Get Boy," "Love, Love, Love, with Apologies to Tchaikovsky," "Marital Rifts," or "Why Didn't You Tell Me This When We Were Back in Prairie City?" "I Hate You! I Hate You! I Hate You!" And one called "Pseudo Love, Pseudo Kiss" for young couples who are just monkeying around.

United World Federalists will be happy to know WOR has a bridge entitled "Brotherly Love: Better World," and labor will be delighted to know that it has two bridges devoted to it, entitled respectively "Hard Labor—C. I. O." and "Hard Labor—A. F. of L." "Hard Labor—A. F. of L." is not as hard as "Hard Labor—C. I. O." because the music department belongs to the A. F. of L.

The original purpose of bridge music was not so much to change the mood as to change the scene. There are a lot of bridges which are just scene-shifters. WOR has one bridge called "Big City," another called "Bigger City." One of its best all-purpose scene-shifting bridges is entitled simply "From Here to There without Fireworks." Or WOR can get very specific with "Slow Taxicab in a Traffic Jam" or "Coming Out of Waterful Music."

Sometimes the bridges mix scene and mood at the same time. "Menacing Humor to Racetrack Background," for example. My particular favorite in this line is one called "Light Confusion—and Then Down the Stairs in a Hurry."

As for mood, the radio dramatist can settle for "Background—Nostalgic" and carry on from there. Or, if he likes music behind his words, he can get "Background Nostalgic—Tender into Ye Rude Awakening." Ye Rude Awakening, in this case, is simply a sad chord of a sort known in the trade as a "stab." You've heard hundreds of stabs if you listen to the radio much. Not all stabs are bad news, though. WOR can also provide you with a hopeful stab called "Things Are Looking Up."

If you pay much attention to mystery stories, you've certainly heard this one: "Sudden Tumultuous Departure, into Motor. Then Abrupt Arrival. Ominous." That's a rather general bridge that can be used for all sorts of occasions. However, WOR has a few highly specialized ones for highly specialized occasions. My favorite in this category is one called: "Mommie! Mommie! Mommie! Daddy's Suitcase Is Gone!"

Psyche Me, Daddy
[DECEMBER 2, 1949]

SOME YEARS BACK, there was a psychiatrist who turned a cold psychoanalytical eye on "Alice in Wonderland." Found it full of unmentionable neuroses of one sort or another. You'd be surprised what a sex fiend Alice really was. As for that Rabbit . . .

Well, anyhow, WNEW, the perky New York independent, has now employed a psychoanalyst, man named Nandor Fodor, to turn his attention to popular lyrics. (Psyche me, daddy, eight to the bar.)

"A song," says Dr. Fodor severely, "ees not a private emotion. Eet becomes a national matter when eet ees put over de radio as eemportant examples of de American subconscious."

With that introduction, WNEW, whose income is derived primarily out of popular tunes rather than psychoanalysis, spun Joe E. Howard's ancient tune "I Wonder Who's Kissing Her Now?" (breathing sighs, telling lies).

"Self-centered like all lovaires," declared Dr. Fodor irritably. "Vundering how much he vass a liar himself. Otherwise why should he accuse de man who hass succeeded heem of telling lies. Probably de emotional deestress of somebody who may not be eequeeped to love."

Fine way to talk to a man of eighty-three. (Or maybe eighty-eight. It's a little hard to find out how old Joe Howard is.) I find it hard to believe that Joe ever bothered about his successors. He was too busy succeeding others. Why, way back in '25—hardly a man is now alive—Howard passed DeWolf Hopper for the All-American matrimonial sweepstakes with a total of six wives.

"Why do they all marry Joe Howard?" asked a newspaper man of one of his wives. The fourth, I believe.

"He's so fascinating and such a perfect lover," she emitted for posterity.

Dr. Fodor passed hurriedly on to another song known as "Oh, Daddy!" This is the one where a winsome lass pleads to daddy for—among other things—a brand new car, champagne, caviar. In short, the best of everything.

"Dees girl ees making terrible mistake," said Dr. Fodor gravely. "Fadder feexation. Cause uff great unhappeeness een later life." It was all right, said he, to yearn for champagne, caviar, but it should come from a sweetheart, not a father.

Now wait, doctor! (He's from Hungary and probably unacquainted with local semantics.) In this country we've got two kinds of fixation. The Daddy, or My-Heart-Belongs-to-Daddy, fixation and the straight, ordinary, run-of-the-mill, you-meet-'em-every-day father fixation. Two different kinds of girl entirely. Two different kinds of treatment. Psychiatry may be all right for the second kind. For the first—champagne, caviar is the only treatment known. Lot of research been done on this. Nothing else works.

The only lyricist who got a passing grade from Dr. Fodor was Irving Berlin for his "Homework" from "Miss Liberty," a lament from a young gal who'd rather be home crocheting (and meekly obeying) than working in an office. However, Berlin got his lumps for writing that old favorite, "Alexander's Ragtime Band."

Is this the ragtime band of Alexander the Great, because of the bugle call to war? inquired the doctor suspiciously. (I'm trying to keep this in English.) An aggressive and militant note. (He continued.) Bands may become dangerous. A threat to international peace. A secret weapon. Why not leave out the bugle call? The triumph of mind over meter, but more treason than reason.

WNEW better keep the good doctor away from "Over There." That one is downright subversive.

A Low Bow All Around
[DECEMBER 2, 1951]

THE FIRST OPERA ever written for television, Gian-Carlo Menotti's "Amahl and the Night Visitors," is one of the most basic of Christmas Eve stories, the story of a miracle of faith and of hope and of charity—all three of the most elemental Christian virtues. Mr. Menotti, as a matter of fact, was gravely concerned about it, feeling that he hadn't any new ideas.

He needn't have worried. Menotti simply can't do anything badly and, while "Amahl and the Night Visitors" is hardly his best work, it was a deeply moving and extraordinarily powerful piece of musical drama. Menotti's great virtue, one that has shown up in "The Consul" and "The Medium" and all his work, is a simplicity and integrity of purpose which leads him straight to the heart of the matter; he deals in the fundamental emotions, fundamental human needs, and he writes about them with a terrifying directness.

"Amahl and the Night Visitors" is, briefly, the tale of a crippled boy who sees the Star of Bethlehem and hobbles home to tell his mother about the wonder he has seen. "A star—this long. Well, maybe only this long." She's much too obsessed with their poverty —there's not a bite to eat nor a stick of wood in their hut—to pay much heed. Presently the three Kings visit the hut and mother and son learn of the birth of the Saviour. They have no gifts to offer the new-born Christ except the boy's crutches. He offers these and suddenly, the miracle, he can walk.

It's the sort of story that could have been drenched in sentimentality, and Menotti, because he is unabashed by the outer trappings of sentiment, because he writes directly about mother love, about poverty, about crutches, about miracles, somehow purifies them and transforms them into genuine and profound emotion. This is a very great gift indeed, the quality of candor, and one which Menotti, almost alone, seems to possess these days.

But Menotti, of course, is much more than candid. He is an enormously skilled and subtle dramatist as well as a magnificent composer, and the two arts, music and drama, go hand in hand with him. He can hardly write a line of music which doesn't seem exactly suited to the particular moment of the drama, inflaming the mind and the heart simultaneously and intensifying the dramatic effect to an almost unbearable degree.

The opera opened, quietly and simply, with the crippled boy—played by twelve-year-old Chet Allen, whose singing is a miracle of sweetness—playing his pipe in the marketplace, all alone, a scene of wondrous freshness like the bouquet of a newly opened wine. There were many other wonderful scenes. Three times the boy peeps out the door at the newly arrived Kings. "Mother, mother, come see what I see!" Three times his mother refused to believe anyone was there, charging the atmosphere with a rising and terrible excitement.

Then there was the procession of the Kings into the hut, reflected like silver balls in the shining eyes of the boy. They were very human Kings, even a little stupid, but very kindly. "Have you royal blood?" whispered the boy. "Yes." "Can I see it?" "It's no different from yours." "What good is it?" Has ever a small boy's heart and mind been so tenderly exposed?

Menotti drew his inspiration from the fifteenth-century Flemish painting, "The Adoration of the Magi," by Bosch, and much of the staging and especially the lighting, which was altogether superb, captured the quality of Flemish art—its composition, its opulence, its rather earthy reverence.

Menotti's music, so powerful in "The Consul," was marked here, I thought, by a rare melodic sweetness completely in harmony with the breathless sweetness of the tale he unfolded. Besides the boy, a low bow is due also to Rosemary Kuhlmann for her performance and singing as the mother, to Samuel Chotzinoff, who produced it, to N. B. C., who commissioned it and who, I hope, will revive it many times.

As for Mr. Menotti, I can think of no higher praise than to say that everyone who saw it was a little better as a person and as a Christian than he was an hour earlier.

CHAPTER 16

Homicide, Plain and Fancy

The King's English
[JANUARY 17, 1947]

AFTER TOO MANY sessions with the stainless steel, highly abbreviated dialogue in the hard-boiled school of detective drama, you'll find it a healthful change of diet to turn to "The New Adventures of Sherlock Holmes," where, in spite of that word "new," the conversation is as leisurely as it was forty years ago. The estimable Holmes and the good Dr. Watson still address each other in a sonorous prose decorated with precise and crusty verbs, each as carefully turned as the gingerbread on a Victorian chair.

The other night Sherlock and Watson got mixed up, more or less against their will, in a little mystery called "The Devil's Foot," or, to put it in Watson's terms, they were "precipitated into the middle of gruesome and nerve-wracking events," a phrase that would never ocur to Dashiell Hammett.

Mr. Holmes had a visitor, man by the name of Tregenis, who had just had a grievous experience. He had discovered his sister dead and his two brothers stark mad in the "libr'y." "They were beside the fire, the candles quite gutted out," said Mr. Tregenis, who, despite his agitation, never omitted a comma in his recital of the unfortunate affair. "It's uncanny, that's what it is! Something came into that room and killed my deah sistah and dashed the light of reason from the minds of my two poor brothahs. It's devilish, that's what it is." Strong words, particularly that last adjective, but of course it was an unsettling experience.

To the average American, steeped in the dialogue of Dick Tracy, this manner of discussing a rather serious breach of the law may seem redundant and even a little heartless. Just the same, it adds a touch of surprise to even the most routine detective-story talk. For instance, at one point Holmes asked a question which has resounded through virtually every mystery story ever written. "What time was it?" he inquired.

"The clock on the steeple was just chiming twelve," said Tregenis, a man of the old school who has probably not yet recognized the word "midnight."

Anyhow, Holmes informed Tregenis that he'd let him know if any ideas occurred to him, only he didn't say it like that. "Should anything occur to me, Mr. Tregenis, I shall communicate with you." Holmes, I decided after this remark, would make an excellent writer of memoranda to the troops, an opinion which was confirmed a few moments later when he boasted, "I have every hope of bringing this affair to a satisfactory termination."

Another great difference between Holmes and the deadpan school of American mystery is that it is not considered bad form to betray excitement, providing, of course, it's put in suitable English. Even Holmes, normally an exceptionally cool customer, will ejaculate in moments of deep stress something like "Great Scott!" Watson, a less stable personality, goes much further. "Ghahstly! Ghahstly!" he exclaimed at one point, and later he emitted what sounded in phonetic English like "Haddible!"

Frankly, I like this grave, rounded talk. It gives homicide a degree of dignity notably lacking in the American production. Tom Conway, of the movies, has taken over the Holmes role from Basil Rathbone. He's had a lot of prior experience solving things as the Saint and the Falcon in the movies. Conway isn't as urbane as

Rathbone, but then virtually no one is. Nigel Bruce has been playing Watson for years, and still is.

Greatest of Them All
[MAY 4, 1950]

SAM SPADE is described on the program of that name as the "greatest private detective of them all" and his originator, Dashiell Hammett, as "America's outstanding detective writer." Sweeping as those claims are, they'd have a good chance of standing up in court, though, of course, there'd be strenuous objections from the Erle Stanley Gardner mob.

If you like tough private eyes, you might as well get an earful of the original one, which is what Mr. Spade is. The Spade caper, which sometimes threatens to revolutionize the speech habits of the nation's young, is a fairly standardized operation, not necessarily a bad thing. At the very outset the telephone rings. Effie, Mr. Spade's secretary, answers. Mr. Spade is on the other end.

"Scurry right down to the apartment, my love," commands Mr. Spade. "And bring along a recording of 'Bongo Bongo Bongo, I Don't Want to Leave the Congo,' two cups of coffee and two voodoo drums. We'll sit on the drums, play the record and drink the coffee."

The great man always subjects Miss Effie to this kind of whimsy, but she has never quite grown used to it. "Oh, Sam!" she wails. Mr. Spade's odd, laconic requests take on some semblance of meaning when he gets down to describing his latest caper. It seems this girl—eyes like smoke, a sheath of satin, a calendar figure—walked into his office, unannounced. "Lie down," invites Mr. Spade, "we'll have a good talk."

"Drop dead," snarls the girl.

"I never argue with a redhead with a gun," Mr. Spade confides to the audience. "Blondes you can reason with. Redheads, no. So I dropped dead—or a reasonable facsimile. Unfortunately, I tipped over the desk and also the redhead. Then we wrestled, an interesting experience."

"I could keep this up all day," he says to the redhead. "You know any other good holds?"

Anyhow, that's typical of the Spade formula, a shrewd mixture of sex and violence. The redheads (or blondes or slinky brunettes) don't always walk into the story at the opening. Sometimes Spade finds them bending over him when he opens his eyes, his head throbbing from the pistol butt blow he received on the noggin in the alley outside.

"I love those low-cut dresses from this angle," murmurs Mr. Spade.

Spade is always getting conked with pistol butts, so often, in fact, that he shakes off the effects in a matter of moments and concentrates on the surroundings, especially those low-cut dresses. Considering the fact that he's the "greatest private detective of them all," he is terribly careless about letting thugs slip up behind him. He's easily the most battered private eye in the business. The pistol butts on the head are routine. To avoid the monotony of a single crack on the skull, he frequently manages to get himself thoroughly beaten up by two or three rough guys. On any other program this would be deplored as brutality. With Spade it doesn't bother you any more than all those wicked doings in Grimm's fairy tales. Spade shrugs off a beating with the jauntiness of the average man dismissing a mosquito bite.

Dashiell Hammett no longer has anything to do with Sam Spade beyond collecting a good deal of money each week. It is written by a number of Hollywood characters who have closely studied his style and, above all, the original story ingredients. While they can't match the old master, they do pretty well.

For one thing, the stories are fairly fresh and hold together remarkably well—as radio detective stuff goes. There are few holes in the plots. The thugs, the girls, the minor characters, even the unfortunates who get murdered, are pungent, tough and uniformly reprehensible, thus carrying out the Hammett theory that everyone has himself in mind at all times. And the narration is about as brisk and laconic as it can get. One of my favorite bits concerned Spade trying to get into someone's room, where he had no business to be.

"Found the landlady, made the pitch, flashed the license, got the key."

"Mr. District Attorney" Disapproves of Crime
[NOVEMBER 5, 1947]

IN ONE OF those horrid little dramas on "Mr. District Attorney" the other night, a football coach suddenly discovered—or thought he discovered—the infidelity of his wife. He got quite angry about it. "I feed you! I clothe you! And you do this to me," sobbed the coach. Then the full enormity of the sin struck him and he added brokenly: "And during football season, too!"

The curious sense of values implicit in that bit of dialogue is characteristic of the whole philosophy behind "Mr. District Attorney," whose enormous and long-standing success is one of the mysteries of broadcasting. Shortly after I started this column I heard one of the "District Attorney" programs which struck me at the time as possibly the most reprehensible piece of trash ever dramatized. "The only other thing in my notes," I wrote at that time, "is a string of adjectives including trite, cheap, degrading, overacted, lachrymose, hypocritical and what looks like implausible, but may be incredible."

That seemed sufficient to wrap up Mr. D. A. for all time. However, since a great many of my early opinions have been somewhat modified by time or because the shows have changed or because I have, I've been looking into "Mr. District Attorney" again. In this case, neither of us has changed a bit.

"Mr. District Attorney" is no bloodier than many other crime shows on the air but in several respects it is vastly more irritating. In the first place, its crimes are indescribably sordid; in the second, and more importantly, they are presented with consummate hypocrisy as a sort of public service. At any rate, there are a lot of virtuous noises at the opening of the show indicating that the purpose here is the exposure of rackets. The rackets come out of the newspapers and in that respect the show touches the fringe of reality, but the details are almost incredibly preposterous. The one about the coach was a dilly.

A couple of gamblers were trying to fix a football game. To accomplish this they bribed an assistant coach and then went to work to drive the head man nuts by means of a series of phony telephone calls concerning the extra-marital activities of his wife. This so distracted the athletic Othello that he lost all zest for his work and was even persuaded to rush home in the middle of the big game. Deprived of his magic presence, the team immediately lost —a situation which might amuse a good many gamblers, though I doubt whether they'd bet on it. The fixing of football games is a lot more complicated than that, Mr. D. A.

Incidentally, the coach's wife, who was as innocent as Desdemona, wound up in the same position, murdered, though in this case there was no particular reason for doing her in except to liven things up with a little bloodshed. She screamed quite a bit before she expired.

It may seem a little unfair to get so exercised over one program when there are so many others which have no great qualms about bloodshed. Mr. D. A., I think, deserves special treatment: (a) because the show has been around so long with no perceptible signs of improvement; (b) because it has the highest Hooper rating of any crime show (17.5); (c) because it lacks wit, taste and imagination. There are a great many slayings on the air (there are now forty-two crime shows on the four networks), but, in defense of some of the best of them, they have acquired the knack of rubbing out the victims with an air of innocence and unreality, like the wolf eating Little Red Riding Hood's grandmother. They are not expected to be taken seriously.

Mr. D. A., on the other hand, is introduced with high moral tone as the "champion of the people, defender of truth, guardian of our fundamental rights to life, liberty and the pursuit of happiness," all of which I find vexing. He even gives a little speech deploring crime. He disapproves, in case you're interested, of bank robbery, arson and matricide.

I seem to have another string of adjectives in my notes, this time concerning Mr. D. A.'s voice. A few of them are pompous, complacent, sonorous, humorless, dogmatic, unconvincing and—I don't know how this one got in here—superfluous. Mr. D. A., to put it more succinctly, sounds like a bad Shakespearean actor in an empty auditorium.

CHAPTER 17

An Era for the Ear

History by Ear
[NOVEMBER 22, 1948]

"THE THIRTEEN YEARS from the beginning of 1933 to the end of 1945 was an era for ear. The first and perhaps the last. Future great happenings will be televised and be remembered visually as well as in the mind's ear."

The most important and moving sounds of that era of massive history, in which radio only coincidentally came of age, have been superbly condensed by Edward R. Murrow and Fred Friendly in an album of five records now on sale in book and record stores. The paragraph above is part of the introduction. It explains better than I could the purpose and importance of the album, called "I Can Hear It Now," possibly the first volume of aural history ever produced. Murrow and Friendly, in what they describe as a labor of love, spent two years poring over 500 hours of recorded noises, most of them taken off the radio. Out of the 500 hours came forty-five minutes of the most significant oratory and other sounds of our time, pulled together, explained and introduced in a running commentary by Mr. Murrow.

All the famed voices are here—the heroes, the villains, the mountebanks, the clowns. "We hold the distinction of being the only nation that ever went to the poorhouse in an automobile," declares that drawling, mocking voice from the past—Will Rogers, wisecracking about a not-very-funny depression in 1932. And 1933. "We have nothing to fear but fear itself." The radio technique of the greatest radio orator of them all had not then been perfected, and it's interesting to watch the development of President Roosevelt's confidence and mastery as the thirteen years roll by.

There is a babble of lesser voices in the middle years. La Guardia, playing Falstaff to Roosevelt's Henry IV, boasting he hasn't a friend among the county bosses. Huey Long redistributing everyone's bank account. The Biblical imprecations of John L. Lewis. A former king of England telling a hushed world he can no longer carry the heavy burden without the help of the woman he loves.

"We take you now to Lakehurst, New Jersey . . ." Herbert Morrison of WLS, Chicago, describes the great airship Hindenburg approaching its mooring, almost motionless in the sky. Then: "Oh . . . Oh, it's terrible. It's terrible." This incoherent babble is possibly the most frightening single broadcast in the album.

Adolf Hitler's sing-song ranting seems from this distance remote and ridiculous, but there is still a note of menace in the massed and organized Sieg Heils that greeted every other sentence. Then the precise, spinsterish voice of Neville Chamberlain after Munich: "He told me privately that [Sudetenland] is the end of his territorial claims in Europe."

"The only defeat the Nazis suffered that year," comments Murrow glumly, as Clem McCarthy counts out Max Schmeling in the first round of his second Joe Louis fight.

In 1940 and '41, the pace quickens, the babble of sound increases in fury. Charles A. Lindbergh at an America First rally at Madison Square Garden: "If we enter a war to save democracy abroad, we may lose it at home." Roosevelt in Chicago: "The hand that held the dagger has stuck it in the back of its neighbor."

"I speak to you for the first time as Prime Minister." He had nothing to offer but blood, toil, tears and sweat. There isn't as much Churchillian oratory as I'd like but there is enough to remind us again that language was used more effectively on both sides of this conflict than at any time since Demosthenes.

"Let us brace ourselves to our duties and so bear ourselves that, if the British Empire and its Commonwealth last for a thousand years, men will still say, 'This was their finest hour.'"

Princess Elizabeth and Margaret Rose piping to evacuated British children during the Battle of Britain: "Good night, children, and good luck to you all." At Elwood, Ind., a drawling, deeply earnest voice in unmistakably Mid-West accent accepts the nomination for an office he persistently called "the Prezdunt."

"We interrupt this program to bring you a special news bulletin." John Daly delivered the bulletin in such matter-of-fact tones it's just possible he didn't realize its significance. "The Japanese have attacked Pearl Harbor. . . ."

"Yesterday," said the famous voice, now tired and profoundly sad, "December 7, 1941, a date which will live in infamy. . . ."

And presently the then unfamiliar voice from SHAEF headquarters: "People of Western Europe, a landing was made this morning on the coast of France. . . ."

Roosevelt's voice is heard a last time, after his return from Yalta before a joint session of Congress, a sick, listless, exhausted voice unrecognizable as the same one that thirteen years earlier had declared ebulliently: "We have nothing to fear but fear itself."

After that the sounds, though important, seem anticlimactic. The death of F. D. R., the swearing-in of President Truman, the successive announcements of V-E Day, the atom bomb, V-J Day were great news stories but they produced no thunders comparable to the early ones. The great voices—heros, mountebanks, clowns and villains alike—had with few exceptions been stilled forever.

Television at the Convention
[JUNE 23, 1948]

JUST BEFORE MIDNIGHT, after the long day of the Republican National Convention, Edward R. Murrow, looking wilted, bored and exhausted, slouched in front of a C. B. S. television camera, chatting fitfully with two of his C. B. S. news colleagues. "It must be the heat," he remarked. "Here are three reporters. We've been here ten minutes and all we've said is that nothing much happened today or, if it did, we don't know about it."

That pretty well sums up the first day of television's greatest event. The convention was broadcast over eighteen East Coast stations all day long; nothing happened before the cameras; and, in spite of it, television put on a great show. All day long notables and others who have small claim to that word paraded before the cameras, nobody saying very much but always bringing the expectation that they might; there was an intolerable amount of handshaking between radio reporters and delegates. ("Well, glad to have talked to you, Senator. Drop around again.") And many times interviews were conducted with a spirited opening and closing of mouths, and no sound came.

We were given glimpses of girls wearing four-leaf-clover ties bearing Taft's initials, of Stassen neckties, of rubber elephants and live elephants. We observed the dress of Virginia Davis, daughter of band leader Meyer Davis, which carried portraits of the four leading candidates and watched with interest as she lifted her skirts to show her real choice, a portrait of Stassen emblazoned well up on her thigh. Charles Collingwood, C. B. S. reporter, crashed the Union League Club with microphone and camera and went through the receiving line to the dismay and anger of Senator Edward Martin, of Pennsylvania. Another C. B. S. man parked five Hawaiian ladies in front of the camera, singing for dear life for ten minutes, while he scurried about trying desperately to get somebody—anybody—to interview. Another reporter interviewed an Indian in his native costume and native language.

Mary Margaret McBride sparred aimlessly with Mrs. Martha Taft for forty-five minutes about women's hats, the woman's place in politics and nothing at all while they waited for Senator Taft to appear. He never did. "I can't tell you how much I wish Bob Taft were here," sighed Mary Margaret when, ten minutes before the broadcast ended, the feminine conversation ground to an almost complete halt.

The intimacy of television is going to be a problem both to candidates and to the reporters. We got spectacular close-ups of the faces of delegates who choose our Presidents, many of them frightening, others—to be honest—reassuring. A glimpse of Speaker Martin with his shy, predatory smile, saying: "Of course, no one could refuse a summons like that." Governor Dewey, radiating confidence, his smile firmly pinned on, sidestepping questions put by Joe Thorndike, managing editor of "Life" (even one as to what he planned to do with that front porch on the White House). Young boy delegates gazing brightly into the eyes of young girl delegates with dawning and wholly unpolitical interest. Senator Vandenberg, scratching his cheek and trying valiantly to summon up some interest in Governor Green's keynote address.

Altogether, television brings you the babble, the heat, the crowds, the chaos, the confusion without—at least on that first day—bringing you much information. But it's a wonderful show, and its shortcomings are the fault of national conventions, not of the broadcasters.

"Life" magazine and N. B. C., which have teamed up for the event and "Life" seems to get top billing in this arrangement—easily ran off with the honors, both in programs and in a technical sense. The "Life" N. B. C. team seemed beautifully organized, knew where—with some exceptions—it was going from minute to minute and succeeded in luring an impressive number of the more important people in front of its cameras. Its kinescope films—that is, movies that were taken directly off a television receiver—were remarkably clear and well edited. These edited films of the daytime activities were shown to the nighttime audience so skillfully that one might easily get the impression he was seeing the actual convention.

One of the most pertinent remarks of the day, incidentally, was made by former Governor Alf Landon of Kansas. Landon said that convention speeches were once two or three hours long. Radio, he said, succeeded in cutting the oratory down by about two-thirds. Television, he continued, may cut it a third again. After listening and looking at Governor Dwight Green of Illinois for a long, dull hour, I find myself for the first time in my life in complete agreement with Governor Landon.

I may be one of the few surviving humans who saw the 1940 Republican convention televised on the old 441-line television sets. As I recall, there were great stretches of that broadcast during which we were presented with the spectacle of an empty table flanked by two empty chairs. In this one, they succeeded in putting people in the chairs, and by 1952 the people in the chairs may conceivably have something of interest to say.

Dewey on Television

[NOVEMBER 9, 1950]

WELL, GOV. THOMAS E. DEWEY won re-election handily in spite of the Hanley letter, and television certainly helped. Just how much it helped, no one will ever know. But no one can dispute that Dewey is the first man to exploit television politically, the first candidate to understand—he appears to have stumbled on this by accident—how to use television properly.

There has been a lot of talk about television's effect on political candidates almost since the birth of the medium. A great many politicians have employed television as a sort of rostrum. But, to my knowledge, no one has ever fully understood what television is exactly. The late President Roosevelt was a radio personality, conceivably the Number One radio personality of all time. It seems to me that all subsequent candidates have used television as if it were radio. They stood in front of a microphone and delivered a speech as mellifluously as possible, hoping that the pancake make-up would conceal their double chins.

Dewey threw the script away. He answered questions, as it were, from the floor—the floor being a dozen street corners all over the State of New York. He spoke extemporaneously; he moved from spot to spot, picking up state reports and documents; he sat on the edge of his desk (never once did he sit behind the desk); he scratched his head, put his glasses on, took them off, wiped them; he posed for photographs and he introduced his wife when someone wanted to look at her. Essentially, though, he answered questions—hundreds of them—questions about state taxes, housing, veterans' benefits, hospitals and a dozen other complex questions. He answered them in awe-inspiring detail, spouting figures and facts without hesitation, and rarely—except in obvious slips of the tongue—making mistakes.

This form of campaigning had a two-fold effect. First, it humanized Thomas E. Dewey as he had never been humanized before. Dewey will never exactly compete with Arthur Godfrey in charm, but it certainly gave the voters the most intimate glimpse of Tom Dewey they'd ever had. Secondly and more importantly, it eliminated the normal pomposities of political rhetoric. A man thinking on his feet is likely to blurt out the truth rather than the well-rounded, wind-filled phrase.

In any case, the old-fashioned campaign speech with a man reading from a script in front of a hall full of people is a dead form of oratory on television. (The Democrats did it on several occasions.) The candidate is in the voter's living room and the voter doesn't want oratory. It had also better be done in short takes. Dewey's eighteen-hour marathon on Monday and his other fourteen local television appearances were mostly done in fifteen-minute segments.

This was a shrewd move. Before radio came in, campaign speeches ran on as long as four hours. Radio drastically reduced these orations. It looks as if television will reduce them even more. And when a candidate is cut down to fifteen minutes, he had better marshal his facts in the most concise form.

Of course, very few candidates—Sen. Robert A. Taft is one of the few others I can think of—could dare undertake this form of campaigning. Dewey knows more about state government than any man since the late Alfred E. Smith. In essence, he was conducting the same kind of campaign—"Let's look at the record."

The Dewey headquarters is convinced that his television campaigning was largely instrumental in holding down the normally overwhelming Democratic plurality in New York City to a record post-depression low. Dewey's advisers also believe that he has invented a type of campaigning which other candidates will be forced to follow. If they do, it will be at their peril. Television throws a merciless white light on phoniness. The candidate had better know what he's talking about and he had better not try to evade a question. The candidate, I'm convinced, could be ugly as a hedgehog; it is not his looks that television puts under scrutiny; it is his ability.

In so far as the voter is concerned, the form of campaigning has its pitfalls, too. Many of the questions hurled at Dewey seemed rigged; all of them were certainly screened; the embarrassing ones were probably eliminated. Television is not entirely a substitute for the old town meeting. Just the same, a television personality—and Dewey is not necessarily the ideal one—is likely to be the politician of the future. The change on the whole is for the best.

The Duke of Windsor Speaks Again
[JANUARY 13, 1947]

"AT LONG LAST I am able to say a few words of my own," said the Duke of Windsor in a broadcast heard the world over on Dec. 12, 1936. All London stopped to listen. People gathered wherever there was a radio, in streets, homes, pubs and theaters to hear the words of their abdicated monarch.

"A few hours ago I discharged my last duty as King and Emperor and now that I have been succeeded by my brother, the Duke of York, my first words must be to declare my allegiance to him. This I do with all my heart." In New York City, it was 5 o'clock in the afternoon, but the midtown streets, usually full of office workers hurrying home, were strangely deserted. People departed a half hour early or remained in their offices huddled around radios. Telephone switchboards, usually jammed with calls at that hour, fell strangely silent from 5 to 5:10 P.M.

"You all know the reasons which have impelled me to renounce the throne. But I want you to understand that in making up my mind I did not forget the country or the empire which, as Prince of Wales and lately as King, I have for twenty-five years tried to serve."

The words echoed from loudspeakers throughout England, across the length and breadth of the United States (where they were carried by both N. B. C. and C. B. S.), across oceans and jungles to the farthest reaches of the British Empire. They were heard both in the original and in hastily whipped up translations in Spain, Norway, Sweden, Denmark, Finland, Austria, Hungary, Czechoslovakia, Germany, Portugal, the Netherlands, Belgium, France, Italy, Switzerland, Argentina and the Dutch East Indies.

Throughout the English-speaking world, no single event has ever transfixed so many people at a single moment in time. No matter what the time zone, 10 P.M. in London, 5 P.M. in New York City, 3:30 A.M. in Bombay, 8 A.M. in Sydney, all other activities ceased to have any importance as radio listeners everywhere gathered around their radios. A reverent hush fell over a substantial portion of the globe.

"But you must believe me when I tell you that I have found it impossible to carry the heavy burden of responsibility and to discharge my duties as King as I would wish to do without the help and support of the woman I love." In London women burst into tears at that last phrase.

It is almost exactly ten years ago that the former King delivered his famed explanation, apology and farewell to the British people. A lot of history has intervened and there have been other celebrated pronouncements over the air, dealing with the beginning of wars and the end of wars. Many of them were far more important than the abdication of a constitutional monarch. Yet none of them was listened to by anything like the same world-wide audience; none of them generated one-tenth the interest. The Duke of Windsor's speech was heard by at least 250,000,000 persons and there are those who consider that a conservative estimate. That's the all-time record radio audience and may never be surpassed.

The only reason for reviving this faded and, from this distance, somewhat anachronistic bit of history is that the other night the Duke of Windsor delivered another radio address, the first, according to The Associated Press, to be heard in this country since his abdication speech. It was a routine piece of oratory in which the former King appealed for public support of the Salvation Army drive.

"Comfort to the weak and saddened. Help to the poor. These are the aims of decent men and women the world over. In such efforts the mercies and contributions of the Salvation Army are well known to all," said the Duke. "From my youth forward, in my homeland and throughout the world, this unselfish organization has been an inspiration to me."

It was a reserved, carefully modulated, and very British, speech—a little dull, in fact—but indubitably a sincere effort in an admirable cause. The Duke of Windsor still possesses as fine a radio voice as you'll find anywhere. The nervousness and the pronounced emotional strain which were so noticeable in his abdication speech, and which, in fact, made that speech so intensely dramatic, were, of course, lacking in this one. The former King sounded a little tired but he was completely at ease.

At the American Broadcasting Company, which carried the speech, officials said they had no idea how many people listened to the Duke's speech. Privately, they admitted that it was doubtful whether His Highness attracted many listeners. In fact, the network had no idea how many, if any, of its other stations carried the appeal.

Two Oceans at Once
[NOVEMBER 23, 1951]

"THIS IS AN old team starting a new trade," remarked Edward R. Murrow at the outset of "See It Now," C. B. S.'s enormously impressive new television news show. He was seated in the control room of Studio 41—a logical spot, he explained, to start out from—and presently he called on Camera 1 to bring in the Atlantic Ocean.

The Atlantic Ocean, a small wet segment of it, swam into view on one monitor screen. Then Murrow called on the crew in San Francisco to show us the Pacific. The Pacific, overhung with San Francisco's customary fog, was a less telegenic body of water, but we did catch a glimpse of it. Then Murrow, more or less acting as quarterback, called on his crews to show us first the San Francisco Bay Bridge, then the Brooklyn Bridge, the New York skyline, then San Francisco's skyline—all on live television.

"We are impressed," said Murrow, "by a medium in which a man sitting in his living room has been able for the first time to look at two oceans at once."

I am, too. I am also impressed by the intelligence of the men—chiefly Murrow and his producer, Fred W. Friendly—who dreamed up this simple trick to bring home to the viewers the wonder of this electronic miracle. "See It Now," which has been in preparation for six months, is the logical extension to the highly successful album of records, "I Can Hear It Now," and to its radio counterpart, the Peabody award-winning "Hear It Now." It is not—and is not intended to be—a complete review of the week's news; it is, instead, an almost entirely new form of journalism, "told in the voices and faces" of the people who made the news; a technique that offers a deeper insight into the headlines and the people who make them—who they are and what sort of people they are.

There was, for example, a film of Winston Churchill during his London Guildhall speech, an aged, aged Churchill, the great voice dimmed by time, the prose style—though a great improvement on Clement Attlee's—subdued into just a whisper of its former thunder. A deeply revelatory picture it was. There were other pictures —of Eden in Paris telling Vishinsky to stop laughing and read the disarmament proposal, of Sen. Taft purring with a cat-like contentment while Sen. Dirksen told an assemblage what a great candidate he was.

Murrow—handsome, relaxed, urbane—sewed the pictures together with a running commentary which, I should say, neither overplayed nor underplayed the significance of the events, and also conducted interviews with some of the C. B. S. news staff members—Eric Sevareid, in Washington; Howard K. Smith, in Paris. (Smith remarked good-naturedly of the relations between Russia and the West that "the mutual ill-will is entirely unimpaired.")

Then Mr. Murrow shifted us to Korea for one of the most intimate and instructive glimpses into that battleground that I have yet seen. This bit was especially remarkable in its avoidance of all the newsreel clichés. There wasn't a single shot of a soldier yanking a lanyard on a 105-mm. cannon, no shots of bombers tearing great holes in the Korean real estate. Instead, the cameras concentrated on the soldiers of Fox Company of an infantry regiment, catching them as they ate and slept and gambled and groused and joked, catching the tedium of warfare, the waiting, the humor of an essentially unhumorous occupation, the humanity of an essentially inhuman profession.

We followed Fox Company as they took position in the front line on a mountaintop and left them there, anticipating trouble that had not yet come. Evening had fallen; the rocket flares were out; a few shells sounded their cricket calls in the distance; the Chinese were astir; but nothing had happened yet. It was a dramatic close. "We wanted," said Mr. Murrow, "to narrow the distance between those of us sitting comfortably at home and those in the line." The news of the week from Korea was the murder of 5,500 captive American soldiers. This was the other side, more dramatic in its sheer uneventfulness.

I think they have the feel of the thing already, but I expect it'll get better as it goes along, that Mr. Murrow and Mr. Friendly have the simplicity of mind and the sweep of imagination to understand what television can do best in the news field and what television cannot do and should not attempt.

A Jury of 20,000,000 Persons
[MARCH 23, 1951]

THE KEFAUVER COMMITTEE hearings in New York were sponsored by "Time" magazine over a nineteen-city television network (and were broadcast unsponsored over a good many other stations) to an audience estimated at twenty million persons.

I bring up the size of the audience because it is probably the most controversial point raised by the televised hearings on a number of counts. The fact that millions of persons were viewing the proceedings sharply modified the answers and the behavior of witnesses. Ambassador O'Dwyer at one point in his testimony protested that he wanted the record on a particular matter made very clear because so many people were watching. The implication was plain that he wouldn't have cared so much if the cameras weren't on him.

The question of invasion of privacy was brought up several times by James Carroll, of St. Louis, who wouldn't testify before the cameras, and by Frank Costello, who wouldn't allow his face to be shown. On strictly legal grounds, it's hard to justify the question of privacy. Public hearings have been held in this country since earliest times and, in the nation's infancy, were held in a meeting house where the whole community could crowd in and watch. In a city of 7,500,000 that's no longer possible, but television has taken us a long way toward making it so.

On the grounds of strict logic, it's also hard to understand why O'Dwyer shouldn't be interested in keeping the record straight whether 20,000,000 onlookers were watching or not. But—let's face it—the audience *does* make a difference, and a very large one. The difference is one of emotion. A great deal of the testimony and the "revelations" were old stuff which had been heard by many grand juries and had been printed many times in newspapers and magazines. But the fact that they were being restated before so great an audience has charged them with emotion, not all of it rational.

The Kefauver committee is the No. 1 topic of discussion in New York and, for all I know, in large parts of the rest of the country, too. Suddenly everyone is an expert on organized crime, a problem that has been with us quite a while now, and what to do about it. All sorts of sweeping, ill-advised and certainly hasty suggestions are being made on how to cope with the problem and are being made by so many people at once that, just possibly, some of them might be pursued.

Some of the reactions have been decidedly curious. Even Sen. Kefauver noted with some alarm that large segments of the populace showed a tendency to sympathize with the witnesses, no matter how shady their past. Similarly, Sen. Tobey, God's Angry Man, and Rudolph Halley, the coldly relentless inquisitor, were not universally popular with the masses and were decidedly unpopular with many people. In fact, the one person who appears to have won universal acclaim after a stint before the cameras was Virginia Hill, which suggests that this isn't so Puritan a country after all.

To be quite honest about it, we have been conditioned by the movies, by the theater, by books to dislike the prosecutor who is trying to send poor Barbara Stanwyck to jail when we all know she's just shielding her idiot brother. The feminine audience especially has a tendency to confuse some of these hoodlums, the well-dressed and successful ones in particular, with Humphrey Bogart and to romanticize them accordingly. In the suburbs the well-heeled matrons have picked Sen. Kefauver as their matinee idol, a sort of Laurence Olivier with a briefcase.

Television, in short, has contributed not only to popular enlightenment but, more importantly, to public maturity. But we've still some distance to go before we can view such a hearing with anything like the cool skepticism and judicial impartiality it deserves. Television is a wonderfully potent instrument for arousing the populace, and in this case it's arousing it against organized crime, a fairly non-controversial thing. Next time, though, the question might not be anything so open and shut as our opinions on criminals; it could conceivably be a question such as foreign policy. Then we'll have to judge the proceedings not on the physical attractions or personal problems of the witnesses but, of all things, on what they have to say.

CHAPTER 18

Hollywood and Other Foreign Lands

This Is—London
[MAY 21, 1951]

LONDON.

THE SUN HAS broken through the clouds, lighting up the wings of the Pan American stratocruiser like silver fire. Inside the cocktail lounge, a great debate is raging. Is that streak of earth down there Ireland or is it not? The plane drunk—there is always one—proclaims firmly that it is not Ireland. "I was born in Ireland. I ought to know," he declares. It is pointed out to him that the speck of land under scrutiny is hardly large enough to be identified from so great a distance.

"If it were Ireland I would feel it here," says the drunk, clutching his breast dramatically. We ask the stewardess. "Ireland," she says. She was born in Brooklyn.

And presently we are in London. Almost immediately we run up against the language barrier. English. I don't speak it. At least not this curious variety of the language. The cadences rise when you expect them to fall, fall when you expect them to rise. The juxtaposition of words in a British sentence is entirely different from that in an American sentence. It is very confusing, altogether a foreign tongue, more comprehensible than Spanish, but not much. I ought to explain that any variations in inflection throw me for a loss. I was once stationed at Savannah, Ga., back in my Army days and it was six months before I understood a single word that was spoken to me.

We are in London, my traveling companion and I, to unblock a pound. Or rather to unblock a lot of pounds. I have never seen a pound unblocked before and I was curious to see how it was done. "Go unblock a pound," I told my companion. "Let's do our bit to free world currency." Well, he freed about eighty pounds from British domination and turned them over to the Pan American people where they were instantly reblocked. It's very difficult to keep a pound unblocked for more than a minute or two.

Europe is full of people thawing out frozen currencies in strange ways. A Briton, for example, who wants to go to Switzerland, is allowed five pounds to take out of the country. That would keep him comfortably in Switzerland for about two days. So he goes to a Swiss banker who liberates a hatful of Swiss francs. Later the Swiss banker goes to London where the Briton unblocks some pounds and pays him back. This means that the world traveler, along with waiting interminably in air terminals and customs offices, can devote most of the rest of his time sitting in the outer offices of bankers or black market currency operators. This chews up so much of his time that he is effectively prevented from getting into the night clubs, the resorts and other pleasure spots where he might get into trouble. You see what a healthy system it is.

Another vexation to the air traveler is his stomach. You arrive in London after an all-night trip from New York. Your stomach tells you it is 7 A.M., time for breakfast. Big Ben insists that it is noon, time for lunch. The trans-Atlantic stomach, one that can adjust itself to any time zone in the world, has not yet been perfected and may not be in our lifetime. Even my watch revolted against this five-hour loss of time. I tried to set it ahead to London time. It promptly stopped. It is strictly a New York watch. Refuses to have anything to do with European time.

I turn on the radio. "Lay on, Lords of France," cries an actor. Shakespeare. Shakespeare in the middle of the afternoon. Or by New York time—Shakespeare at 9 A.M. This my stomach refused to countenance. I switched to another channel. Here a girl is pleading with the most famous dancer in Europe. She wants to be his partner and become the most famous ballerina in Europe. He is telling her she will never make it, though some instinct tells me she will. It is not exactly soap opera, but it is close enough. I begin to feel at home.

The only thing that is missing is the commercial. "Tide gets clothes cleaner than AN-N-Y-THING!" I feel that some message of this sort should be in there somewhere, if only to stop that would-be ballerina from sobbing for a minute. Later, though, we are walking along the embankment and I see a huge sign. McClean's Toothpaste. "Did you McClean your teeth today?" Britain will pull through all right if she has advertising men who can write copy like that.

The French Language
[MAY 23, 1951]

PARIS.

FRENCH IS AN eloquent language which must be seen to be fully understood or sometimes even to be comprehended at all. That is why the telephone has always defeated the French. The shrugs, the gestures, the rolling eyes, the expressive hands are missing on le telephone, which means the nuances—the essence of the message to be conveyed—are missing, too. Sometimes two Frenchmen can't understand each other on le telephone.

That means that radio is not for the French. The machine talks, yes, but it doesn't really talk. About 30 per cent of the French language cannot be conveyed by a box which simply stands there motionless. The box has no soul. The French, therefore, have simply walked away from radio as we know it and employ it largely as an instrument for the diffusion—which is the French way of saying broadcasting—of music.

The three national French networks—Programme National, Programme Parisien, and Paris-Inter (only God and the French know what Paris-Inter means) sound to these untrained American ears pretty much like WNEW and WQXR in New York. You get a mixture of popular and classical music on all three, though Programme National is likely to be a little heavier in density than the other two. Apart from news, you won't hear much talk, which is all right with me.

Turn a radio on in a French hotel and you'll think you're home again. In comes Mlle. Judy Garland singing "I'm Tired of the City" *en cette langue barbare, l'Anglais.* American popular music is just as popular here as it is in America. Of course, it's not always sung in English. One of the most exquisite experiences I have yet had in Paris is listening to "Bewitched, Bothered and Bewildered" sung in French. (I'm going to learn how to sing "Bewitched, Bothered and Bewildered" in French if it kills me.)

The great thing about "Bewitched, Bothered and Bewildered" sung in French is that the mood of the song is completely transformed. It becomes *une chanson Parisienne*—haunting, delicate and somehow more elegant than the love song Rodgers and Hart had in mind when they wrote it. I might add that this applies equally well to American songs sung in English—if sung by the French. A French chanteuse singing "The Lady Is a Tramp" in English—or what she thinks is English—is as French as the Rue de la Paix. In fact, it would be more comprehensible if she sang it in French.

As for the Voice of America, it is, according to all evidence, not heard in Paris. That does not mean it is not broadcast in Paris. It *is* broadcast here but, as I say, not heard. An acquaintance of mine expressed it aptly: "You can always tell when the Voice of America is on the air by leaning out the window. You'll hear the click of radios being turned off all over Paris."

The French simply don't understand what the hell the Voice of America is talking about. They find the "Voice" not only bewildering but faintly ludicrous. I'm inclined to agree. One program, for example, is called "Ici New York" which is roughly comparable to "And now—we give you San Francisco." Or, in this case, New York.

This is likely to start out with some such vital message from the American people as this: *"Nous voici au Stork Club. M. Billingsley nous dit bon soir, et puis voici une Francaise. On la reconnait par le chic Parisien de son chapeau. Je vous presente Morton Downey. C'est un fameux chanteur de ballades Irelandaises."*

The average Parisian doesn't know what the Stork Club is and couldn't care less about M. Sherman Billingsley. Much of the "Voice's" message here consists of records, and the French complain bitterly about the quality of the records. They are very old records, many of them Negro spirituals. The French have a great fondness for our spirituals, know a great deal about them and feel strongly that the "Voice's" selections couldn't be worse. One Frenchwoman told me that every time she turned on the "Voice," all she got was "Ol' Man River."

"As for the rest of it—discussion programs," she said. "A bunch of people sitting around a table discussing what goes in Arkansas. You know, M. Crosby, I don't *care* what goes in Arkansas."

Happy Birthday
[MAY 30, 1951]

PARIS.

The American people have been cordially invited—by poster, by advertisement, by all the marvelous resources of the American press agent—to visit Paris on its 2,000th anniversary. We have always been sentimental about birthdays and are more than ordinarily susceptible to antiquity, having so little of our own.

The combination of a birthday and 2,000 years is a powerful lure and a very clever one. However, if I were you, I wouldn't fall into discussion with a Frenchman on the subject. I never met one who ever heard of this 2,000th anniversary. Parisians are not only unaware of their city's birthday but inclined—when told about it—to be a little skeptical. Paris is a very old town, all right, but it'd be awfully hard to put your finger on the exact date when it was founded. It was first a Gallic town, then a Roman town called Lutetia for a couple of centuries, and it didn't acquire the name Paris until the third century.

The designation of 1951 as the 2,000th anniversary of Paris is completely arbitrary, but I'll play along. Perhaps it was exactly 2,000 years ago that Paris was founded. If the British can have a Trade Fair, Paris can have a 2,000th birthday. Let's spread the tourist dollar around. Happy birthday, Paris. Next year it will be somebody else's turn. I suggest my own home town of Oconomowoc, Wis. It was exactly 2,500 years ago next year that an Indian named Okeeboje fell to fishing in the Oconomowoc River, decided it was a nice place to stay and built a teepee there, thus founding the town, which has not grown much bigger since. Drop in on us next year, fellows. The fishing is still pretty good.

To pass on to other matters, let us discuss the French child, whom I found fascinating. We are all aware of television's grip on our own young and it is, I think, instructive to inspect the whelps of another nation where a television set is so mercifully expensive that few French children have ever seen one. It'd be just as well if they never did.

The French child, I notice, is a very imaginative child. He is not overladen with toys as our own are (or if he is, he doesn't carry them into a public park). Three or four French children with only a stick to draw circles on the ground can invent their own games and play for hours. They don't need the blessings of a Hopalong Cassidy suit, a pair of revolvers, a bicycle or wooden dogs that bark when you pull them. The play, in other words, is provided by the child, not by toys or machines. He is a very active participant.

This applies to his entertainment. In one of the parks on the Champs-Élysées you'll find a Punch and Judy show known as *le Vrai Guignolet*. You'll have no trouble finding it because the shrieks from the children will guide you to it. Here, small children of from two to five watch the puppets spell out the misadventures of M. Guignol. Most of the children have seen each show ten or twenty times, know the plots by heart, and shout advice, lamentations and encouragement to the hero and the villains.

For the children, the show is M. Guignol. For the adults, the show is the children. If you have ever watched a bunch of kids sitting passive as dolls in front of a television set for hours, it is refreshing to see some youngsters enter into the game personally, become a part of it and draw some faint intellectual stimulation from it.

Maybe television can give a child the same emotional and intellectual release. But I doubt it.

One American Conquest
[MAY 28, 1951]

ROME.

THE MOST SUCCESSFUL export we have made to Europe and one of our best ambassadors in every country is our dance music. It's rather odd when you think about it a bit. The world's great music sprang from Europe but the Europeans, at least the current crop, don't seem to understand how to compose a popular song.

You can wander all over Europe and never get out of hearing distance of "Ol' Man River," "Begin the Beguine," "Night and Day" and "Smoke Gets in Your Eyes" which are conceivably the four most international songs in the world. The French, the Italians, the Danes—well, name anybody—prefer our old popular songs, the older the better. At Grosvenor House in London you will find the English, a sober race, jiggling up and down sedately to "Bye Bye Blues." And at that football field of a dance floor in the Grand Hotel in Stockholm, you'll find a different crowd but the same tune.

Move over to Helsinki, which has been aptly described as the Tim Costello's of the north—there's only one night club there—or at the Wunderbar in Copenhagen you'll hear an awful lot of "After You've Gone." In Berlin at the Golden Horseshoe, where the customers ride horses around a sanded ring for reasons which were never made clear to me, you'll encounter that old-time tune, "Avalon."

In Vienna, at the Moulin Rouge, at this very moment I bet anything you'll find a couple of professional entertainers tap-dancing to "Tea for Two," which, of course, is the tune people have been tap-dancing to all over the world ever since it was written. In Rome, there is a wonderful restaurant and night club called the Hosteria dell Orso in an edifice that was standing there in Dante's day. And the tune we danced to there—"Yes, Sir, That's My Baby" which came along only a few years after Dante.

In Paris—this paragraph may just confuse you a bit at first but stick with me here—the Metro, the subway, contains some of the most glamorous names in France as station stops. One line contains in order the following subways stops—Louvre, Palais Royal, Tuileries, Place de la Concorde and Champs-Élysées. I took this line once, stopped off at the Lido on the Champs-Élysées and got there just in time to hear a girl sing "Take The A Train," which can hardly mean anything to the French. You'd think the French would write songs about their own subways. But no.

I was in that enchantingly beautiful city, Bruges, during the Whitsun holiday, which is strenuously celebrated in Belgium.

There were carnivals in all the city squares. Blaring from one of the merry-go-rounds, competing with and almost drowning out the thirteenth century bells of the Cathedral of St. Sauveur, was Hoagy Carmichael, old gravel-voice himself, croaking "Am I Blue?"

"Stardust," "Penthouse Serenade," "Time on My Hands," "September Song"—they'll ring in your ears everywhere this side of the Iron Curtain and conceivably on the other side, too. We Americans have not succeeded very well in exporting ideas. We are not very well understood anywhere and neither is democracy or capitalism. It has occurred to me that one device for selling our ideas might be the popular song. Let's get Irving Berlin, Cole Porter, Rodgers and Hammerstein and the rest of them to wrap up a few American ideas in good popular dance tunes. They'll be sung all over Europe.

The G.I.s took the jitterbug, which has pretty well passed out of the picture in America, to Europe during the war. It's still there, though not just everywhere. At the Vieux Colombier in Montparnasse, where the Sorbonne students hang out, you'll hear some of the best American jazz in the world and also see some of the most amazing jitterbugging and Big Apple—a dance which has completely died back home. In both cases, the French have formalized the dances. There is less abandon, less improvization, and more precision and formal movement, though they are still danced at the speed of light.

Home Again
[JUNE 1, 1951]

IN MOST EUROPEAN countries—on our side of the Iron Curtain, at least—the customs, a highly developed form of international confusion, are reasonably perfunctory. Fifteen minutes in London. About ten in Paris. Possibly seventeen in Rome. Then you arrive back in New York and the situation changes radically. The Europeans of tourist lands welcome travelers with money in their

Home Again

pockets. The United States Immigration Service is hostile to the idea of letting anyone into this country whether he lives here or not.

The way I understand it, an immigration official gets ten points if he can delay a traveler an hour, twenty points if he can hold him up two hours and 100 points or jackpot if he can deflect you to Ellis Island. My man did his best. He scowled at my passport for a minute or so, turned all the leaves, then said:

"What were you doing in Belgium?"

"Well," I said. Then I stopped. I did a lot of things in Belgium, not all of which I'd like to spread around even to Immigration officials. "I played roulette," I told him. I added hastily: "I know Senator Kefauver wouldn't approve, but it's quite all right over there, you know. It's legal."

"What else did you do in Belgium? Why exactly were you in Belgium? Where were you in Belgium?"

I explained that I was in a little seaside resort called Knokke, a sort of Flemish Fire Island, that a good deal of my activities were shrouded in a sort of haze that envelops me from time to time and that my demeanor, while not entirely above reproach, was hardly subversive.

"You weren't in Czechoslovakia? Poland?"

"Why would anyone want to be in Czechoslovakia? Who in his right mind would want to go to Poland?"

"You're sure?"

I said I was absolutely positive. There was an occasion when, to my very great surprise, I woke up in Providence, R. I. But I have never wakened up in Czechoslovakia or Poland and I hope to God I never do. My man appeared unconvinced. He ruffled through the passport—there are pathetically few stamps in it—and then gave up. I was released into the protective custody of the Customs people.

The Customs officials have all your luggage neatly arranged alphabetically. I found my bags under Q, removed them to the C counter and waited. An hour passed. Customs officials passed. No one tarried except the passengers—the Cs, the Bs, and one forlorn Q whom I suspect of being a misplaced C. Finally, a man appeared before the woman next to me—a B girl—and gave her a bad time over a watch she had procured in Switzerland. I had better luck. The Customs man took one look at the dirty shirts, decided not to soil his hands on such alien filth and shot me through.

Well, I suppose it's a good system. We can't go letting American citizens back into the country indiscriminately. They might come back harboring germs or conceivably even opinions. But don't look at me. I tossed all my opinions overboard at the three mile limit. They sank like stones.

In a bar that night, I had my first look at American television in a month. Bert Parks in "Stop the Music." A long-legged girl was tap-dancing. This gave me an excellent opportunity to compare European culture with our own. In Paris the showgirls are in general draped handsomely from the waist down to the toes, undraped from the waist up. Here we drape them topside, undrape them extensively from there down. On the whole I think our own is the better system, that it puts the emphasis on the proper end of a female.

Bert Parks, I'm happy to report, is still draped all over except for his teeth, which appear to be in wonderful condition except for a slight discoloration on the ulterior bicuspid. Anyhow, it's nice to be home and this column will resume its more normal operation—that of estimating the quality of television and radio programs—immediately.

The British Mania for Railroads
[NOVEMBER 9, 1951]

THE ENGLISH HAVE unloosed some pretty wonderful movies in this country—"Hamlet," "Henry V," the early Alfred Hitchcock masterpieces, to name only a few—but they have also committed some pretty dreadful things on celluloid, all of them now doing the rounds on television. The Washington correspondent of "The Economist" of London not long ago wrote that a favorite dinner table discussion in America was the worst television show anyone had ever seen. British films, he lamented, frequently led the list.

A really bad English film, though, retains certain British eccentricities quite foreign to our bad films, which, heaven knows, have enough peculiarities. The British—I'm judging them largely through their films, which is largely how they judge us—are entranced by transportation. I don't know who originally taught our English cousins that a train is terribly photogenic (Hitchcock, probably), but at any rate it's been almost impossible to get the British off the train ever since. I don't think I ever saw a British film which didn't have a train tearing through the English countryside, emitting its feminine peep-peep and spewing pretty clouds of steam.

A train is a wonderful substitute for emotion, on which the British are low, and also a fine cover-up for plot deficiencies, creating the illusion that something eventful is taking place simply because the actors are going from here to there. Occasionally, the story line falters after a spell on a train and then a really ingeniously bad English director will shift all his characters on to a ship. Ships are photogenic, too; they belch forth even more smoke than trains; and they make a far more impressive noise.

The other night on the "Late Show," one English film fell so hopelessly in love with all forms of transport that it almost exhausted the possibilities. Besides a good deal of train travel, we embarked twice on boats—one regulation ocean liner, one fishing boat—engaged in a bit of plane travel, darted around in taxicabs for quite a spell, and ascended to the top of a mountain on a funicular which is more popularly known over here as a cable car. What little footage was left after all these extensive explorations was spent on skis, the heroes and villains tearing down a magnificent procession of slopes in pursuit of one another.

About the only conveyance they managed to avoid in this—I can't seem to suppress myself here—vehicle was the bicycle. I can't think how they got around the bicycle, which is easily the most popular form of locomotion in all England. Just possibly it landed on the cutting room floor.

The plot? You know, I really couldn't tell you. Something about counterfeiters. But I never quite figured who was guilty of what, being left breathless by all this tearing around. The chase is one of the oldest devices known to the cinema. It was probably invented by Mack Sennett, who ended all his early comedies with a lot of cops chasing the comedian. No one has ever figured a better ending for a movie than a chase, and it has been employed in some very good ones ("The Third Man," for example, where it was laid in a sewer) and just about all the bad ones, including all the cowboy pictures ever shot.

Just the same the chase shouldn't comprise the whole movie. There should be an interval in there where the actors get off the trains, the boats, the airplanes, the ski lifts, stretch their legs and talk things over, just possibly establishing a reason why one set of actors is chasing the other set of actors.

Inside a Gag Writer's Mind
[JANUARY 25, 1949]

HOLLYWOOD.

RADIO GAG WRITERS are a very specialized branch of the Vertebrate family, dealing as they do almost exclusively in the old switcheroo. After years of turning jokes and phrases upside down, they become as fast and agile with a switcheroo as a con man with three shells and, as a matter of fact, some of them look a little like a con man, too.

Jack Douglas, who has written comedy for half a dozen programs, including Jimmy Durante's and Jack Carson's, is the specimen I happen to have at hand and he possesses as fine a bundle of eccentricities as anyone in the profession. Douglas won't drive on Balboa Avenue because he's afraid he might run over a dog. There aren't any more dogs on Balboa Avenue than anywhere else, but you can't convince him.

He has a vast and improbable house at North Ridge which he designed himself by cutting out magazine pictures of rooms that caught his fancy. The driveway is dotted with signs that get progressively more insulting—"No Trespassing," "Keep Out," "Go Away," "Get OUT of Here." There was and still is some talk of putting an alligator farm next door, so Douglas thoughtfully painted a sign—North Ridge Lion Farm—at the foothills of his estate. Behind the sign is a loudspeaker from which emerge recorded lion roars.

Once Douglas was chatting with a sponsor after a script conference when another writer approached and said he'd like to speak to him. "Go ahead," said Douglas.

The other writer glanced nervously at the sponsor and muttered: "Not in front of the client."

"Well," said Douglas, "spell it."

Douglas likes to tell people that he never had a mother. "We were very poor," he explains. Despite this omission, the first chapter of his book is entitled "Mother" and the word appears frequently in the text. ("Horace pawned his mother and bought a revolver.")

The book, named "No Navel to Guide Him" (With Dirty Pictures by Currier & Ives), carries on its cover the legend—"This Book Bans Boston"—and is altogether as fine a collection of switcheroos as you'll find anywhere. The book has a little of everything—anecdotes about his great-uncle Cosgrave ("He's the one with the nest of robins instead of hair"), luncheon suggestions, geography and history.

Some of the chapter headings are "Moonlight, Magnolias and Juvenile Delinquency," "For Men Only," "Hold a Lighted Match behind This Page," "How to Train an Aardvark." Page 57 consists of just one line, "Disregard preceding two pages—letter follows."

"A chapter about India," writes Douglas in his chapter about India, "would be incomplete without extensive mention of Mahatma Gandhi, therefore let us consider this chapter incomplete, shall we?"

"In 1863," another chapter starts, "my uncle Rodney was shot by a firing squad. It seems that while serving with the army at Shiloh my dear uncle had fallen asleep on guard duty and Lincoln had to draw the line somewhere."

In the travel section, Douglas reports with surprise that the Taj Mahal is a tomb: "And, incidentally, the only tomb I know of with a men's room. It has jade stalls with 'Out of Order' spelled out in rubies."

Well, that ought to give you an idea of the inside of a gag writer's mind, where nothing is ever forgotten and everything is upside down.

Children of Hollywood
[JANUARY 27, 1949]

HOLLYWOOD.

THIS PLACE TEEMS with children of movie and radio stars and the other big shots of the entertainment world, some of the most beautiful and pampered children in the world. They are rather odd customers, these children, and I'm not at all sure how they'd adjust to any other society but this.

Out in Brentwood where movie folk are thick as oranges, there is a hierarchy of governesses whose standing in the community is governed rigidly by the nature of their charges. The children in this caste-conscious community rank in the order of their illustrious parents, a producer's children, for example, outranking an actor's children. This automatically puts the governess in a somewhat higher bracket—no matter what her earnings are—and naturally she views a lesser governess with some constraint like a Boston dowager meeting one of the younger set whose ancestors didn't get here until 1712.

"We had a governess once and there were only certain children she'd let ours play with," Groucho Marx explained. "This governess had worked for a lot of important people in pictures and she had a position to maintain."

The governesses and their small fry run into one another frequently at schools or at parties and on these occasions they introduce the kids by the name of their parents rather than by their own. "These are Dore Schary's children." Or: "This is Judy Garland's little girl." Miss Garland is Mrs. Vincente Minnelli, but she gets top billing, of course. This practice of associating the children with the biggest marquee name is sometimes taken to extremes. There are a couple of nice kids who are known here as Walter Pidgeon's nephew and niece.

At parties the caste system sometimes wreaks havoc since children everywhere enjoy showing off. After one party a small girl was discovered crying bitterly. She was the only child in the room whose parents didn't have a projection room. All important film stars and producers have projection rooms and the kids quickly pick up the idea that a projection room is one of the ordinary necessities of life like a Cadillac.

There is an exchange agreement between studios whereby important stars or executives can obtain almost any feature film for home consumption. If a child has been good all day, he gets an hour of Rita Hayworth the way the rest of us used to be told bedtime stories.

Early in life the children pick up the patois of the studios as children everywhere pick up grown-up speech. The following snatch of conversation between two eleven-year-old girls was taken down verbatim by a feminine accomplice of mine in the ladies' room of a country club: "Her father would be making westerns if it weren't for my father. Why, daddy gave him screen credit in three pictures he had nothing to do with."

The whelps of the famous are surrounded by coaches of all varieties—swimming instructors, boxing instructors, tennis instructors. One day Chico Marx's little boy was playing with George Burns's youngster and displayed a marvelous agility climbing trees.

"Who is your climbing instructor?" inquired the small Burns.

Nevertheless the celebrated citizens of Hollywood are sincerely crazy about children and they may yet restore the large family to national popularity. Don Ameche, for example, has six children. Twenty years ago a family of that size would have doomed him to obscurity. Charles Correll, the Andy of Amos 'n' Andy, has five kids. Almost every office is littered with pictures of children and most of the famous parents carry photographs which will be thrust on you almost immediately.

In fact, it's wise to carry pictures of your own progeny in self-defense.

CHAPTER 19

"But Seriously, Though . . ."

Leadership in Broadcasting
[JULY 25, 1946]

ADDRESSING THE SIXTH Imperial press conference in London recently, Sir William Haley, director general of the British Broadcasting Corporation, said: "The secret of leadership in broadcasting is that of always being ahead of the public, yet not so far ahead as to be out of touch. A broadcast has no purpose if it is not listened to. Our task is to draw more and more listeners to all that is worth while."

In three sentences, Mr. Haley unwittingly summed up the greatest weakness in our own commercial broadcasting system. When they are assailed for the low level of current broadcasting standards, our own broadcasters invariably retort that 80,000,000 persons listen to the radio in this country and like what they hear. The public, say the broadcasters, create a demand for certain types of programs and the broadcasters fill that demand.

That's a spurious argument. In the late fifteenth century, Ludovico Sforza commissioned an artist to paint a mural in a church in Milan. The painting was "The Last Supper." Sforza was the public who created the demand. Leonardo da Vinci was the artist who filled that demand. Sforza probably would have been content with a far lesser work, but the artist himself was not even content with his own painting. It is the responsibility of the artisan to elevate public tastes, not vice versa.

The public has created a demand for entertainment, education, music and news on the radio but the quality of that product should be determined by the broadcasters. George Jean Nathan, I think it was, summed it up very neatly about ten years ago in commenting on the unlooked-for success of Lillian Hellman's "The Children's Hour," a distinctly unusual play. The public, he said, doesn't know what it wants until it gets it. Somebody else—I forget who—put it another way. The public, he said, knows what it wants but doesn't know what it is.

That's why a Hooper rating is very misleading. There may be dozens of unproduced programs with potential Hoopers of twenty points or higher, but they never will be produced if the broadcasters wait for the public to ask for them. Only in the fields of politics and radio is leadership expected to come from the grass roots rather than the other way around. Both fields suffer severely from this upside-down notion.

The concept of industry's leading the public is practiced even in Hollywood where it is only imperfectly understood. The motion-picture industry can hardly be held up as great purveyors of culture. Yet, strangely, it is, because even former button-hole manufacturers suffer from a creative urge. The result is pictures like "The Informer" and "The Long Voyage Home." Those pictures would never have been made if the producers had waited for a ground swell of public demand.

It's a curious but heartening fact that Hollywood, almost against its own will, has elevated the dramatic standards of the entire country. I doubt if any picture today is as bad as the tent shows of my early youth. The movies have elevated the public's standards of acting to such a degree that the ham actors who toured backwoods regions in fifteenth-rate road companies would not be tolerated in the same regions today.

Only in radio has the curious belief persisted that the public will sicken and die if it is fed rich food or if it is fed something it never tasted before. As Mr. Haley pointed out, broadcasters can't get too far out in front. But they certainly should be out in front.

I don't want this plaint to be construed as an indorsement of the British government-controlled B. B. C. The B. B. C.'s performance is not nearly as high as its intentions. Recently the House of Commons voted to keep British broadcasting a government monopoly for another five years and to exclude commercial radio.

At that time Herbert Morrison, majority leader in the House, stated: "Nothing I have heard or read so far has convinced me that the American or Australian listener gets such consistently good entertainment as he does in this country."

A lot of American soldiers who were stationed in Great Britain during the war would argue with Mr. Morrison about that. As a matter of fact, a great many Britons disagree too. Recently, in a nation-wide poll, 45 per cent of the British public said it would prefer both commercial broadcasting and the B. B. C. in place of the present government monopoly.

If the listeners in this country were forced to hear a full day of B. B. C. programs in place of American programs, the outcry would be louder than anything that ever went up over our own soap operas. The public doesn't quite know what it wants, but it definitely knows what it doesn't want.

Just the same, Mr. Haley's concept of industry leadership is a refreshing change from the Hooper-ridden philosophy of our own broadcasters.

Censorship on the Air
[JULY 29, 1946]

A NEW PROCEDURE in the Army used to originate in the ranks, where it would start as a good plan to correct, let us say, a current abuse.

In its progress from higher authority to still higher authority, the plan would be modified by each man who got his hands on it, until, by the time it reached the War Department, the original plan had lost much of its original meaning and acquired a lot of new and useless trimmings. Once incorporated into Army doctrine, this new, distorted plan would start downward toward the ranks again, this time acquiring different interpretations at every step. By the time it reached the starting point, the ranks, the plan would have little to do with the original abuse or with anything else. Still, it was inflicted on the men as gospel and the men wearily accepted it as another sample of Army snafu.

Censorship on the air is pretty much the same routine, the misuse of an originally sound purpose. The broadcasters, quite understandably, don't like to offend individuals, minority groups, religious orders, advertisers or members of other nationalities. There is nothing particularly wrong with this desire to please except that in many cases it is pursued to such lengths that radio programs are robbed of much of their vitality. The intentions are good but the administration is ridiculous.

Possibly the most censored man in radio is Fred Allen. Allen gets his ideas from current news. His jokes are invariably pointed, and pointed jokes usually sting somebody. As a result, Allen's fourteen years in radio have been an almost continuous battle with censors and he has lost many an engagement. After fourteen years of this, Allen is a little bitter toward radio censorship. Recently he left for a vacation in Maine and in his suitcase was a collection of notes which he refers to as his "white paper" and which he plans to turn into a "Saturday Evening Post" article during his vacation.

Before he left, Mr. Allen graciously let me run through that part of his notes concerning censorship, and, as a sort of preview of that "Post" article, with Mr. Allen's permission, I should like to give you some examples of the jokes that have been cut out of Allen's scripts and the reasons they were cut out. This should give you some idea as to why humor on the air is usually as bland

and innocent of the life around us as an Edgar Rice Burroughs novel.

Let us first consider salaciousness. Off-color jokes are not allowed on the air and that, in itself, is a good idea. However, the man who censored Allen's scripts at the National Boadcasting Company— let's call him Pincus, although that's not his name—pursued this noble aim with a zeal which would have alarmed even Savonarola. Mr. Pincus suspected any word he didn't understand, particularly in a boy-girl context, of being a dirty word.

Allen, for example, had a terrible time getting the adjective "saffron" on the air because Pincus suspected it had sexual connotations. With the aid of Funk & Wagnalls, Allen got the adjective approved. On another occasion a character in an Allen show called Bear Mountain a "strip tease crag." Mr. Pincus was horrified, and it took hours of arguing to convince him that "strip tease" could hardly be offensive when applied to a mountain.

Pincus also objected to the phrase "pitch a little woo." Believe it or not, he'd never heard it before and Allen had quite an argument convincing him that the phrase was current usage among the young folks. Although he yielded on that point, the censor refused to budge on another phrase about "pizzicating" a woman's lavaliere. It brought up a distressing mental image, said Pincus.

A decent respect for religion on the air is hardly open to comment. Still, Mr. Allen's censor took it to lengths which any sensible minister would consider rather silly. Once Allen brought in a gag about a judge, recently deceased, "going to a higher court." The joke was blue-penciled. "Higher court" implied heaven and you can't make cracks about heaven. Then there was a joke about a man named Stickney S. "for Stickney" Stickney who got that name because the minister who baptized him stuttered. It was cut out, too. Mustn't make fun of ministers.

Another Allen line read, "She promises to love, honor and lump it till death do them part." Absolutely not, said Pincus, the marriage ceremony is not a suitable topic for comedy.

Allen has complained for years because he is unable to mention or even hint at the existence of another network. "Darn," he said once, "is a word invented by N. B. C., which doesn't recognize either hell or the Columbia Broadcasting System." Here again the ban is invoked to incredible lengths. For instance, Allen once spoke of smoking "that cigarette that grows hair, fixes up your nerves and fumigates the house." N. B. C. objected to the phrase "fixes up your nerves" because it sounded a little like Camel's current advertising campaign. At that time, the Camel show was on C. B. S. and not even by so remote a connection as a single vague phrase did N. B. C. want to call attention to its powerful network rival.

[JULY 30, 1946]

FRED ALLEN's fourteen-year battle with radio censorship was made particularly difficult for him by the fact that the man assigned to reviewing his scripts had little sense of humor and frankly admitted he didn't understand Allen's peculiar brand of humor at all. This censor, whom I've been calling Pincus, which isn't his name, invoked each of N. B. C.'s censorship rules with the zeal of the Civil Liberties Union defending the Bill of Rights.

You can't, for instance, defend individuals in a comedy show, which would be a reasonable rule if sensibly administered. However, Pincus extended this ban to include virtually everyone living or dead and sometimes even imaginary people. Allen, for instance, once gagged about an imaginary society matron named Mrs. Biddle Pratt. Pincus wouldn't allow it until Allen had combed all the Blue Books and Social Registers in the country to make sure there wasn't a real Mrs. Biddle Pratt. He did and there wasn't. Then there was a gag about Senator Guff of Idaho. Even after a search of past and present Congressional directories failed to reveal the names of any Senator Guffs of Idaho, Pincus was not fully reassured. He approved the line with considerable misgivings because, after all, there might some day be a Senator Guff of Idaho.

However, Allen was forbidden to use the harmless line "Brenda never looked lovelier" at the time of the Brenda Frazier wedding without the permission of the Frazier family, which could not be obtained. Another time, Allen tacked a cockney accent on a character identified as the first mate of the "Queen Mary." This had to be changed because Pincus said the first mate of the "Queen Mary" was quite a cultured person in his own world and might not like a cockney accent affixed on him.

All networks are, of course, extremely careful to avoid offending any racial or religious group. No one can possibly quarrel with this but their caution is sometimes taken to outlandish lengths. You might be interested to know that Allen had a terrible time winning approval for the current Minerva Pious character, Mrs. Nussbaum. N. B. C. was fearful that Jewish-dialect comedy might offend all Jews. Wearily, Allen and his representatives pointed out that Jewish-dialect comedy had been in vaudeville and burlesque for thirty years without offending anyone.

Since N. B. C. is a national network, it must be careful about hurting the feelings of towns or regions, which are sometimes even more sensitive than individuals. Allen once wrote a sketch concerning a town called North Wrinkle, a name he thought up all by himself. N. B. C. objected on the ground there might somewhere be a North Wrinkle whose inhabitants might not like Mr. Allen's humor. A radio executive was unloosed on this problem and after considerable research, turned up with a deadpan report which I print below as an example of the radio mind at work.

"The most comprehensive list of towns in the United States is the United States Postal Guide. No North Wrinkle is listed there. The United States Post Office knows of no such town. However, they state that there is a possibility that there is such a community without a post office, but that there is no way in which they can check further unless we suggest a given state in which case they could make a more intensive search. I believe that it is safe to use North Wrinkle."

Allen not only couldn't poke fun at individuals, he also had to be careful not to step on their professions, their beliefs, and sometimes even their hobbies and amusements. Portland Hoffa once was given a line about wasting an afternoon at the rodeo. N. B. C. objected to the implication that an afternoon at the rodeo was wasted and the line had to be changed. Another time, Allen gagged that a girl could have found a better husband in a cemetery. Pincus thought this might hurt the feelings of people who own and operate cemeteries. Allen got the line cleared only after pointing out that cemeteries have been topics for comedy since the time of Aristophanes.

Anything that might conceivably hurt the feelings of an advertiser or even a potential advertiser is, of course, scrutinized with extraordinary care. The incredible Pincus, for instance, objected to the line, "The zoo keeper told mama the mongoose was seeing aspirin." Pincus was under the impression aspirin was a trade name. The line was cleared after Pincus was told that aspirin was not the exclusive property of the Bayer people.

Allen once wrote a sketch in which a woman character named the Widow Kane said she had forgotten to turn off the gas in her Kansas home before coming to New York.

"Good heavens," said Allen. "Attention, Soup Ladle, Kansas. Go to Widow Kane's home. Turn off the gas." A few moments later the program was interrupted by a mock news flash. Soup Ladle, Kansas, has been blown off the map. N. B. C. deleted the entire sequence because the gas companies objected to calling attention to the explosive properties of their product.

[JULY 31, 1946]

PINCUS WAS A MAN of little if any humor but he was a stickler for "truth, the whole truth and nothing but the truth." In one script, Allen remarked that Schopenhauer was a sustaining program for years under the name of Pick and Pat. That, said the distressed Pincus, simply wasn't so. Schopenhauer, said Pincus, died in 1860 and was never on any radio program. Allen finally succeeded in convincing Pincus that it was a joke, son, and the line was cleared.

Censorship on the Air

The veteran comedian was not so lucky in convincing the radio censors that radio itself is a suitable topic for comedy. Of all radio's sacred cows, radio itself is the most sacred, and, while Allen has repeatedly lampooned the industry that pays him $20,000 a week, he has also lost many a battle to the censors.

In 1938, for instance, after Orson Welles scared the daylights out of half the Eastern seaboard with his invasion from Mars, Allen wrote an introduction to his program which poked a little fun, not at Welles, but at the people who ran all over New Jersey looking for the Martian invaders.

"'This is a comedy program,'" wrote Allen. "Any sound effects or dialogue you hear during the hour will be purely imaginary. If you hear a phone ringing (and he demonstrated) don't answer it. If you hear a knock on the door (another demonstration), don't rush to open the door. Just sit back and relax. Nothing is going to happen."

N. B. C. not only blue-penciled the entire introduction but flatly refused to allow Allen to make any illusion to the Welles incident, which had frightened the entire broadcasting industry. Allen carried his appeal up the chain of command at N. B. C., all the way to Lenox Lohr, then president of the network. The appeal was rejected. N. B. C. didn't want to hear any more about the Welles invasion, particularly over the air.

Probably the funniest battle Allen ever lost involved a sketch about the movies. One line in the sketch read: "Motion pictures are your best entertainment." No greater uproar could have been caused if a Mahometan had called the faithful to prayer in St. Patrick's Cathedral. Even a hint that there is any other form of entertainment, especially a better one, than radio is blasphemy in broadcasting circles.

The line caused a small war at N. B. C. Allen and his representatives argued the point from executive to executive right up to Mr. Lohr and got nowhere. The broadcasters refused to concede that it was a joke and even if it was a joke, they didn't think it was funny. The line was thrown out and, to my knowledge, no such sacrilegious sentiment has ever been expressed over N. B. C.

Naturally, over a period of fourteen years, this stifling censorship has aroused considerable bitterness in Allen, one of radio's great wits. This is only too apparent in his shows. In the last few years there have been repeated and biting references to N. B. C. vice-presidents. ("The man with the mould on him is a vice-president.") The network has never issued any flat ultimatum to Allen to stop this but N. B. C. executives have pleaded unsuccessfully with him for years to lay off the vice-presidents for the sake of N. B. C.'s dignity.

Allen continues to make fun of the N. B. C. vice-presidents, and no wonder. Another of Allen's pet peeves is the automatic cut-off at N.B.C. While other networks will allow a big show to run a minute or two past its time and will make it up to the next show, N. B. C.'s cut-off is operated by an automatic clock which stops the show exactly on the hour or half hour. Even those chimes are mechanically operated.

Once, to work off a little steam at both the N. B. C. executive staff and at that automatic chime, Allen inserted a line in his script in which a stooge remarked: "I must balance my chime report. Lenox will be furious." Even Allen had no hope of getting such a crack at the N. B. C. president on the air and, of course, it was cut out. The comedian finds some consolation in the fact that he has outlived, or at least outlasted, three N. B. C. presidents and he may outlast the present one.

Among the more recent excisions from an Allen script was a reference to an imaginary summer resort named Gromyko's Grotto. N. B. C. deleted the line on the grounds it might offend the Russians.

"My God," said Allen wearily, "everything else has offended the Russians. We're the only thing left. We might as well offend them too."

[AUGUST 2, 1946]

IN HIS CHAPTER on forbidden words in the brilliant work "The American Language," H. L. Mencken wrote: "The radio is almost as prudish as Hollywood. Late in 1934 its syndics actually forbade the verb 'to do' in songs, feeling that it was a bit too suggestive."

The verb "to do" actually started the censorship of lyrics in radio, a practice which has been carried so far that many song publishers now issue two sets of words, one for the radio and one for night clubs, records and you and me. It was Cole Porter who started all this with his song "Let's Do It." ("Birds do it, bees do it. . . . Let's do it, let's fall in love.") This was on the air for some time before someone decided it sounded nasty. Banned from the air with it were a couple of other "do" numbers such as "You Do Something to Me," another Porter number, and "Do It Again."

Porter's sophisticated lyrics have been a headache for the song-clearance departments of radio networks for years. Many of his lyrics have had to be laundered for radio and others have been banned outright. Remember "Get Out of Town"? "When you are near, close to me dear, we touch too much" is the way Porter wrote it. Over the air it somehow came out "When you are near, close to me dear, the spell's too much."

Then there was Porter's "I Get a Kick Out of You," which had the line "I get no kick from cocaine." Mention of drugs is absolutely taboo on the air. The line was changed to "Perfume from Spain." As a matter of fact, the way perfume advertisers are running rampant these days perfume also may be a forbidden word any day now.

The broadcasters took a long, long look at "My Heart Belongs to Daddy" before it was allowed on the air. Then, for obscure reasons of their own, they decided young ladies could sing it but young men couldn't. Several other Porter songs, "Miss Otis Regrets," "Miss Lowesborough, Goodbye" and "You've Got That Thing," just couldn't be cleaned up, short of rewriting them entirely, and were banned in toto.

Sex or any implication of that horrid business is No. 1 on the strike-out parade in songs. The late Lorenz Hart, Richard Rodgers's lyric writer, was frequently too outspoken for broadcasting circles. Hart's lyric "Have You Seen Miss Jones?" contained one line which read "The nearest moment that we marry is too late." It had to be change to "No other couple are as much in love as we," which didn't rhyme with anything in particular but included that non-inflammable word "love," which has nothing to do with sex, at least over the air.

Irving Berlin, that gentle little songwriter who never had a thought you couldn't fry an egg on, has run afoul of the censors, too. His song "These Little Things Remind Me of You" carried a couple of lines which had a vaguely salacious sound to the censors. "Gardenia perfume, lingering on a pillow" was changed—and never mind the meaning—to "a seaplane rising from an ocean billow." Another line, "silk stockings thrown aside" was, of course, strictly taboo. It became "a glove you threw aside." Gloves are something you dispense with in the living room. Stockings are generally removed in the bedroom and the networks want the songwriters to stay out of the bedroom as much as possible.

In fact, the very word "bed" is not well liked by the song censors. The classic example of all song censorship was "Let's Turn Out the Light and Go to Bed" which became "Let's Turn Out the Lights and Go to Sleep," the reasoning being that you can't get into any mischief when you're asleep. The censors probably don't know it but the substitution of a euphemism for "bed" is also widely practiced by mountaineers in the Ozarks where no one goes to "bed." In the Ozarks they "lay down."

A moment ago, I said you can't get into trouble asleep but as a matter of fact, songwriters have to tread carefully around slumber too. A few years back there was a torch song called "Billy" in which a young lady confided, "And when I sleep I always dream of Billy." What sort of dreams, asked the censors, Freudian dreams? They took no chances and the line was changed to "I want you to know I love him so."

A song called "Thank Your Father," which was more or less a paean of praise to procreation, had to be thoroughly cleaned and pressed before airing, particularly the lines: "Though your father's name was Stanley, thank heaven he was manly."

The networks don't always see eye to eye on a song's acceptability. N. B. C. couldn't see anything wrong in a Negro spiritual called "Satan, I Give You My Children," but C. B. S. thought the title was sacrilegious. The title, and of course the entire meaning, was changed to "O Lord, I Give You My Children," but C. B. S. still refused to pass on it.

Research and Hysteria
[DECEMBER 16, 1947]

A RESEARCH COUNSELOR named William A. Yoell has announced a radio survey technique which purports to show not only what is being listened to but whether the listener actually WANTS to listen or has been forced into it by his wife and child. The Yoell index determines what the listener was doing when the set was turned on, who turned the program on and how far each individual is from the receiver. (A man twelve feet away presumably is less susceptible to the blandishments of Dreft than one six feet away.)

Down in Washington James Seiler, director of research for WRC, was dissatisfied with all the other surveys, because, he said, they paid too much attention to where the radio was tuned (and whether it was on or off) and not enough to what the individual was doing while the program was on. He conducted a survey which uncovered the striking information that lots of men go to work and lots of children go to school between the hours of 8 and 9 A.M.

and they must be counted out in subsequent listening even though the radio stays on.

From Oklahoma City comes word of a mobile audience survey device. You drive this thing around and it records whether the radios in the houses you are passing are turned on and what station they are tuned to.

Recently George Gallup conducted an intensive survey of listeners concerning their feelings about eight potential radio performers, only one of whom had a sponsored program at the time. In other words, we are being asked not only what we like on the air, but what we like that isn't on the air. It won't be much longer before they ask us to write the scripts.

In addition to being thoroughly analyzed on our program preferences, our station preferences are also subjected to minute examination. Broadcast Measurement Bureau, an outfit supported by all four of the major radio networks, issues a set of figures each year which shows how great an audience each station has. From these figures each network draws a comforting picture of its own fitness for the advertiser's dollar which conflicts sharply with that of the other three networks. The Mutual Broadcasting System, dissatisfied with the B. M. B. survey, has produced its own survey, which —if I understand it correctly and I'm not at all sure I do—shows how many people could listen to Mutual if they wanted to. (Mutual is trying to prove that, if Jack Benny were on its network, more people could and presumably would listen to him than now do on N. B. C. N. B. C. violently disagrees.)

Well, that's enough to illustrate that broadcasting has gone research crazy (or Hooper-happy, as they say in the industry). Radio is no longer guided by research; it's enslaved by it. Recently Edgar Kobak, president of the Mutual Broadcasting System, declared in some alarm that the industry was wasting millions of dollars in research; that the innumerable surveys were only confusing the industry rather than enlightening it.

In even stronger terms, Walter Weir, New York advertising executive, denounced the research hysteria as a Frankenstein's monster which threatened to destroy the industry. Research, he said, had become a means rather than an end. These evidences of common sense within the industry are heartening and, I trust, they are the beginnings of a return to sanity.

It has always seemed to me an imposition on the listeners to determine what is broadcast. The responsibility of providing good radio programs belongs to the professionals in the industry, not the amateurs outside it. No amount of slavish obeisance to public taste and no amount of complicated machinery will produce a good radio program or even a popular radio program.

Also, with all respect to the listeners, their likes or dislikes should not be the arbiter of what goes on the air. They are not equipped for such a task, and the only common level they could agree on would be one of impossible mediocrity. Sean O'Casey's magnificent play, "The Plough and the Stars," caused riots when it was first produced in the Abbey Theater. If the playgoers had been equipped with Program Analyzers, they would have kept the red button pushed down throughout. They were not given that chance.

None of the popular arts can be run according to what a cross-section of the public wants to see or hear or read. If a newspaper were run that way, a good many of the grim headlines would be eliminated; a newspaper would be a more cheerful sight but it wouldn't be a better newspaper. Entertainment can't be measured and it sneers at statistics. At best, the public can only set up certain loose standards, but even those can be destroyed over night when a great creative intellect comes along and kicks them over and sets up his own new standards.

If radio would stop taking its own pulse every five minutes it might get well.

One of Our Last Great Natural Resources
[NOVEMBER 27, 1950]

ONE OF THE nation's great natural resources goes on the block today. The Federal Communications Commission is opening hearings on the question of reserving 20 per cent of the remaining 400 stations in the VHF television band and roughly 2,000 stations in the ultimate UHF band for educators. This is the last amount of spectrum space available in the foreseeable future. If educators are to get any of it, they had better get it now.

Virtually no one is opposed to this proposition—at least, openly—except the educators. The educators are not exactly against television; they are simply apathetic to it. They would, I'm convinced, be secretly relieved if these channels would go in perpetuity to commercial interests, in which case they could, in perpetuity, blame television for its commercialism, its effect on the young, its mediocrity.

Educators are the hardest people in the world to educate. They have been using a blackboard and eraser since the University of Bologna was founded in the twelfth century; they accepted with some reluctance the invention of type and, with even greater reluctance, the development—used with such great success by the Army, Navy and Air Force—of visual education. Television is the greatest challenge ever presented to an educator. It demands of an educator imagination, integrity, resource and plain hard work. All these things the educator has demanded of radio, lately of television. Failing to find them, he has heaped scorn on radio and now television for the lack of qualities which he has himself neglected to provide.

In the hearings opening today, there will be no representatives from Yale, Harvard, Princeton, Columbia; there will be few representatives from any of the great educational institutions of this country. They are letting go by default the greatest educational medium ever devised as they let radio go by default to the commercial interests. In the early 20's a great deal of the broadcasting was done by educators, and radio was greeted as a great educational tool. Between 1921 and 1936, 202 licenses were granted to operate educational radio stations; in the same period, 164 licenses either expired or were sold to commercial interests.

Neither the state legislatures, which support the great public schools, nor the boards of trustees, which control the funds supporting the great private schools, had much interest in paying radio's bills. More importantly, the educator never seriously grappled with the demands of aural education.

Television has at least fivefold the impact of radio and, at the same time, presents five times the problems. It would be no easy task for an educator to make history, literature, poetry, astronomy as arresting as Milton Berle. Rather than meet such imposing problems, the educators—most of them, anyway—have decided simply to walk away from them.

Television is the greatest tool put into the hands of an educator since the invention of print. But to get him to use it will take the outraged cries of the community at large. Who, says the educator, will pay for it? F. C. C. Commissioner Frieda B. Hennock, who has crusaded almost singlehanded for the setting aside of TV channels for education, points out that $7,000,000,000 in public and private funds were spent on education last year. Why can't some of it be spent on TV? Expensive as it is, television is the cheapest means of bringing the greatest teachers into the homes and classrooms of the most people. Given just a few hundred millions of the money spent annually on football stadiums and gymnasiums, television could bring the most lavish and thorough courses in every known subject to your children.

Before that happens, some sort of revolution will have to take place in the educational system; a great explosion will have to take place in the minds of educators. In the meantime, though, the channels will have to be set aside while the educators educate themselves. Once these channels are lost to commercial interests they will never be recovered.

As Gen. Telford Taylor, counsel for the Joint Committee on Educational Television, declared: "It may be five years—or thirty years—before educational networks become a vital force but, meanwhile, the country cannot risk loss of a just share of the radio spectrum for education."

If you have any interest in seeing to it that these channels are conserved for educational purposes, write or wire Frieda B. Hennock, Federal Communications Commission, Washington, D.C. She needs a lot of help.

The Man without a Radio
[APRIL 25, 1947]

THE COLUMBIA BROADCASTING SYSTEM, which takes a morbid interest in statistics, has just issued some more figures, most of them running into the millions. Here we go, hang onto your hats. Thirty-six million homes or 93 per cent of all American homes have radios, 52,000,000 of them. The discrepancy in these figures is because lots of people have two radios, one out of every three families to be exact. One out of five families bought a new radio in 1946, 30 per cent of whom were poor and presumably should have spent the money on something else.

Those are all substantial but fairly understandable figures. Right here it gets hard. Total listening time per day is up 4,600,000 hours or 525 years or roughly twice the elapsed time between Alexander the Great and the Roman conquest of Greece. That, you understand, is the increase in listening, not total listening, which probably exceeds the history of mankind from the ooze to Truman.

Just what effect these 525 years of increased listening have on our culture, it's hard to tell. There are great gaps in these figures.

The Man without a Radio

If we spent 525 years every day—you'll just have to get used to the way we statisticians figure things—our state of culture depends largely on how many centuries we spent on Milton Berle as compared with, say, the N. B. C. Symphony. Just a hundred years or so of "Invitation to Learning" should generate at least 2,000,-000,000 foot pounds of culture (centigrade) or enough to drive a locomotive from here to San Francisco and back.

Each family which has a radio (93 per cent of us, remember) spends 233 minutes a day listening to it or 3 hours and 45 minutes. Right here is another big and, in this case, ominous gap in the figures. What do these people do with the other 20 hours and 17 minutes of the day? Let's say they spend eight hours at work, eight hours asleep, maybe an hour getting to and from work, and two hours for meals. That leaves an hour and 17 minutes wasted somewhere, probably reading the newspaper or fixing the screen door to the kitchen. We'll have to tighten up here.

But the biggest gap in these statistics is that 7 per cent of families or people who don't have radios in use. (C. B. S. counted only those that worked.) Well, I'd like to fill in this particular gap. I know one of these guys, C. B. S.; he has a radio which doesn't work and he hasn't any intention of fixing it either.

He is a non-conformist, this fellow, and he messes up statisticians every time they come around. The Gallup people almost went out of their mind recently when they tried to pin him down on the '48 elections. Well, this fellow views Truman with suspicion and Dewey with cold distaste and all the others with a mixture of sorrow and contempt. Still they couldn't put him in the "Don't know" column because he does know and, in fact, lectured the Gallup man on everything from high prices to the Greek loan.

What, you ask, does he do with those 3 hours 48 minutes he should be listening to the radio? Well, he fritters away a lot of his time reading and he spends one or two centuries every day in a saloon, usually telling the man next to him what he thinks of Senator Robert A. Taft. In fact, every way you look at it, he's a dangerous individualist and it's disturbing to find out that there are 7 per cent of such people in the country, puttering around the garage when they should be listening to Art Linkletter. They sure mess up the percentages.

AFTERWORD

My first radio was a small portable. I used to lie out on the sands at Fire Island, alternately listening and dozing. When the soap operas got a little turgid, I'd turn it off altogether and dive into the Atlantic Ocean which was very cold that summer. It was at Fire Island that I first got acquainted with Arthur Godfrey, whom I used to listen to every morning. After Godfrey I'd go to the village and get the papers. After the papers were devoured I'd write the next day's column.

Life was a lot simpler then, and writing a column seemed the easiest thing in the world. I'd been at it only a few months. Hal Boyle, who had been in the column-writing dodge a lot longer than I had, used to grin a little sardonically when I exclaimed how easy it all was. "Wait," he'd say. "Just wait a bit." I know now what he means. Column-writing gets to be hard work—it can be the hardest work imaginable—the better you get at it. It sounds like a paradox, but the fact is that the more you learn the higher your standards become and the harder you are to please. Today, six years and a million words later, Arthur Godfrey is still on at the same time, same station, but I no longer find him as pleasing as I once did. I'm just harder to please. Or perhaps just older.

The persistence of Mr. Godfrey (as well as everyone else who hits the big time in radio or television) is the worst obstacle in this business. Radio entertainers never retire and there are grounds for suspicion that they never die. They don't—like General MacArthur—just fade away, either. They just go on and on and on—defying the columnist to find something new to write about them. After you have poured out your innermost thoughts about Arthur Godfrey (or Faye Emerson or Jack Benny or Burns and Allen) four or five times, you find you have exhausted the subject. Mr. Godfrey's personality is, God knows, one of the most extensive in all recorded history. But there are limits even to him. And after you have had your final say on the subject of Godfrey, you can't squeeze out so much as another acerbic adjective on the issue.

Looking back on it all, I'm surprised I've managed to squeeze out so much wordage on Mr. Godfrey. Or on anyone else. The entertainers who provided me with the most wordage, I note, were not necessarily the best entertainers. Frequently, they were the worst. The most agreeable columns— to me, at least, in retrospect—have been the most savage ones. I find this deplorable. I remember writing "Lotsa Fun, Lotsa Laughs, Lotsa Loving," which you'll find well forward in this volume in a total elapsed time of twenty minutes, propelled to this furious outburst by a feeling of hopeless exasperation. On the other hand, a column on Gian-Carlo Menotti's "Amahl and the Night Visitors"—you'll find it under Music—took hours. My admiration for this work was so boundless that it struck me dumb. This is a terrible state of affairs. I find that I—and most critics—are incoherent in our admiration but afflicted with a formidable coherence when we disapprove.

This is a sad commentary not just on critics but on humans in general. The most interesting part of the dinner table chatter is not when you are talking about that nice Mrs. Barnes who is so wonderful with her children; it is that bit of sulphur about that Smith witch who is always making passes at someone else's husband. This is the nature not only of writers, but of readers. The most popular columns, alas, have also been the most damaging.

I bring it all up to correct what might be a serious misapprehension in the hearts of those of you foolish enough to have read this far. The general air of disapprobation which rises like miasma from so many of these pages might mislead you into unnecessary and unwarranted sympathy. "The poor bastard"—

I can hear you saying—"has had a hell of a time. Imagine having to look at Milton Berle for a living."

I haven't really. On the whole I've had a wonderful time with Mr. Berle and Mr. Godfrey and Miss Emerson and Ed Sullivan and old Ben Grauer and all the rest of them. The fact is—deplorable as it may sound—that I greatly enjoy those things of which I most heartily disapprove.

INDEX

Able Day, 4
Accents, 176
Account executive, the, 149-150
Ace, Goodman, 50-52
Ace, Jane, 50-51
Adair, Yvonne, 64
Adams, Joey, 104
Addams, Charles, 49
Ad men, our ingenious, 146-147
Advertising, amazing but true, 141-143; leisurely class, 147-150; nature isn't always right, 143-145; our ingenious ad men, 146-147; our tragic sense of smell, 137-139; Soviet hucksters, 136-137; the Girl, 139-141
After Many a Summer Dies the Swan, Huxley, 85
Age of noise, 1-3
Aherne, Brian, 19
Alexander, Joan, 88
Allen, Chet, 228
Allen, Fred, 31-33, 35, 43-46, 194, 272-278
Allen, Gracie, 50
Allison, Ada and Peggy, 180-181
"Amahl and the Night Visitors," 227-229
Ameche, Don, 167-170, 268
American Broadcasting Company, 85, 121, 184, 247
American Language, Mencken, 279
"American Town Meeting of the Air," 207-209
"America's Number 1 columnist," 194
"Amos 'n Andy," 16, 50
Amsterdam, Morey, 33
Andrews Sisters, 201, 202
Animal kingdom, 210-217
Animal stories, 212-213
"Another Part of the Forest," 79, 80
Anthony, John J., 25-27, 43
"Appalachian," U.S.S., 6, 7
Arlen, Margaret, 96

Arthur, Jon, 115
"Arthur Murray Show," 59-61
"As the Girls Go," 207
Atomic bomb tests, Bikini, build-up, the, 3-6; let-down, 6-9
Attlee, Clement, 248
"Author Meets the Critics," 160-163

Baby-talking baby, 220-222
"Backstage Wife," 71-72
Bairnsfather, Bruce, 55
Bankhead, Tallulah, 35, 43-46
Barber, Red, 144-145
Barker, Lex, 10-11
Barnum, P. T., 64
Barrie, Wendy, 97-98
Barry, Jack, 108
Barrymore, Diana, 104
Barrymore, John, 129-130
Barrymore, Lionel, 15, 85
Barton, Chuck, 176
Battle of titans, 27-29
Beck, Mrs. Martin, 103
Behrman, S. N., 188
Bell, Don, 7, 8
"Bell, Book and Candle," 109
Benchley, Robert, 200
Bendix, William, 163
Bennett, Frank, 203
Benny, Jack, 24, 33, 56, 67, 107, 131, 147, 149, 186, 212, 282
Bergen, Edgar, 193
Berle, Milton, 27, 33, 36, 52-54, 56, 103, 115, 145, 176, 181, 285, 287
Berlin, Irving, 226, 260, 280
"Better Half, The," 165-166
Bickering Bickersons, 167-170
"Big Show, The," 35
Bikini atom bomb tests, build up, the, 3-6; let down, 6-9
Billingsby, Sherman, 37-38, 63-64, 145, 256
Bing Crosby Enterprises, 176
Blackmer, Sidney, 102

293

Blandy, W. H. P., 6, 7
"Blind Date," 175
Block, Ray, 221
Blyth, Ann, 80
Bogart, Humphrey, 145, 251
Booth, Shirley, 188
Brassiere industry, 61-63
Brattleboro (Vt.) *Daily Reformer*, 213
Breakfast programs, 43-46
"Bride and Groom," 174-175
Bridge music, 222-224
"Brief Encounter," 94
"Brighter Day, The," 70
British Broadcasting Corporation, 108, 110, 133, 178, 269, 271
British films, 262-263
British mania for railroads, 262-264
Broadcast Measurement Bureau, 193, 282
Broun, Heywood, 43
Brown, John Mason, 182
Brown, Pamela, 110
Bruce, Nigel, 232
Bruges, Belgium, 259-260
Buka, Don, 88
Burns, George, 107, 268
Burroughs, Edgar Rice, 276
Burrows, Abe, 99, 100, 104
Business man in fiction, 187-188
Byfield, Robert S., 207-209

"Caesar and Cleopatra," 109
Cagney, James, 163
"Cakes and Ale," 81
Caldwell, Erskine, 182
Caldwell, Taylor, 41
"Call Me Madam," 34
Caniff, Mrs., goes to town, 153-155
Cantor, Eddie, 52, 53, 131
"Captain Midnight," 122
Carroll, James, 250
Carroll, Madeleine, 188
Carson, Jack, 265
Censorship on the air, 271-281
Chalk players, 213-216
Chamberlain, John, 187
Chamberlain, Neville, 238
Chaplin, Charlie, 56
Chaplin, W. W., 5, 7-8

Chapman, Ceil, 10
Chapman, John, 195-196
Charlotte (N.C.) *News*, 176
Chase, Ilka, 99-100, 160
Chesnuts are in bloom again, 91-93
Children of Hollywood, 266-268
"Children's Hour, The," 79, 270
Children's programs, enfant terrible, 118-119; experts and, 119-121; influence of, 115-116; ministers, psychiatrists and, 122-124; modern boyhood, 116-118; radio research, 113-115
"Child's World," 185-186
Chotzinoff, Samuel, 229
Christmas broadcasts, 15-17
Churchill, Sarah, 36
Churchill, Winston, 238-239, 248
"Cisco Kid," 122
Clark, Bobby, 208
Clemens, Samuel L., 124
Clift, Montgomery, 97
Clooney, Rosemary, 221
Close, Upton, 187
Coleman, Carol, 99, 100
Colman, Ronald, 15
Collingwood, Charles, 240
Collins, Ted, 101, 102
Columbia Broadcasting Company, 7, 62, 109, 132, 192-194, 240, 263, 281, 286
Comedian and the cause, 52-54
Commercials, 136-149; singing, 218-220
Communism in Hollywood, 19
Compulsive drinker, 218-220
Conn, Billy, 8
"Consul, The," 227, 228
Contest programs, 151-160
Convention, television at, 240-242
Conversation, a dying art, 189-190
Conway, Tom, 231-232
Copenhagen, 259
Corey, Wendell, 95
Cornell, Katherine, 38, 103
Correll, Charles, 268
Costain, Thomas B., 182
Costello, Frank, 250
Cotsworth, Staats, 88
Count of Monte Cristo, Dumas, 174
Coward, Noel, 94-95

Index

Craig, Nancy, 96
"Creative Impulse, The," 81
Crime Prevention Week, 184
Crosby, Bing, 17, 19, 27-28, 31, 54, 56, 107, 143, 202
Crosby, Cork, 42-43
Crosby, Cricket, 42-43
Customs officials, 261-262
"Cynara," 111

Dahl, Arlene, 10-11
Daily Worker, 195
Dalby, W. Barrington, 133
Daly, John, 239
Dance music in Europe, 258-260
Darcel, Denise, 103, 104
Davenport, Marcia, 161-162
Dave's Dream, 5, 7, 8-9
Da Vinci, Leonardo, 269-270
Davis, Joan, 85
Davis, Meyer, 240
Davis, Virginia, 240
Day, Dennis, 147, 163
Daytime television, 57-59
Deane, Martha, 96
Death in the afternoon, 71-73
"Death Stays the Hand of the Sculptor," 42
De Gasperi, 13
De Mille, Cecil B., 21
Dempsey, Jack, 64, 131
Denny, George V., 209
Detective stories, 230-236
Detroit Symphony Orchestra, 34
Deutsch, Karl, 181
"Devil's Foot, The," 230-232
Dewey, Thomas E., 241, 242-244
Dialogue writers, guidebook for, 89-91
Dickens, Charles, 160, 188
Dickens Inn, 195
Dietz, David, 5
DiMaggio, Joe, 108
Dining, a dying art, 190-191
Dirksen, Senator, 248
Disenchanted, The, 87-89
Dockstader's Minstrels, 25
"Double or Nothing," 107, 155
Doubleday, Abner, 127
Douglas, Jack, 265-266

Downey, Morton, 256
Downs, Bill, 7, 8
Dreiser, Theodore, 187
"Duffy's Tavern," 46-49
Dumas, Alexander, 174
Dunphy, Don, 133
Durante, Jimmy, 265
Dying arts, two, 189-191

Easter parade, 13-15
East Side, West Side, Davenport, 161
"Easy Aces," 50
Eden, Anthony, 248
Edison, Thomas Alva, 22, 127
Education, range reserved for, 284-286
Educators, children's programs and, 122-124
Edwards, Ralph, 73-75, 158-160
Einstein, Albert, 3
Eisenhower, Dwight D., 3, 19, 128, 206, 239
Electronics, wonder of, 174-176
Elliot, Win, 125-126
Elizabeth, Princess, 176-179, 239
Embittered liberal, 186-188
Emerson, Faye, 97, 102-104, 104-106, 106-107
English literary romance, 93-95
English sportscasters, 133-135
Erlanger, Gloria, 50
Euripides, 109-110
Evans, Maurice, 83-84
Experts, children's programs and, 119-121
Exquisite Form Brassiere Co., 62

Farley, Jim, 38
"Father, The," 167
Faye, Alice, 16, 193
Federal Communications Commission, 284-286
Ferber, Edna, 71
Fesperman, Tom, 176
Fidler, Jimmy, 17-20
Fights broadcasting, 128-129, 133-135
Fire Island, 9

"First Hundred Years, The," 76-77
Fitzgerald, F. Scott, 87
Fitzgerald, Zelda, 87
Flanagan, Edward, 19
Flea position, 216-217
Flynn, Errol, 217
Fodor, Nandor, 225-226
Foley, Red, 16
Ford, Corey, 203-205
Forrestal, James V., 3
Fortune magazine, 187
Fox Company in Korea, 248-249
Francis, Arlene, 175
Franco, 13
Frazier, Brenda, 274
French language, 254-256
French networks, 255
"Freshman, The," 55
Friendly, Fred W., 237, 248, 249
Frisch, Frankie, 131

Gable, Clark, 174, 212
Gabor, Eva, 217
Gag writers, 264-266
Gallup, George, 282
Gambling, John, 213
"Gangbusters," 183-185
Gardner, Ed, 46, 48-49
Gardner, Erle Stanley, 232
Garland, Judy, 197, 255, 267
Garroway, Dave, 29-31, 32, 108
Gehrig, Lou, 144
General Electric Company, 172, 195
Gilbert Youth Research Organization, 113-114
"Give and Take," 153-155
Giveaway programs, 151-160
"Glamor-Go-Round," 98-100
Glendenning, Raymond, 133-135
Godfrey, Arthur, 27-29, 30, 100, 102, 107-108, 144, 176, 212, 213, 243
"Goldbergs, The," 32
Goldmark, Peter, 107
Gomez, Vernon (Lefty), 129-130
"Goodbye, My Fancy," 188
Goodson, Mark, 151-152
Gould, Jay, 27
Grant, Cary, 90

Grauer, Ben, 13-15, 16, 17
Greater New York anniversary, 163-164
Greb, Harry, 130
Green, Dwight, 241, 242
Guest star appearances, 107
Guide book for dialogue writers, 89-91
"Guiding Light," 70

Haley, Sir William, 269, 271
Halley, Rudolph, 251
Halop, Florence, 50
"Hamlet," 262
Hammett, Dashiell, 230, 232, 233
Hardy, Thomas, 81
Harris, Phil, 16, 193
Hart, Lorenz, 280
Haskell, Jack, 31
Hayes, Helen, 95
Hayes, Peter Lind, 64
Hayworth, Rita, 4, 99, 268
Healy, Mary, 64
"Hear It Now," 248
Heatter, Gabriel, 42
Hellman, Lillian, 79-81, 167, 188, 270
Helsinki, 259
Hemingway, Ernest, 182
Henie, Sonja, 131
Hennock, Frieda B., 285, 286
"Henry V," 262
Herlihy, Ed, 16, 17
"High Button Shoes," 99
Hill, Virginia, 251
"Hilltop House," 70
Hindemith, Paul, 5
History by ear, 237-239
Hitchcock, Alfred, 262
Hitler, Adolf, 238
"Hit the Jackpot," 151-153, 157
Hi-V Corporation, 27
Hollywood, celebrates a New York anniversary, 163-164; children of, 266-268; communism in, 19
Holm, Celeste, 37-38
Home again, 260-262
Homicidal wives, 166-167
Homicide, plain and fancy, 230-236
Hooper rating, 270

Index

Hoover, Herbert, 131
Hopalong Cassidy, 36, 258
"Hop Harrigan," 122
Hope, Bob, 16, 27, 33, 52, 53, 56, 85, 114, 143
Hopper, DeWolf, 225
Hopper, Hedda, 9-11, 99, 163
Howard, Catherine, 108, 110
Howard, Joe E., 225
"Howdy Doody," 36, 176, 195
Huckleberry Finn, Twain, 123-124
Hume, 35
Hunch players, 213-216
Huston, John, 25
Huston, Walter, 25, 80
Huxley, Aldous, 1, 85, 87
Hysteria, research and, 281-283

"I Can Hear It Now," 237-239, 248
Impact of television, 195
"Informer, The," 270
Institute of Radio Engineers, 195

"Jack Armstrong," 122
Jackpot takes up culture, 151-153
James, Dennis, 57-59
James, Jesse, 127
Jamieson, Samuel, 175
"Jazz Singer, The," 25
Jessel, George, 104
Jet-propelled news, 11-13
"Johnny Olson's Rumpus Room," 67-69
Johnson, Nunnally, 91
Joint Committee on Educational Television, 286
Jolson, Al, 19, 23-25, 53, 176
Jones, Bobby, 131
Journalism, modern, Ross's contributions to, 199-201
"Just Plain Bill," 70
"Juvenile Jury," 118-119

Kabloona, de Pochin, 161
Kaltenborn, H. V., 16
"Kate Smith Evening Hour," 100-102
Keaton, Buster, 56

Kefauver, Estes, 250-251
Kefauver Committee hearings, 249-251
Kilgallen, Dorothy, 110
King, John Reed, 153-155
King's English, 230-232
Kinoy, Ernest, 86
Kintner, Bob, 97
Kirby, Durward, 99
"Kiss and Tell," 111
Kobak, Edgar, 282
Koestler, Arthur, 188
Kuhlmann, Rosemary, 228-229
Kwajalein, 5, 7, 8-9

Ladd, Alan, 16
"Ladies Be Seated," 192
"Lady's Not for Burning, The," 110
La Guardia, 238
Lahr, Bert, 61
Laine, Frankie, 35
Lamarr, Hedy, 18, 21, 23, 141
Lamour, Dotty, 99
Landi, Elissa, 162
Landis, Carole, 23
Landon, Alf, 242
Langdon, Harry, 56
Langford, Frances, 167-170
Lardner, John, 23
Lassie, most versatile actor, 210-212
Last secret thought, 185-186
"Late Show," 263
Lattimore, Owen, 206
Laughs Unlimited, 176
Leadership in broadcasting, 269-271
Le Gallienne, Eva, 88
Leigh, Vivien, 4
Leisurely class, 147-150
Levant, Oscar, 119
Lewis, Fulton, Jr., 19
Lewis, John L., 238
Lewis, Robert Q., 104
Liebling, A. J., 200
"Life Begins at Eighty," 108
"Life Can Be Beautiful," 71
Life magazine, 3, 33, 241
"Lights Out," 166
Lincoln, Abraham, 127
Lindbergh, Charles A., 238

Linkletter, Art, 16, 43, 172-173, 288
"Little Foxes, The," 79, 167
Lloyd, Harold, 55
Lohr, Lenox, 277
London, 252-254
"Lone Ranger," 122
Long, Huey, 238
"Long Voyage Home, The," 270
Look magazine, 33
"Lorenzo Jones," 72
Louis XIV, 147
Louis, Joe, 131, 238
Lunacy on twentieth-century kinescope, 158-160
Lux Theater, 79, 80, 146

MacArthur, Douglas, 19
Mailer, Norman, 187
Man Gets Around, McNulty, 213
Man without a radio, 286-288
Mann, Arthur, 177
"March of Time," 165
Margaret Rose, Princess, 239
Marriages, sponsored, 172-174, 174-175
Marshall, George C., 19
Martial relations, 165-175
Martial status, advertising, 180
Martin, Edward, 240, 241
Martin, Mary, 35, 55
Marx, Chico, 268
Marx, Groucho, 267
Mason, Noah M., 48
Maternity, perils of, 69-71
Matthews, Joyce, 145
Mature, Victor, 21-23
Maugham, Somerset, 81-83, 87, 182-183
Mauldin, Bill, 55
Maxim-Mill fight broadcast, 133-135
Maynor, Dorothy, 35
Mayo, Virginia, 38
McBride, Mary Margaret, 67, 96-97, 241
McCaffrey, John K. M., 161-162
McCambridge, Mercedes, 104
McCarthy, Clem, 238
McCrae, Gordon, 16
McElhone, Eloise, 97

McGraw, John, 131
McGuire, Dorothy, 83, 84
McNellis, Maggi, 13-15
McNulty, John, 213-216
Mechanical joke, 54-56
"Medium, The," 227
"Meet Corliss Archer," 110-112
Mencken, H. L., 3, 279
Menjou, Adolph, 151
Menotti, Gian-Carlo, 227-229
Merman, Ethel, 24, 35
Metropolitan Museum of Art, 42
Milland, Ray, 191
Miller, Merle, 161
Ministers, children's programs and, 122-124
Minute Maid Corporation, 28
Montgomery, Robert, 163
Moore, Tom, 192
Morgan, Henry, 31, 163, 164, 172, 205-207
Morgan, Russ, 221-222
Morley, Christopher, 183
Morrison, Herbert, 238, 271
"Mt. McKinley," U.S.S., 6, 7
"mr. Ace and Jane," 50-52
"Mr. District Attorney," 234-236
Mueller, Merrill, 177-178
Multiplicity, 106-108
Munn, Carrie, 180
Murray, Arthur, 60-61
Murray, Mrs. Arthur, 60-61
Murray, Jan, 222
Murrow, Edward R., 177, 237, 240, 247-249
Mutual Broadcasting System, 121, 282

Nalle, Bill, 99
Nathan, George Jean, 270
National Broadcasting Company, 5, 6, 16-17, 29, 35, 43, 100, 101, 126, 137, 192-194, 203, 229, 241, 273-278, 281
Networks, French, 255; two biggest, 192-194
"Nevada," U.S.S., 8
"New Adventures of Sherlock Holmes," 230-232
New York Daily News, 11, 195-196

Index

New York Herald-Tribune Book Review, 182
New York Mirror, 11
New York Times, 196
New Yorker, 54, 76, 199-201
Nimitz, Chester W., 3
"Nobody Lives Forever," 146
Noone, John J., 157-158
Norris, Kathi, 65-67
"No School Today," 115

O'Brien, Pat, 130
O'Brien, Mrs. William, 130
O'Casey, Sean, 283
O'Dwyer, Ambasador, 249, 250
Off-colored jokes, 276
"Okay, Mother," 57-59
O'Keefe, Walter, 107, 155
Old-fashioned boyhood, 15-17
Olivier, Laurence, 251
Olsen, Johnny, 67-69, 101-102
"1,000,000 B. C.," 21-23
O'Neill, Eugene, 95
O'Neill, Eugene, Jr., 161
Opper, Frederick, 177, 178
Orlan, Dickie, 118-119
"Our Gal Sunday," 70

Palmer, Lilli, 109-110
Parent-Teachers Association, 120, 122, 123
Paris, 259; anniversary, 256-258
Parks, Bert, 143, 212, 262
Parks, Larry, 176
Parsons, Louella, 9-11, 16
Pegler, Westbrook, 19
Pemberton, Brock, 196
"Pennsylvania," U.S.S., 7
"People Are Funny," 174
Pep, Willie, 21
"Pepper Young's Family," 70
Perry, Freda, 158
Peterson, Elmer, 8
Phelps J. Halder, 146
Pinza, Ezio, 55
"Playhouse of Stars," 94, 95
"Plough and the Stars," 283
Pochin, Contran de, 161
Porter, Cole, 260, 279

"Portia Faces Life," 42, 67, 72
Pot and the Kettle, 17-20
Powers, Jimmy, 134, 135
Press, Henry Morgan views, 205-207
Price, Vincent, 80
Psychiatrists, children's programs and, 122-124
"Pulitzer Prize Playhouse," 95
Putnam, George F., 11-12, 13

Quaker Oats Company, 121
Quick magazine, 65
Quiz contest programs, 151-160
Quiz Kids, 16, 118

Radio, age of noise, 1-3; on not listening to, 41-43; research, 113
Radio Daily, 147
Raft, George, 18
Rathbone, Basil, 231-232
Rawson, Mitchell, 25, 221
Rayner, Billy, 216-217
"Red Ryder," 122
Reed, Florence, 84-85
Religion on the air, 276
Remarque, Erich Maria, 188
Republican National Convention (1948), 240-242
Research, radio, 113-115; hysteria and, 281-283
Rice, Grantland, 130
Rich, Irene, 104
Rinehart and Company, 152
Ripley, Dillon, 4
Roach, Lavern, 129
"Robbins Nest, The," 62
Roberts, Ken, 51
Robinson, Jackie, 19, 128
Rockne, Mrs. Knute, 131
Rodgers, Richard, 35, 255, 260
Rogers, Will, 238
Roller derby, 131-133
"Romeo and Juliet," 83-85
Rooney, Mickey, 131, 214
Roosevelt, Eleanor, 19, 131
Roosevelt, Franklin D., 128, 206, 238, 239, 243
Ross, Harold, 199-201

Royal wedding, 176-179
Russell, Audrey, 178
Russell, Connie, 30
Ruth, Babe, 131

"Safety Last," 55
Salvation Army, 246
"Sam Spade," 193, 232-234
"Samson and Delilah," 21
Santa Anita, 23-24, 214
Sardi's, 36
Saturday Evening Post, 197
Savold, Lee, 21
Schmeling, Max, 238
Schulberg, Budd, 87-89
Schwartz, Arthur, 99, 100
"Second Mrs. Burton," 71, 72
"See It Now," 247-249
Seiler, James, 281
Sennett, Mack, 264
Sevareid, Eric, 248
Sforza, Ludovico, 269
Shakespeare, William, 83, 95
Shaw, George Bernard, 81, 109, 187-188
Sheldon, Herb, 14
Sherwood, Robert E., 188
Shoppers' programs, 65-67
Shore, Dinah, 128-129
Shriner, Herb, 35
Sigma Delta Chi, 205
Sinatra, Frank, 16, 17, 19, 130, 195
Singing commercials, 218-220
Siodmak, Robert, 110
Skelton, Red, 32, 149
"Sky King," 122
Small, George, 129
Smith, Alfred E., 244
Smith, Howard K., 177, 248
Smith, Kate, 100-102
Snow White, 123
Snowstorm of 1948, 201-203
Soap operas, 69-71, 71-73, 76-78
Song writing, 220-222, 279-281
"Songs for Sale," 221-222
"South Pacific," 55
Soviet hucksters, 136-137
Spaatz, Carl, 4
"Space Cadet," 144
Sponsored marriage, 172-174, 174-175

Sporting events broadcasting, 125-133
"Sports Newsreel," 126
Stalin, Joseph, 13
Stanwyck, Barbara, 251
Stark, Mrs. Claire, 151
Steinbeck, John, 21
"Stella Dallas," 42, 69, 72, 147
Stereotypes, radio, 186-187
Stern, Bill, 16, 126-128, 129-131
Stevens, Mark, 18
Stevens, Samuel N., 121
"Still Life," 94-95
"Stop the Music," 143, 158, 212, 262
"Stork Club," 36, 37-38, 42, 63-64, 145, 256
Strindberg, August, 167
"Studio One," 166-167
Sullavan, Margaret, 95
Sullivan, Ed, 97, 101, 217
"Summing Up, The," 83
"Superman," 122
Surveys, 281-283
"Suspense," 191, 197
Swancutt, Major, 9
Swarthout, Gladys, 38
Sydney, Sylvia, 102
Syracuse University, 180-181

Taft, Martha, 241
Taft, Robert A., 241, 244, 248, 287
Taylor, Henry J., 209
Taylor, Telford, 286
Telephone quiz contests, 156-158
Television brain, 131-133
Television Guide, 103, 104
Telford, Frank, 95
"Teller of Tales," 81
"Tello-Test," 156-157
"Tennessee Jed," 122
"Terry and the Pirates," 120, 121, 122
Textron, 140
"Third Man, The," 264
Thomey, Myrtle, 175
Thorndike, Joe, 241
"Those Websters," 121
Three Musketeers, Dumas, 174
Thurber, James, 76, 194
Time magazine, 34, 249

Index

Tin Pan Alley, 222
Tito, Marshal, 13
Tobey, Senator, 251
Todd, Larry, 7, 8
Todman, Bill, 151-152
"Tom Mix," 122
Tom Sawyer, Twain, 123-124
Tone, Franchot, 64
"Tonight at Eighty-Thirty," 94
Totalitarian individual, 79-81
Toynbee, Arnold, 182
Treasure Island, Stevenson, 123
Trends, small, 180-182, 191-192
Truman, Harry S., 19, 56, 197, 239
Truman, Margaret, 34-36
"Truth or Consequences," 73-75, 158-160
Twain, Mark, 124

Understatement, 125-126
United States Immigration Service, 261
University of the Air, 85-87
Untapped billion dollars, 113-115

Valentine, Lewis J., 183-184
Vandenberg, Arthur, 241
Vanderbilt, Cornelius, 27
Vienna, 259
Viper in the jackpot, 157-158
Vishinsky, Andrei, 248
Voice of America, 255-256

Walker, Mickey, 130
Walker, Stanley, 88
Wanamaker, Sam, 188
Warren, Neil D., 120
"Wash on the Air," 147
"Watch on the Rhine," 80
Watson, Arthur, 212
"We, the People," 191
Webb, Clifton, 47-48
Weir, Walter, 282
Welles, Barbara, 96
Welles, Orson, 277
"When a Girl Marries," 191
Whitman, Walt, 5
"Whiz Quiz," 151
Wilde, Oscar, 119
Wilson, Earl, 193-194
Winchell, Walter, 19, 193
Windsor, Duke of, 238, 245-247
"Winner Take All," 153
"Winter Cruise," 81-83
Wolfson, Mrs. Norman, 175
Wood, Major, 9
Woollcott, Alexander, 38-40
Working hours of authors, 182-183
Wrightson, Earl, 104

Yoell, William A., 281
Young, Brigham, 40
Young, Loretta, 174
"Young Dr. Malone," 70
"Young Widder Brown," 70, 72

ABOUT THE AUTHOR

JOHN CROSBY *was born in Milwaukee, graduated from Phillips Exeter Academy and passed a couple of years in the freshman class at Yale University before beginning what he considers his real education—newspaper work. His first newspaper job—his first job of any sort, for that matter—was on* The Milwaukee Sentinel *where he covered courts and police headquarters. In 1936, he came to New York for five years, covered police stations and general assignments for the* New York Herald Tribune, *wrote a play which was optioned to five producers and produced by none of them, and finally went off to war as a private with New York's Seventh Regiment (National Guard). It was five years before he got back to the* Tribune. *The editors didn't know quite what to do with him, the place being aswarm with reporters fresh out of uniform, and as a sort of emergency measure, asked him to write a radio column. He'd never owned a radio, had listened to it rarely, but took the job until something better showed up. So far nothing has. The column,* RADIO & TELEVISION, *is now syndicated from coast to coast to an audience of more than 18 million readers. In his spare time, Crosby turned out a novel, read it and instantly decided to suppress it. He would like to write another play. He is married and the father of two children, Mike and Maggie.*